EDUCATION
FOR THE PUBLIC SOCIAL SERVICES

Education

FOR THE

Public Social Services

A REPORT OF THE STUDY COMMITTEE

AMERICAN ASSOCIATION OF SCHOOLS OF SOCIAL WORK

CHAPEL HILL

THE UNIVERSITY

of North Carolina

PRESS

List of Committees

Jane M. Hoey	Social Security Board ·
John Ihlder	Alley Dwelling Authority, District of Columbia
Walton C. John	Office of Education, Federal Security Agency
Winthrop D. Lane	Trenton, New Jersey
William M. Leiserson	National Labor Relations Board
Katharine F. Lenroot	U. S. Children's Bureau
Earl J. McGrath	American Council on Education
Joseph L. Moss	Cook County Bureau of Public Welfare, Chicago, Illinois
Walter W. Pettit	Advisory Committee on Training and Personnel to the Bureau of Public Assistance and U. S. Children's Bureau
Flora L. Slocum	American Home Economics Association
Frederick F. Stephan	American Statistical Association
Walter West	American Association of Social Workers

STUDY COMMITTEE

Robert T. Lansdale, Chairman	New York School of Social Work
Edith Abbott	University of Chicago, School of Social Service Administration

George C. S. Benson	University of Michigan, Curriculum in Public Administration
Fred K. Hoehler (ex-officio)	American Public Welfare Association
Margaret Johnson	Western Reserve University, School of Applied Social Sciences
Dorothy C. Kahn	American Association of Social Workers
Leila Kinney	University of Denver, Department of Social Work
Hertha Kraus	Bryn Mawr College, Department of Social Economy
Karl de Schweinitz	Pennsylvania School of Social Work

EXECUTIVE COMMITTEE, 1938-1940

Roy M. Brown	University of North Carolina, Division of Public Welfare and Social Work
Arthur Dunham	University of Michigan, Curriculum in Social Work
A. Gordon Hamilton	New York School of Social Work
Florence W. Hutsinpillar	University of Denver, Department of Social Work

List of Committees

Arlien Johnson — University of Southern California, Graduate School of Social Work

Anna E. King — Fordham University, School of Social Service

Margaret Leal — New York School of Social Work

Wilber I. Newstetter — University of Pittsburgh, School of Applied Social Sciences

Alice L. Shea — University of Minnesota, Graduate Course in Social Work

R. Clyde White — University of Chicago, School of Social Service Administration

Elizabeth Wisner — Tulane University, School of Social Work

Helen R. Wright — University of Chicago, School of Social Service Administration

RESEARCH STAFF

George C. S. Benson   Dorothy C. Kahn

Marion Hathway

Preface

THIS INQUIRY has been an adventure of a high order.
As originally conceived, the undertaking appeared
fairly simple and certainly limited in its extent; but
when the Committee fully comprehended the implications of a study which would attempt to analyze the
skills and knowledge required for the proper administration of a wide variety of public social services and to
appraise the adaptation of educational programs to
those needs, the task seemed too enormous to undertake with the available resources. At this point it sud-
denly became clear that the thing to do was to make a
beginning. It was perfectly evident that these services
were dynamic, that requirements would constantly be
undergoing change, that educational institutions were
not static either, and that adjustment between service
requirements and educational programs would be an
ever-evolving process.

The limitations which had to be placed upon the
range and intensity of the study are indicated in the report and need not be repeated here. It is important,
however, to stress the fact that the Committee looks
upon this as the completion only of a first stage in the
consideration of the educational needs of the public
social services. Several lines of further activity immediately suggest themselves. First and foremost is discussion of the findings and recommendations of this report
by groups of administrators, educators, professional
workers, and students assembled in local, regional, and

national conferences. Studies in other fields of public welfare should be undertaken as soon as possible. Even within the area covered by this project there is need for further work, particularly to determine the effect of the merit systems upon public assistance and child welfare service and to examine the changes in the character of the old age and survivors' insurance program resulting from the 1939 amendments and a longer period of experience in making benefit payments. The American Association of Schools of Social Work will endeavor to stimulate these and related activities, but leadership is also anticipated from other professional bodies as well as from the services themselves.

Although fully aware of how much more needs to be done, the Committee is by no means apologetic for the results of its efforts up to this time. Rather it feels justified in expressing considerable satisfaction in having moved as far ahead as it has in the undertaking. The findings of the staff speak for themselves. The Committee can merely add a word of appreciation for the ingenuity and industry of Miss Dorothy C. Kahn and Mr. George C. S. Benson, who did the major work on the study of the personnel requirements of the services, and for the patience, courage, and skill of Miss Marion Hathway, who not only conducted the study of the schools but also knit together the two aspects of the study into an integrated final report.

For the summary of findings and recommendations, the Committee assumes full responsibility. In drawing up this summary the members of the Committee sought to bring together what they considered to be the chief issues revealed by the staff reports and to point out the significance of these issues in terms of action by administrative and educational leaders. In the process of drawing up this statement, the members of the Committee subordinated individual differences of opinion to the end of achieving a consensus of opinion which would as nearly as possible express the beliefs of the majority. Thus it may be said that the interpretations of findings and the suggested courses of action which constitute the summary would not be endorsed in full by any one member of the Committee, but rather that they represent the dominant opinions of the group as a whole.

Robert T. Lansdale
Chairman, Study Committee
October 1, 1940

Contents

List of Committees   v

Preface   ix

I. INTRODUCTION: PUBLIC SOCIAL SERVICES
IN A DEMOCRACY   3

II. SUMMARY AND RECOMMENDATIONS   11

III. THE STUDY: ORGANIZATION AND METHOD   31

IV. PROFESSIONAL EDUCATION AND THE SERVICES   44

V. PUBLIC SOCIAL SERVICES: THE OPERATING
LEVEL   66

VI. PUBLIC SOCIAL SERVICES: SUPERVISION AND
ADMINISTRATION   105

VII. PERSONNEL POLICIES   124

VIII. THE SCHOOLS OF SOCIAL WORK:
THEIR PROGRAMS   170

IX. RELATIONSHIP OF THE SERVICES
AND THE SCHOOLS   221

Appendix A: Additional Services   246

Appendix B: Tables   282

Index   317

EDUCATION

FOR THE PUBLIC SOCIAL SERVICES

Chapter One

INTRODUCTION:

PUBLIC SOCIAL SERVICES IN A DEMOCRACY

As THE SOCIAL and economic setting of a democracy changes, the responsibilities placed upon a government "of the people, by the people, and for the people" are modified correspondingly. In a simple economy the task of such a government is to regulate private initiative so that the individual has the opportunity for an independent solution of his problems. A philosophy of neighborliness or interdependence is developed, and human needs are met with comparative ease. In a complex economy it becomes the responsibility of the government to make provisions for the protection and security of individuals whose problems are impossible of independent solution.

The last century of our history has witnessed a shift from a land to a money economy, from a domestic system of production to a factory system, from hand labor to machine labor, and from a population that was principally agrarian to one that is principally urban. Unemployment or under-employment, industrial accident and industrial disease, the hazards of poor housing and congested urban living have accompanied these changes and have become social risks to which a large portion of our population is now exposed. During the same period, the responsibility for protection against these risks has gradually been accepted by the state, and institutional forms which make it possible for the individual to function as a member of a democratic society have emerged. The citizen needs security if he is to function adequately, and it is in the spirit of developing a citizenry competent for the operation of a democracy that a system of corporate responsibility for social risks has been established and guaranteed by law.

As needs have been more clearly understood, the scope of governmental responsibility has expanded. Public health has moved from concern for the protection of the community against communicable disease to a consideration of the individual, provisions for medical care, and preventive services. Now it includes a broad program of maternal and child health care, social hygiene, industrial hygiene, and health education. Public recreation programs first limited to the provision of corner playgrounds now comprise camping, music, and dramatics, parks and recreational developments. Public school systems first limited to the task of educating youth now include provision for nursery schools, adult education, special classes for various groups, vocational guidance, and employment counselling.

At the turn of the century, assistance to families and individuals known as "poor relief" was still the responsibility of local government units. The obligation for the care of the mentally ill and for defective and delinquent groups had been accepted by the states. Preventive work for these groups was still in the hands of the local authorities. A partnership of federal, state, and local authorities in anything resembling a national welfare program was then unknown. The beginnings of a federal employment office system were established in 1907,[1] the first workmen's compensation act was passed in 1910,[2] the first mother's assistance act in 1911,[3] and the first old age pension act in 1914.[4] Twenty-five years later, through the instrumentality of the Social Security Act,[5] the states and the federal government were linked together in the administration of public assistance to the aged, to the blind, and to dependent children, in the provision of special services to children, and in the development of unemployment compensation and employment office administration,[6] and the federal government had assumed responsibility for a national system of old age insurance. Low cost housing had been extended under a program of federal, state, and local coöperation. A public works program for relief to the employable and a program of aid to unemployed youth were also carried by the federal government. Assistance to the unemployable and to those not otherwise provided for remained in the hands of local authorities. Workmen's compensation, still a state responsibility, had been extended to all but one state jurisdiction, with federal legislation covering special groups.[7] The administration of these services now

1. In the Bureau of Immigration. The first State Employment Service had been established in Ohio in 1890. Raymond C. Atkinson, Louise C. Odencrantz, and Ben Deming, *Public Employment Service in the United States* (Public Administration Service, Chicago, 1938), p. 19.

2. I. M. Rubinow, *Social Insurance* (New York, Henry Holt and Company), 1912.

3. Missouri (limited to one county), and Illinois (State wide), Emma O. Lundberg, "Mother's Pensions," *Encyclopedia of Social Sciences*, Vol. XI, p. 54.

4. Arizona. I. M. Rubinow, "Old Age," *ibid.*, Vol. XI, p. 460.

5. 49 *Stat* 620, August 14, 1935.

6. Wagner-Peyser Act, 48 *Stat* 113, June 6, 1933.

7. United States Employees' Compensation Act, 39 *Stat* 742, September 7, 1916; Longshoremen and Harbor Workers' Compensation

constitutes an important arm of governmental activity.

Nature and Objectives.—In every social service, public or private, it is possible to identify the objectives of the service, the present content of the job, and the setting in which the service is rendered. The objective of all public services in a democracy is to serve the citizens of the state in an effort to promote the "greatest good to the greatest number." Public health, public education, public safety, and public recreation are all social services in this sense, dedicated to the good of the body-politic in its broadest significance. The public social services in the sense used in this study are less easily defined because of their varied and changing scope. Yet an underlying concept may be identified. The administration of certain benefits to individuals, either as persons or as members of groups, and to assist in their normal functioning within society can be accepted as the primary objective of these services.

Conceivably, effective administration of many of the public services involves the recognition of special responsibility for particular groups of individuals. For example, to function properly as an instrument of education for children in a democracy, the public schools need to command several skills in addition to the classroom teaching and educational leadership. Vocational guidance, visiting teacher service, and the study and treatment of behavior disorders are social services which promote the normal operation of the educational process, and they may be cited as illustrations. Similarly, to function adequately the courts should utilize groups of special services to individuals, including medical, psychiatric, and social case work.

Act, 44 *Stat* 1424, March 4, 1927, amended to cover private employees in the District of Columbia, 45 *Stat* 600 on May 17, 1928.

These services can be distinguished from the administration of low-cost housing for the use of disadvantaged
groups, from the administration of unemployment insurance and the employment services, and from the
administration of public assistance for those in need.
The care and treatment of juvenile delinquents and the
assistance to the aged embody a concept of service to the
individual as a person which is not involved in the administration of a police department for the protection of
life and property in the community. Such services carry
definite responsibilities for individuals and are organized to help them in a peculiar way. They must be administered in a way that embodies the understanding of
how to help people.

 The Philosophy of Service.—It is sometimes suggested
that within these public social services a further distinction can be made, according to whether the service is intended to administer benefits on the basis of individual
need or of individual right. Individual need has been the
basic criterion in the administration of public relief, or,
to use the later term, "public assistance." As the broad
general language of many early statutes will indicate, the
early poor laws, also, were designed to meet individual
need. Yet the "pauper concept" in the administration of
the poor law is an established fact.[8]

With the gradual passing of the philosophy of a *laissez
faire* economy and the emergence of a philosophy of col-
lective responsibility, a new concept of assistance to the
individual appeared. It took the form of protecting him

8. In searching for a reason, the student learns that the social setting
in which the poor law was administered accounted for much of its
failure to develop a concept of adequate service to the individual. The
social philosophy of the community, state or national, is a powerful
determinant upon the content of the service administered.

against the social risks of normal living. His right to this protection began to be recognized and was first embodied in workmen's compensation legislation. Yet the history of the administration of workmen's compensation is sad evidence of failure. Not only are the benefits provided in many of the statutes quite inadequate, but as the right to protection emerged as a principle there was a failure to see that the individual right was also a "right in terms of individual need." The mere payment of the cash benefit did not recognize the need for rehabilitation service, and the individual often returned to society no more able to function than he had formerly been, except that he was assured the limited security of compensation.

Mother's assistance did, however, embody the idea of "right in terms of need." The right of every child to security and protection had been stated by the first White House Conference in 1909. As the states first accepted this principle of right two years later, they began to incorporate the concept of individualized service in the systems of aid to mothers of dependent children. However, in spite of the fact that legislation and administration embodied this concept, appropriations frequently resulted in the same failures noted in workmen's compensation administration. The acceptance of the principle was not sufficiently frequent to establish a precedent. The administration of mothers' aid in Pennsylvania, for example, embodied this idea from the very beginning.[9] Right and need began to converge as rights were established and needs were clearly understood.

The administration of old age assistance supplies another illustration of this development. Early regarded as

9. See *Manual: Mothers' Assistance Fund of Pennsylvania,* established in 1913.

an annuity which would discharge society's responsibility to the aged person and thus remove him from the crowded labor market, it now embodies in many state administrations a concept of the "good life" for the aged person. This does not mean any attempt to reform or modify life-long habit patterns of the aged to which certain advocates of old age pensions have raised such strong objections. Rather, it means the assurance that assistance is granted to the eligible person in a way which will make his functioning in society constructive to himself and to the community as well.

Does this discussion suggest that in every service administering benefits the understanding of the individual is a *sine qua non* if the mistakes of the poor law and of workmen's compensation administration are to be avoided? The answer of the present study is in the affirmative. Yet the understanding of individual need should be distinguished from an acceptable manner in greeting people. Though the gracious reception of a person who asks for direction is a recognized part of any good office procedure, a deeper insight is necessary for the administration of special services to individuals. This understanding is the result of special preparation and special study of individual behavior and its relation to environmental conditioning. It is only this understanding which secures the use of discretion and judgment in the service. It distinguishes professional service from "over-the-counter administration of doles."

Individualized service is the essence of professional practice in the social services of public assistance, child care, employment service, unemployment compensation, and old age insurance with which the present study is concerned. The concept of how to provide individualized service is based on the fundamental conviction that the relationship of the individual to society is dynamic and that knowledge and skill have been developed which, when applied to an individual situation, can effect a constructive association. This body of beliefs has from the beginning been associated with modern social work practice.

The profession of social work developed around concern for the individual and his adjustment to society. Understanding of the individual's need and environmental control of the forces that tend to thwart his effective adjustment in society have thus become the dual objective of social work. The professional practice of social work is thereby distinguished from the custodial care which was the first provision for defective groups and from the dole system characteristic of early poor relief administration. The discoveries of medical science and of the social sciences have provided a subject matter and experience upon which has been developed a system of professional practice recognized by certain leaders as the only sound basis for the administration of services to individuals whether under private or public auspices.

Education for professional practice is offered in schools of social work against a background of brief experience, for only forty-one years have passed since the first formal program for education in the field was established.[10] The relation of existing programs in these schools for the preparation of personnel at the professional level to the skills and knowledge needed in a group of social services in their present and future development constitutes the point of orientation for the following study.

10. The New York School of Philanthropy, now the New York School of Social Work of Columbia University, was established in 1898.

Chapter Two

SUMMARY AND RECOMMENDATIONS

THE FOLLOWING STUDY of education for the public social services, sponsored by the American Association of Schools of Social Work under a special grant from the Rockefeller Foundation, represents an attempt to analyze the training needs of the social services established or expanded under the Social Security Act and to evaluate the role of the schools of social work in the preparation of personnel for these services. A Study Committee of the Association, in consultation with an Advisory Committee representing federal and state agencies and national private agencies, carried the responsibility for the general direction of the investigation, which was conducted by a special research staff appointed for that purpose. The findings of the staff have been accepted by the Study Committee as a basis for the formulation of recommendations from the Committee to these agencies and to the schools. Committee recommendations have been reviewed by the schools and by the agencies, and the final step in the study process will provide joint consideration by the two.

Believing that the materials of the study will be more useful as supporting data if viewed against the findings and recommendations, the Study Committee presents in the following paragraphs a summary which embodies the general findings and the recommendations resulting therefrom.

I

The services established or developed under the Social Security Act which are included in this study comprise old age insurance, unemployment compensation and the employment service, public assistance (under which are administered old age assistance, aid to the blind, and aid to dependent children), and child welfare services. Within the services studied, the approximate number of personnel, exclusive of clerical employees, was as follows: old age insurance, 1,163; unemployment compensation and the employment services, 36,246; public assistance, 25,000; and special child welfare services, 550. Typical positions at the operating, supervisory, and administrative levels in these services were reviewed, but the positions of consultants and special staff assistants were excluded. The levels reviewed provide a sample cross-section of personnel employed in the general administration of these agencies.

The administration of public assistance and child welfare services at the operating, supervisory, and administrative levels requires the application of a body of knowledge and skills, as well as a discretion and judgment, which can be best attained through professional preparation for the field of social work. The administration of specific services to individuals, as in old age insurance, unemployment compensation, and the employment service, involves discretionary action which requires a similar body of knowledge and skills. If the direction in which

the services are moving rather than their present level
of development is used as a basis for judgment, a preparation comparable to that for public assistance and
child care is justified.

Recommendation: In the public social services studied,
the rendering of specific services to individuals constitutes a professional function. The skills and knowledge
which distinguish this function are more easily identified
in some services than in others, on account of the nature
of the particular task to be performed. A clearer definition of the function in terms of the knowledge and skills
required is urgently needed.

II

The skills and knowledge required in the administration of specific services to individuals in old age insurance, unemployment compensation and the employment
service, in public assistance and child welfare, constitute
the elements of an educational program basic to all the
services. The analysis of the operating jobs in the services reveals the same elements which are variously emphasized in the several programs, but which in themselves
are inherently a part of the equipment necessary for the
jobs.

The common training needs at the operating level are
a knowledge of the organization of the social services and
their place in the structure of government; a knowledge
of agency function; an understanding of social, political,
and economic forces in the community; a professional
attitude; the understanding and use of the knowledge of
behavior; and the comprehension of and ability to utilize the principles of administration. The common training needs at the supervisory and administrative levels

include those just indicated and, in addition, the following: the ability to work with administrative groups; knowledge of resources and methods of planning, direction, and budget operation; a knowledge of social research methods and their place in administration; and skill in public relations. The supervisor carries primary responsibility for staff development and the administrator for executive direction and planning.

Recommendation: The nature of the jobs established in the services studied demands the knowledge and skills of social work and indicates the need for professional education at the graduate level. Although two years of professional study appear ultimately desirable and can be justified, such a period cannot be required in all instances, considering the present stage of development of both the services and the professional schools. In public assistance and in child welfare, complete professional preparation is accepted as essential, in spite of the fact that such requirement cannot be imposed at the present time. In old age insurance, unemployment compensation and the employment service ultimate justification of such requirement is based upon the recognition of the needs inherent in the job.

It is recommended, therefore, that two years of professional study be prescribed wherever possible; that one year of professional study be prescribed where two years cannot be specified. Where graduate professional study is impossible, college graduation with broad social science preparation should be used as the basis for selection of personnel, for whom professional study may later be possible. It is further recommended that no consideration be given to the establishment of professional curriculums on an undergraduate basis, or to undergraduate specialization in technical courses. The evolution of a sound policy of selection during the developmental period should be left to the joint efforts of the federal agencies and the schools of social work. For this purpose the precedent of the Advisory Committee on Training and Personnel to the Bureau of Public Assistance, Social Security Board, and the United States Children's Bureau is cited as an example. It is believed that similar committees might be helpful to the old age insurance, unemployment compensation, and employment service.

III

Although the study revealed certain common elements of preparation needed by the personnel, these have not been recognized by the separate services, and variations in personnel requirements accordingly hinder selection of qualified people. In all the services reviewed, however, there is a trend towards establishing higher pre-entry standards for technical positions. Among the services studied, old age insurance is giving most attention to outlining promotional possibilities and to other progressive personnel policies. This service has not given equal attention, however, to the content of the job as related to education. In unemployment compensation and the employment service, a certain minimum of paid experience is required of all applicants for appointment at any level. Because of this requirement, graduates of colleges or professional schools without paid work experience are not eligible to the entering job level in these programs. In public assistance the recognized trend is toward the employment of personnel prepared in schools of social work. Achievement of this entrance standard is hampered by salary levels which frequently do not justify an investment in professional education at the graduate level. In the child welfare services included in the study, considerable progress has been made in the establishment of preparation in professional schools of social work as a minimum requirement for the appointment of professional personnel.

Among the handicaps to the development of desirable standards especially noted in the study are narrow residence requirements for the appointment of personnel. In certain states studied, such limitations have prevented the appointment of qualified personnel from without the state at a time when qualified personnel with residence in the state could not be found or was not available. Preference on the basis of residence was observed as an important factor in the selection of personnel in all the services, even in those which are federally operated. Other handicaps to the establishment of desirable standards have been the absence of sound public opinion supporting and demanding the selection of qualified personnel in the services.

Recommendation: Narrow residence requirements should be removed in the interest of obtaining better personnel.

Salary discrepancies should be eliminated. Specifically, attention is directed to the discrepancy in entrance salaries between local public assistance personnel and local office personnel in old age insurance. Salaries in public welfare should be raised at least to the level of those in old age insurance administration.

Re-examination of present requirements for admission to certain of the services is clearly indicated, with particular reference to unemployment compensation and the employment service. Here, where experience in paid employment is required of all beginning workers, the use of educational leave or the acceptance of suitable field work under supervision as substitutes for experience might be explored with profit. Consideration of these devices by joint committees of educators and administrators is urged.

From a long-range point of view, the establishment of professional certification by national or state authorities in the field of social work will assist greatly in the raising of personnel standards. Certification at a low level will not result in improved standards of social work. The professional associations in the field are urged to consider the problems inherent in certification at the present time and to bend their efforts towards making possible an adequate system of certification with a high level of standards.

IV

Certain components which meet the training needs of the social services studied can be identified in the educational objectives and in the subject-matter of the curriculums of the schools, yet this does not imply that the thirty-eight schools of social work are offering suitable curriculums. With a few exceptions the schools of social work are directing their efforts towards preparing personnel for those public social services which now recognize an educational content necessary to the job. In public assistance and child welfare, the schools have made a special effort to meet the training needs of the services. Here training needs were recognized in relation to professional education and the content of the professional curriculum in social work. So far as old age insurance and unemployment compensation and the employment service are concerned, the schools have made no significant effort to offer preparation for these new forms of public administration. A partial explanation, however, is the lack of encouragement to the schools by these services.

Deficiencies in the curriculum within the subject matter of administration, of economics and government, of health, and with reference to the rural aspects of the programs of the public social services, were especially noted. Around the teaching of basic case work courses were observed the most perplexing problems in curriculum adaptation.

Recommendation: Areas in the curriculum related to special needs in the public social services require exploration and development. Among these are labor economics, medical economics, vocational guidance and aptitudes, occupational classification, industrial processes, and procedural analysis in administration and finance. Preparation for research in the field to enable students to evaluate the need for and the effect of public programs upon individuals is important and should be furthered.

From the standpoint of the public social services, public welfare administration is to be regarded as a basic course which should be required of all students.

Study and re-orientation of methods courses such as case work, group work, and community organization in the curriculum are urgent. Content of courses dealing with methods of administering services to individuals and to groups, should be given special attention. Field training centers should be established in larger number and in a greater variety of settings in which observation, analysis, and interpretation of human behavior can be

carried on under school auspices. Such extension of opportunities for study should include field work placements in the newer fields of public social service.

V

The schools of social work hold that social work is a
profession for which a common educational foundation
is necessary. As new fields of activity appear, curriculum
modifications need to be made in order to preserve this
concept. The process is illustrated by the addition and
enrichment of the content of public welfare administration as the public social services have expanded. The
basic curriculum adopted by member schools of the
American Association of Schools of Social Work has influenced progress towards an acceptable common content
in the professional curriculum, but it has also tended to
standardize the schools recently established to a degree
that may be questioned. This basic curriculum is now
under review, and recommendations for changes are
anticipated at an early date.

Recommendation: Continuous study of the basic curriculum is needed in the light of the changing character of
the field and of developments in related fields, notably
health and education. There should be further recognition of fundamental concepts of practice. The common
content needs overhauling; revision both of subject-
matter and teaching materials, especially in the technical
courses, is important.

As the curriculum develops on a broader basis, further
distinction should be made between the school and the
agency function, so that general preparation is provided
by the school, and orientation to the agency situation

and setting for a particular job is recognized as the responsibility of the agency.

VI

The present efforts of the schools are more effective in some instances than in others, for reasons easily discerned. Schools with a long tradition of interest in the public field are equipped both with experience and resources to improve and to expand present offerings. Administratively, some schools are more flexible than others and thus programs and curriculum changes may be effected more easily. The tradition of a faculty close to practice has aided some schools in evaluating current developments in the field which affect curriculum planning.

Schools were observed which have anticipated certain demands in the field on the basis of their understanding of the nature of the long-range function of the agencies. Others were observed which have made little effort to do this and have concentrated their energies on preparing personnel for existing and demonstrated needs in the agencies. Both the capacity of the school to be responsive to new needs in the service and a close relationship of the school to the public welfare programs are important factors in successful adaptation.

Recommendation: Joint planning between schools and public services can further efforts made by the schools to develop educational programs which meet the needs of the public social services now and in the future. While the educational program is properly the function of the school, it can best be furthered by continued consultation with the agencies in the field.

VII

The extension of adequate facilities for professional education is to be distinguished from a mere increase in the number of schools. The number of schools whose enrollments are small and increasing slowly if at all, indicates that accessibility to a relatively few students in a particular area is being emphasized. This is not a substitute for the enrichment and extension of existing resources and for devices such as educational leave, whereby the student can be given the best in a school of his choice.

Educational resources available to some schools are not accessible to others. The preparation and experience of the professional faculty and the size of the full-time faculty in relation to the full-time student body vary from school to school. Available field work resources in some instances provide a rich experience in field work practice, and in others provide a limited opportunity beyond an experience in general case work practice. Some schools can utilize the offerings of related professional schools and the facilities for graduate study in the social sciences. Others have been established in universities or colleges where these facilities do not exist. In the present stage of development, experimentation in the curriculum has a direct relationship to resources available to the schools.

Recommendation: Schools with small budgets and with limited resources in faculty and field work should re-examine their programs to determine whether they should limit their efforts to offering a well-rounded one-year curriculum for membership in the American Association of Schools of Social Work as a one-year school, rather than attempting a two-year curriculum.

VIII

In expanding their present capacity, the schools are clearly dependent upon adequate field work facilities. The use of "direct supervision," whereby field work supervisors hold full-time appointments on the school staff and are considered as faculty personnel, has increased facilities in some cases and has been utilized as one way of insuring field work with educational content. For certain types of field work experience, such as for advanced students in administration and community organization, where identification with agency program is particularly necessary, this method is not feasible. In the field work program, a close relationship of the school to the agency is always desirable and is especially important when the field work supervisors are provided by the school.

The increasing tendency on the part of the schools to assume a part of the field work supervision cost is apparent, especially in the use of agencies newly developed as field centers. More adequate opportunities for field work in the public agencies have been made available where the "direct supervision" plan has been furthered, and the study indicates that a number of schools committed to the philosophy of supervision provided by the agencies have recently utilized the direct method in public agencies.

In spite of efforts observed, there is clearly evidence that field work opportunities in the public agencies are not available to the schools to a satisfactory extent. *Recommendation:* Joint effort by the schools and the agencies should be made to overcome difficulties of providing field work instruction in the public agencies. An increasing number and variety of such placements are necessary if the schools are to prepare students for the public services. The public agencies should accept greater responsibility for providing field work opportunities for use by the schools and for the development of educational supervision within the agencies.

IX

A professional curriculum which provides a broad preparation for the public social services requires adequate faculty leadership. In the greater number of new faculty appointments made by the schools, emphasis has been placed upon recent and general practice in both public and private agencies, in addition to other professional equipment. The evidence of the study, however, indicates that faculties long conditioned to the needs of private social agencies have not adjusted themselves easily to the needs of the public agencies. Frequently they lack a broad interest in the private as well as the public fields.

Recommendation: A re-orientation of faculties to the significance of expansion in the public social and health agencies is an essential adjunct to the professional competence which is already stressed. In new faculty appointments, broad experience and sound training in the social sciences in addition to professional competence should be emphasized. Further orientation of present staff members in the area of the social sciences should be undertaken by various methods, among which are leaves of absence for further study. Opportunities for additional practice in newer fields should be made possible by provision for leaves of absence. Staff members should be granted leaves of absence for additional experience in new fields of practice as a method of enriching their contribution to the school program. Every effort should be made to keep faculties currently informed of developments in the social services and of social and economic factors which shape these developments.

X

The study reveals evidence that the schools have not always been careful in the selection of students of suitable personality for the needs of the public as well as the private social services. Furthermore, the study indicates that agencies in selecting staff members for educational leave have not always had the requirements of the schools in mind and have not always been careful to recommend those workers who could profit most from the educational experience.

Recommendation: Further and consistent efforts to recruit and select the ablest students for the field should be made by the schools. In granting educational leave and in recommending staff members for further study in the schools, agencies should accept the responsibility of careful selection with the general requirements of the schools and the future needs of the field in mind. Coöperative efforts on the part of schools and agencies should be made toward this objective.

XI

As pre-requisites for admission to the schools are more clearly formulated and more widely accepted, the schools of social work can conserve some of the energy now expended in offering courses to make up for undergraduate deficiencies and can direct it toward the enrichment of content in the professional curriculum.

Recommendation: Study and revision of social science materials and teaching in the liberal arts colleges should be encouraged. An adaptation of these materials to contemporary American culture patterns is needed. Experimentation with a variety of methods or approaches is desirable.

In advising undergraduate students preparing for professional study in the field, college counsellors should stress the importance of a broad liberal arts foundation. The scope of the social sciences as a whole, including economics, history, political science, psychology and sociology, rather than a narrow specialization in one field, is important.

XII

Although adopted by the American Association of Schools of Social Work in 1937, the two-year professional curriculum as a basis for the professional degree is not yet firmly established. Those schools which have autonomy in university administration have achieved this standard more easily than others which are jointly administered with social science departments, for the reason that the professional objectives of the curriculum are in the first case identified and recognized more definitely.

Recommendation: The member schools of the Association which exist as curriculums jointly administered with social science departments should be established as autonomous professional schools within the university framework at the earliest possible moment. The present

policy of admitting as two-year schools only those which
have this status should be maintained.

XIII

The total annual expenditure for professional education each year by the schools of social work is a meager
figure. Education for social work is expensive. The inadequate and uncertain budgets under which the schools
are operating have a direct relationship to some of the
unmet problems of professional education.

Recommendation: To further the public interest in
more competent administration of the public social services, more adequate financial resources should be made
available to the schools of social work. It is recommended that the administrative officers of universities
in which schools of social work are located give
careful attention to the needs of these schools at
this time.

XIV

The schools experimenting with extension courses
offered in near-by communities find such efforts to be
difficult and often productive of few benefits. The slight
provision made for extra-mural courses by the schools,
however, is in contrast to the eagerness of the services
for such provisions.

Recommendation: The entire area of extra-mural or
extension work should be studied by the schools. In any
undertaking of this kind, administrative and educational
controls should be established. The line of demarcation
between extension course work and in-service training
should be maintained, so that the extra-mural program
may be soundly related to professional education and in-

service training soundly related to specific agency demands.

XV

The agencies and the schools are not generally recognizing the significance of post-entry training in the services. Its importance to the schools is indicated by reports from a few of the schools that the percentage of mature students with previous experience in the field is increasing. The needs of these mature students have a direct relation to curriculum planning in the schools. The importance of post-entry training to the public social services is indicated by the extension of merit systems by amendment to the Social Security Act to all personnel employed in the administration of the provisions of the act. Post-entry training then becomes one of the chief methods of improving the competence of staff following selection under the merit system.

Recommendation: The services should accept primary responsibility for post-entry development of personnel. Under such a program of staff development should be included provision for educational leave for study, with and without salary allowance, use of extra-mural courses and of part-time curriculum in the schools and organized in-service training programs.

The schools should coöperate with the agencies in the development of provisions for post-entry education. Such coöperation should lead to a further clarification of the function of the school in developing the formal program of professional education and of the function of the agencies in developing programs of in-service training. A re-examination of extra-mural courses and of courses available to employed personnel should be made. Wherever possible, fellowships should be provided to meet the needs of workers seeking educational leave.

At each point, joint consideration by agencies and schools of the problems of post-entry education is clearly indicated.

XVI

The merit system of selection through a public central personnel agency is the goal towards which operating agencies in the public social services are working. A wide variety of practice was found during the course of the study. Although some experiences in selecting personnel under a merit system were not entirely satisfactory, no evidence of unwillingness to analyze the problems involved and to build constructively upon all experience was revealed.

Recommendation: Merit systems should be comprehensive in their scope, including every phase of a program for selection and retention of qualified personnel. They should be developed on the basis of the acceptance by the operating agencies and by the personnel agencies of uniform qualifications and standards for comparable positions. There should be coöperative selection programs in overlapping geographical jurisdictions.

Positive recruiting programs including continuous access to existing or potential sources of qualified personnel should be recognized as an essential strength in a merit system.

Promotional opportunities should be based on principles of open competition.

Examination programs should be conducted under auspices which insure the services of test experts as well as those of qualified practitioners in the fields in which examinations are held.

Whenever it is possible to do so, examinations should be scheduled to be announced and administered at times when the largest number of qualified personnel is available both from the schools and from the agencies. Sufficient time for final recruitment and for adequate preparation by applicants of application forms should be allowed between the announcement and closing of examinations.

Following and promoting the democratic creed concerning equal opportunity regardless of race, religion, or color should be accepted as a first principle in merit system administration. Organizations promoting extensive preference to peace-time veterans should be kept close to the principles underlying good public administration, and their coöperation should be enlisted in promoting "the merit" in merit systems.

Merit systems should function under formal authorized regulations; they should operate without favoritism to any individual or groups.

Merit systems should be progressive and should continuously review their operations. Whenever necessary, regulations should be changed and adapted to changing programs in the operating agencies which they service.

The schools of social work and operating agencies should give full support and coöperation to the personnel agencies in establishing and maintaining uniformity, integrity, and progression in operations. A closer relationship between the schools and the merit system agencies should be developed so that fuller understanding of each other's problems will lead to mutual helpfulness.   *   *   *

In submitting these findings and recommendations of this study, the Committee wishes to call attention to the limitation in the scope of the study which is discussed in the body of the material. Social research holds an important place in all of the services studied. Its place in the equipment of the administrator is stressed, but no reference is made to the work of the specialist in the field. Likewise, no reference has been made to the place of medical social workers in the Crippled Children's Services or in the Maternal and Child Health Services under the Social Security Act nor to the variety of specialized workers who may function under the program of Child Welfare Services. These omissions resulted from the decision to limit the scope of the study to the typical positions at the operating, supervisory, and administrative levels. Because the work of these specialists has been clearly recognized as professional and because the schools of social work have so generously contributed their resources to the equipment of the personnel in the special fields, their exclusion from the study is of far greater significance than their numbers indicate.

Chapter Three

THE STUDY: ORGANIZATION AND METHOD

THE EXPANSION of the public social services, first on an emergency basis to meet the onset of the depression of the 1930's and later on a permanent basis to afford security against the so-called normal risks of living in present-day society, has created a demand for personnel which is without precedent. In an effort to meet this need, the schools of social work expanded both in number and in enrollment, extended facilities to employed personnel, participated in institutes and short-time courses set up to give some degree of orientation to new recruits, and supplied a variety of other services.

The social services were expanding in numbers and changing in scope of activities. The acceptance of the right to benefits based upon established employment record and of the right to assistance based upon the established need made an important change in the concept of service to the individual. The meeting of mass need and the development of service on a "short contact" basis effected an important change in methods. The schools of social work accordingly began to review their programs in relation to the changes observed in the field. A few schools had made great contributions to the development of professional practice in the public services and had constantly scrutinized their programs in relation to the needs in the field. Others had developed curriculums primarily around the needs of social agencies under private auspices, and had made great contributions to leadership and practice in the private field. A few schools had focused upon special needs in the whole field, as, for example, the need of social case work service in mental hospitals. Others had a religious emphasis. Amidst such diversity of interests, the scrutiny of curriculums assumed a variety of forms.

In the meantime, practitioners in the field of social work, administrators recruited from other fields to carry executive responsibility for these services, and educators began to question the assumption that professional preparation for the field of social work was suitable equipment for the personnel in public social services. Charges that the schools of social work were preparing students for employment in private social agencies, criticism of the basic courses offered in the schools as unsuitable preparation for the "short-time contact" service demanded by these new agencies, and the failure of schools to graduate students who could step into important administrative positions were frequently cited. In increasing numbers, graduates of schools of law and of business administration were seeking employment in the services as new opportunities developed. The case for general administrative training was being advanced by the schools of public administration. The orientation of preparation to the culture patterns of the rural areas was being urged by certain of the land grant colleges. Believing, therefore, that some examination of the field of the social services and the place of professional education in any program of preparation was timely, the American Association of Schools of Social Work sought foundation sponsorship of an undertaking designed to throw light on the present and future role of these schools in the situation.

A grant from the Rockefeller Foundation in April, 1938, made possible a limited study of training needs in the field as a background for the evaluation of the present programs of the schools of social work. Under the sponsorship of the Association, a study committee was appointed to carry the general direction of the investigation.[1] This Committee had the advice and counsel of the General Advisory Committee composed of representatives of federal and state agencies concerned in the field.[2] A special staff began the collection of data in the fall of 1938 and completed the task in the late spring of 1939. The material gathered covered both a scrutiny of needs in the field and a study of resources for professional education in the schools. A brief review of the scope and organization of the sections of the study will clarify the data which follow.

SCOPE OF THE STUDY

Training Needs in the Field.—The field study was limited principally to those services included under the

1. Robert T. Lansdale, Chairman, Edith Abbott, Margaret Johnson, Hertha Kraus, Leila Kinney, Karl de Schweinitz, Arlien Johnson, William Haber, and members of the Executive Committee. In June, 1940, the ex-officio members included Margaret Leal, Martha Chickering, Elizabeth Wisner, Fred K. Hoehler, Alice L. Shea, and R. Clyde White. Dorothy C. Kahn and George C. S. Benson were appointed members of the committee in December, 1939. William Haber resigned in June, 1940.

2. Fred K. Hoehler, Chairman. For membership of committee, see page v.

Social Security Act.[3] Fortunately, this limitation made possible both a review of services in which a tradition of practice had been long established and a review of services in which a content of practice is being newly developed. The administration of public assistance and child welfare services has been greatly influenced by the best traditions of social work practice; while the administration of unemployment compensation and old age insurance has no such heritage. The employment services are closely allied to the insurance programs and to all intents and purposes are a part of the same group.

In addition to these services for which the study assumed responsibility, two coördinate investigations were carried out which were of significance to the undertaking. Under the auspices of the United States Housing Authority a short study of training needs of project management staffs was completed in August, 1939. The use of comparable methodology made this study valuable for analysis. A study of social work services in public medical care programs was undertaken simultaneously by the American Association of Medical Social Workers in coöperation with the American Public Welfare Association.[4] Findings of these two studies are summarized in Appendix A of this report.

3. The amendment to the Social Security Act, August 10, 1939, effected two important changes in the services studied. (1) Old Age and Survivors Insurance replaced Old Age Insurance and (2) principle of merit selection of personnel was made mandatory upon the states after January, 1940. These changes have not been included in the study, but their significance is indicated in certain of the citations. It is hoped that this method of comment will clarify for the reader some of the impact upon personnel policies and practices in the specific services studied.

4. *Medical Social Work in Tax-supported Health and Welfare Services*. A report of the joint committee of the AAMSW and APWA, by Margaret Lovell Plumley. APWA, Chicago, 1940.

The selection of services for the field study was prompted by several additional factors. Limitations of time and financial resources were exacting. Administratively, public assistance and child welfare services were frequently grouped in state and local agencies. Unemployment compensation and the employment services were invariably so grouped. Old age insurance, although federally administered, is coördinated to some extent with public assistance and unemployment compensation through the regional offices of the Social Security Board, although local offices were independent of the others. Important also was the fact that federal leadership either through direct administration or through a system of grants-in-aid was present in all of the services. Stability in administrative practices and the consequent development of standards were possible.

Obviously, there are important omissions in the list of the services reviewed. The reader will wonder about rural resettlement, the works program, vocational rehabilitation, probation and parole services, youth programs, institutional management in the field, and the work of home and school visitors and public recreation. Brief memoranda concerning some of these services have been included in a single chapter.[5] Their omission should imply no doubt that a study of these services would reveal important material. Limitation of scope was necessary here. Later studies may be projected, it is hoped, and the data of the present investigation thus amplified and increased in significance.

The states chosen for the field study were selected upon the advice of federal and state officials and other informed leaders in the field. It seemed desirable to

5. Appendix A.

observe services which reflect the diversity of administration under a federal system, and it was advisable to
select within these regions the better-organized services.
The limitations of time and budget entered into the
final use of these criteria.

As the list of states indicates, however, the coverage
is reasonably adequate and should give a picture of the
problems of personnel in a variety of situations. In
Alabama, California, Connecticut, Indiana, Michigan,
Nebraska, Pennsylvania, Utah, and Wisconsin, all services were studied. In Texas, the employment service
alone was visited; in West Virginia, public assistance
and child welfare services were covered; in the District
of Columbia and Maryland, old age insurance alone
was studied.

Method of the Study: In addition to conferring with
most of the appropriate federal personnel, both in Washington and in the regional offices of the Social Security
Board, the staff usually interviewed several individuals
in the state administrative offices (in all except old age
insurance, which is federally administered). Suggestions
concerning representative local offices were thus obtained, and wherever possible, three or more were visited
in a given state. An attempt was made to include an
office in a metropolitan city, one in a small city, and one
in a rural area within each state.

In each office, interviews included personnel carrying
the direct service to individuals, such as the interviewer
in the employment service, claims examiner or deputy
in unemployment compensation, the visitor in public
assistance and child welfare services. Supervisors and
sub-executives in these services and administrators at the
local and state level were also included. Clerical workers

and technical specialists such as accountants, lawyers, statisticians, home economists, psychologists and psychiatrists, and others in a consultative relationship were excluded. The intent of the inquiry was to focus on the content of service for which the agency was primarily responsibile.

Because of their significance to the findings, the interviewing methods should be briefly reviewed. The term "training need" was used to signify any skill, knowledge, or aptitude essential or desirable for a particular type of position. A check list of approximately 90 skills and knowledges related to the services under consideration was compiled, and some 300 people in 125 local and state offices were asked to indicate which of the items were, in connection with the individual's own position, "essential" or "desirable," and which, in their opinion, would be desirable as a general background for reference purposes. Administrators and supervisors were usually asked to mark a check list not only for their own positions, but also for positions under their supervision. Generally, though not invariably, the list was checked in the presence of a member of the study staff.

The great value of the check list was inherent in its tendency to promote a direct relation of training needs to actual components of the job. Many persons, who obviously had stereotyped views on training needs growing out of their own experience, when presented with the list, checked items which they recognized as necessary for the position but which were not included in the stereotyped statement on training. In order to give a clear view of the training needs as revealed in the interview, the check list material is summarized.

In addition to the controlled interviews conducted

with the check list, "free" interviews were used with two or three hundred other persons. This method permitted a range of evaluation over all aspects of the work without the suggestive effect of the check list. It clarified the results of experience with various types of preparation. Moreover, it was less time-consuming and brought to light the effects of administrative policies on training needs. On the other hand, biases growing out of the interviewer's own preparation and experience were given freer play, and more care was necessary to sift these from the more nearly objective judgments.

Some additional light on training needs was revealed by a study of job specifications and the educational and experience qualifications for examinations, and of in-service training programs. This material was often inadequate and frequently suspect because of the same training biases which appeared in the free interview method; the persons who prepared the specifications for examinations frequently said that they had in mind as much the personnel available for the salaries offered as the ideal preparation for the positions. Despite these drawbacks, these materials represent official statements as to training needs, and hence are important supplementary material for a study of this nature.

A comparison of the background of various individuals now at work with their service ratings or some other measure of performance on the job was not generally used due to two important factors. First, objective criteria are still in the process of development. Service ratings are infrequently used and where attempted they are poorly developed. Other criteria are largely absent in the fields studied. Second, the complete lack in many cases of training backgrounds related to the jobs limits the gains to be made from such studies. In the future, however, improvement of service ratings, development of other criteria, and the establishment of training background may make such a technique more usable. The building of a successful training program involves consideration of many factors. So far as they were available, data on salary ranges, number of positions, and possibilities of promotion have also been included in the report.

Fundamental to the method of the study was the frequent consultation with representatives of the federal and state agencies included in the General Advisory Committee. These officials gave generously of their time and counsel whenever it was sought.[6]

The ready response and coöperation of the state and local public officials in the regions where field work was undertaken was a source of help and encouragement to members of the study staff. Without the continued assistance of these groups, the field inquiry would have been impossible.

Training Facilities Offered in the Schools of Social Work.—The study of the schools of social work was limited to those institutions whose programs have been developed in accordance with the standards of the American Association of Schools of Social Work, which has functioned since 1919 as the organization through which the schools have coöperated in the development of content and standards of professional education for the field. Within the group of 38 member schools,[7] marked differences in educational philosophy may be found, yet the

6. In addition, their comments and criticism were invaluable in the final revision of the material.
7. By December, 1940, the membership included 40 schools.

40   Education for the Public Social Services

tendency over a period of years, as indicated in the present standards for membership, supports broad objectives in professional preparation which will insure a common body of knowledge to all students entering the field as practitioners.[8]

Method: The material gathered for analysis was related to the past and present experience of the schools and to plans under consideration for the future. For this purpose, questionnaires were sent to all member schools of the Association requesting data as of October 1, 1938, concerning the organization and administration of the school, the curriculum offered, the field work facilities, the teaching personnel and character of the student bodies, and to a number of other subjects. Returns were received from 33 of the 38 schools.[9] Although formal data were not received from the University of Cincinnati and Ohio State University, field visits to those schools helped to round out the picture of the entire group.

It was not surprising that the questionnaire returns varied considerably in the care and detail with which material was recorded. The assembling and recording

8. Membership requirements as stated in the Constitution and By-Laws of the American Association of Schools of Social Work, 1939. Appendix B.

9. The analysis of programs was based on returns from 33 schools. The Program of Training for Public Welfare Administration, University of Cincinnati, was terminated in June, 1939, and for this reason the questionnaire was not completed. At Ohio State University, a clearer differentiation between the undergraduate and graduate program was in process, and for this reason the material seemed less applicable and the questionnaire therefore was not completed. Boston University, the University of Toronto, and the Montreal School of Social Work, admitted to the American Association of Schools of Social Work in January 1939, were not included in the study except in a few instances, as the data gathered by questionnaires referred to 1937-1938, the year of experience prior to their admission to the Association.

was a substantial undertaking for schools under-staffed with clerical and administrative assistance. In spite of the precautions taken, it was inevitable that material was obtained more readily from the experience of some schools than from others. The study emphasizes the degree of difference within these schools, and will indicate why the questionnaire was more applicable to certain schools than to others. In general, however, the extent to which the material was usable is gratifying and bears tribute to the generous efforts of all the schools to further the undertaking as planned.

Following the review of questionnaire material, a member of the staff visited each of the schools, spending the days at each school in interviews with individual members of the faculty, or as an observer at joint faculty discussions, reviewing the field work program by means of discussions with field work supervisors, visiting classes, and observing the student body. In almost every instance, it was possible to visit certain local and state agencies to which the school had contributed trained personnel or curriculum offerings available to part-time students employed in the agencies. These visits to the schools served to supplement and vitalize the material recorded in the questionnaires. They also served as a method of discerning opinion with reference to many common problems which the schools face as they attempt to prepare students more adequately for the public field. The extent to which the schools have been successful was revealed in part by the interviews with agencies. No attempt, however, was made to examine the various formal programs in detail with reference to known agency needs.

The responsibility for the study of training needs in the field was carried by a staff selected because of experience with the problem. Dorothy C. Kahn, now Assistant Secretary of the American Association of Social Workers, was formerly Executive Director of the Philadelphia Board of Public Assistance. George C. S. Benson is Director of the Curriculum in Public Administration, University of Michigan. Assisting Miss Kahn and Mr. Benson, who completed the major portion of the field work, were Robert T. Lansdale, of the faculty of the New York School of Social Work and Chairman of the Study Committee, and Saul Bernstein, now of the New York School of Social Work. Marion Hathway, Executive Secretary of the American Association of Schools of Social Work, was responsible for the study of the schools of social work. Frances N. Harrison, formerly Assistant Director of the Graduate School for Jewish Social Work, assisted in the final summary of the staff reports.

ORGANIZATION OF MATERIALS

The following chapters attempt a synthesis of the study of the services and the study of the schools. The focus of the material is on the content of practice in the services studied and on the present and potential role of the schools of social work in the development of personnel for the services. The content of the job for which preparation is needed is indicated by the analysis of the objectives and function of the service and the description of the responsibilities of those who carry out the functions of the agencies. Common elements in the preparation for these services are indicated first, and special needs in terms of the function of the services follow. Personnel practices and personnel problems common to the services are also reviewed. Throughout the analysis there is an attempt to identify the place which general and special education can occupy in the preparation of personnel for these services, so that the programs of the schools of social work can be evaluated as present or potential contributors to these services.

Chapter Four

PROFESSIONAL EDUCATION AND
THE SERVICES

THE PRESENT STUDY had its origin in the desire to know what the schools of social work are doing to prepare personnel for the public social services. Related professional schools of law, engineering, business administration, and public administration have contributed personnel to the services, and no invidious comparison is implied by their omission from the present analysis. Limitation to the schools of social work, it must be recalled, was inherent in the original plan of the American Association of Schools of Social Work for study of its own member schools in relation to the findings of a field staff chosen from without the immediate area of school administration. To understand the role of the schools in preparation for these services, it is necessary for the reader to relate the findings of the study to a setting in which the development of the professional curriculum in social work and the function and scope of the public services are briefly considered. In the following paragraphs, an attempt is made to review briefly certain data concerning the philosophy, organization, and scope of the schools and concerning the responsi-

44

bilities and numbers of personnel involved in the administration of the services examined.

THE PHILOSOPHY OF EDUCATION FOR SOCIAL WORK

Social work accepts as its main objective the adjustment of the individual in society. It views this adjustment as dynamic and changing as individual development takes place and as the social setting is modified. It views the lack of adjustment as originating in the physical, mental, and emotional make-up of the individual and in the environment which conditions his behavior. Thus the profession of social work functions in both areas, utilizing certain skills for service to the individual and others for the control of the environment.

While there are differentia here and there, professional preparation as offered in the schools of social work recognizes this multiple approach and tends more and more towards a general instruction for the field which combines a variety of skills and which is applicable to a variety of situations. In contrast to the early efforts toward formal training for the field of social work which constituted specific training for specific agency jobs, the schools have accepted in substance a basic curriculum that is believed to be applicable to practice in the entire field. The schools then do not attempt to prepare students for particular activities within the framework of social work, but recognize that the entire curriculum should have a substantial content of skills and information which is interchangeable between agencies and programs serving individuals and which has certain traditions which can be carried over experimentally to new undertakings.

46   Education for the Public Social Services

Education for the profession of social work assumes certain skills indigenous to the field, a program of services in which these skills are applied, and a framework of government and of the community in which these services have been developed and to which they are related. The preparation has organic unity. And while, on the assumption that established techniques are not transferable, new developments may bring pressure upon the schools to offer special "training for this or that," the tendency is to withstand this pressure in the confident belief that experience will once more reveal common elements in programs which have the same fundamental objectives in terms of the individual in society.

Professional education for social work is little more than forty years old. By 1910 only five schools of social work had been established: The New York School of Philanthropy [1] in 1898; the Chicago School of Civics and Philanthropy [2] in 1901; the Boston School of Social Work [3] in 1904; the Philadelphia Training School for Social Work [4] and the Missouri School of Social Economy [5] in 1908. The first great impetus to the establishment of the schools grew out of the social service needs of the First World War, when the American Red Cross granted small subsidies to colleges and universities to aid in the establishment of short courses for the preparation of personnel needed in services to soldiers and sailors and their families. By 1928, only ten years later,

1. Now the New York School of Social Work, Columbia University.
2. Now the School of Social Service Administration, University of Chicago.
3. Now Simmons College School of Social Work.
4. Now the Pennsylvania School of Social Work.
5. No longer in existence.

the schools numbered 35, including both accredited and non-accredited institutions.[6] The second great impetus to the development of schools of social work was the effect of the depression of the 1930's and the subsequent expansion of public social services on a permanent basis. The number of accredited schools has increased rapidly during the seven-year period studied. In 1932, twenty-four, and in 1938, thirty-five were reporting enrollment figures.[7] By 1938 [8] there were 38 accredited schools and 14 more known to be working towards accreditment (Appendix B, Tables V and VI). Isolated courses were offered in a large number of colleges and universities.

According to the present standards of the American Association of Schools of Social Work which are acceptable criteria,[9] the professional curriculum in the member schools is based on four years of undergraduate study in a liberal arts college; it is offered by faculty academically and professionally qualified; it includes the basic curriculum and approved program of field work leading to a professional degree or certificate; it is recognized as an autonomous unit within university administration, with defined professional objectives. Two types of

6. Sydnor Walker, *Social Work and the Training of Social Workers* (Chapel Hill, University of North Carolina Press, 1928), p. 132.

7. During this period there were added to the membership of the American Association of Schools of Social Work, Boston College, University of Buffalo, Catholic University, University of Cincinnati, University of Denver, University of Iowa, University of Louisville, Northwestern University, University of North Carolina, University of Oklahoma, University of Pittsburgh, St. Louis University, and the University of Washington. The University of Missouri and the University of Wisconsin were dropped from membership.

8. By December 1940, there were 40 accredited schools and 10 working towards accreditment.

9. Constitution and By-Laws, American Association of Schools of Social Work, amended 1939, Appendix B.

schools offering graduate programs [10] hold membership in the Association. The one-year school provides a one-year professional curriculum for which the certificate is recommended, and the two-year school offers a two-year professional curriculum for which the professional degree is recommended.[11] The essential differences between the two are in the length of the professional curriculum and the teaching and administrative leadership required. The distinction is quantitative rather than qualitative. The one-year schools will, it is hoped, be established only where resources and personnel demands indicate that students will enter the field following a single year of study.

Although the first schools of social work were organized and functioned independently, affiliation with an

10. Although member schools of the American Association of Schools of Social Work are asked to develop the professional curriculum on a graduate basis and to admit students at that level only, special students up to 10 per cent of the enrollment may be accepted. Mature persons with experience in the field of social work who do not meet the full academic requirements of the degree but who may present the equivalent of education in other areas are therefore eligible, though in small numbers.

11. "To be eligible, either as a one-year or two-year member, a school shall offer an organic grouping of relevant courses of instruction into a separate curriculum for the purpose of professional education for social work; it shall be under the direction of an executive head empowered in coöperation with the faculty to exercise control over admission requirements within the limit of university regulations; it shall have an annual budget for teaching and administrative salaries adequate to carry out the program of the school and shall have an assurance of maintenance by the college or university for at least three years following the date of admission. Criteria for determining the qualifications of the director shall include professional experience, graduate study, and familiarity with the problems of education. Instruction in fundamental social work courses and the practice of social work shall be given by persons who have had valid and authoritative experience in social work and it is assumed that instruction in other courses in the curriculum shall be given by persons qualified in their respective fields."—Constitution and By-Laws, American Association of Schools of Social Work, amended 1939.

educational institution of recognized standing was soon accepted as a trend to be encouraged. At the time of the present study all but two of the member schools within the Association were affiliated with colleges or universities.[12] And today no school can be accredited unless a university or college sponsorship is definite and real.[13] The educational auspices under which these schools were functioning in November, 1939 (Appendix B, Table V), and a similar classification of the schools not yet members of the Association (Appendix B, Table VI), indicate a broad basis in the support of professional education for the field of social work. At the time of the present study nine schools were established within state universities,[14] and two within municipal universities.[15] As indicated above, at the time of the study two schools were still independently organized and administered.[16] Twenty-three are within private universities and colleges.[17] Of this group, four are found within women's

12. The New York School of Social Work and the Graduate School for Jewish Social Work. By December, 1940, the New York School of Social Work was affiliated with Columbia University, and the Graduate School for Jewish Social Work had been closed.

13. The one recent exception to this is the Montreal School of Social Work which is independently controlled and financed although utilizing the facilities of McGill University and having a close relationship to it. This presents a very informal type of affiliation.

14. University of California, Indiana University, University of Iowa, University of Michigan, University of Minnesota, University of North Carolina, Ohio State University, University of Oklahoma, and the University of Washington.

15. University of Cincinnati and the University of Louisville.

16. Graduate School for Jewish Social Work and the New York School of Social Work.

17. Atlanta University, Boston College, Boston University, Bryn Mawr College, University of Buffalo, Carnegie Institute of Technology, Catholic University, University of Chicago, University of Denver, Fordham University, Loyola University, National Catholic School of Social Service, Northwestern University, Pennsylvania School of Social Work, University

colleges, three, however, admitting men as well as women students.[18] Three receive a substantial amount of state aid.[19] Recently two Canadian schools which had previously been members of the Association were re-affiliated with the group.[20]

During the present period of expansion in the public social services the total number of students enrolled in the schools of social work has almost doubled. On November 1, 1932, 3112 students were registered in the schools, and on November 1, 1938, 6109 were enrolled.[21] This expansion in enrollment took place by extending facilities within the existing schools and not by an increase in the number of schools reporting. The greatest increase in enrollment within a single year's time was between November 1, 1932, and November 1, 1933, when the total enrollment increased from 3112 to 5255. During the same period the number of schools reporting increased by one (Appendix B, Table VII).

Comparisons of the number of students majoring in social work are more significant, since the total enrollment figures noted above include students electing isolated courses but not specifically preparing for employment in the field. Students from other professional schools or departments taking occasional courses are

---

of Pittsburgh, St. Louis University, Simmons College, Smith College, University of Southern California, Tulane University, Washington University, Western Reserve University, and the College of William and Mary.

18. Bryn Mawr College, Margaret Morrison College of Carnegie Institute of Technology, Simmons College, and Smith College (admits women only).

19. University of Pittsburgh, Pennsylvania School of Social Work, and the College of William and Mary.

20. University of Toronto and the Montreal School of Social Work.

21. On November 1, 1940, there were enrolled 6257.

found in this group. In 1932, as indicated, the total number of students majoring in social work in the 24 schools was 2863. In 1938 the number had increased to 4956, with 35 schools reporting.[22] The peak enrollment of students majoring in social work was reached in 1935, with 5296 students reported (Appendix B, Table VIII).

The trend from undergraduate to graduate enrollment in the schools is a further significant development of the period. In 1937 the American Association of Schools of Social Work voted that by October 1, 1939, all member schools should offer the professional curriculum at the graduate level only. For many years prior to the change in membership requirements, there had been a gradual reduction in the number of schools offering the curriculum at the undergraduate level. Applicant schools had been encouraged to establish curriculums only at the graduate level. This trend is indicated in Appendix B, Table VIII, which shows full-time students majoring in social work increasing from 1534 in 1932 to 2356 in 1938.[23] In 1932, of the 1534, 936 were graduate, 563 were undergraduate, and 35 were otherwise classified, probably as adult specials.[24] In 1938, of 2356 full-time students, 2147 were graduate, 193 were undergraduate, and 16 were otherwise classified.[25]

These trends have paralleled the expansion in the public social services, and their relation to personnel needs is clear. These services have placed upon the schools a demand for personnel which has taxed re-

22. In 1940 the number was 5273, with 40 schools reporting.

23. In 1940, the number was 2672.

24. "Adult specials" are defined as "mature individuals with experience in the field of social work, lacking academic requirements specified for entering students."

25. In 1940, of 2672 full-time students, 2622 were graduate, 38 undergraduate and 12 otherwise classified.

sources. They have also occasioned changes in the character of the student body and thus in the responsibilities carried by the schools.

FUNCTION AND SCOPE OF SERVICES STUDIED

The analysis of the content of the jobs in certain of the public social services and of the training needs for these jobs is the central focus of the present study. Old age insurance, unemployment compensation and employment service, public assistance, and child welfare have been selected for review.[26] The responsibilities of personnel in these services can best be understood when related to the function of the services. The importance of personnel is clearly apparent when the number and classification of employees is reviewed. It is appropriate, therefore, by way of introduction to the substance of the study, to consider briefly the function and scope of the services, and in the interest of clarification this will be done service by service. Subsequently the description of job content and skills and knowledge needed will be presented.

Old Age Insurance.—Under the Old Age Insurance provisions of the Social Security Act, benefits become available to workers who reach the age of sixty-five years.[27] These benefits are limited to workers in the covered industries and depend upon the amount earned in wages during the individual's working years after

26. The services were studied prior to the passage of the amendments to the Social Security Act of 1939, which provided survivors' benefits and changed the title of the Act to "Old Age and Survivors' Insurance Benefits," 53 *Stat* 1360.

27. Social Security Act, Titles II and VIII, 49 *Stat* 620, August 14, 1935, as amended 53 *Stat* 1360, August 10, 1939. Title VIII made a part of Internal Revenue Code.

1936. In case of death, his estate is a limited beneficiary.[28] By amendment to the act in 1939, survivors' benefits were also provided, and the revised program became known as Old Age and Survivors' Insurance.[29] By July 1938 coverage extended to 30,154,024 workers.[30]

The system is federally financed and operated. Eligibility to coverage and the initiation of claims have been decentralized and administered through 327 local field offices under the supervision of twelve regional offices.[31] The maintenance of the worker's identity through a "social security number" and wage record has necessarily been centralized and recorded in the office of the Social Security Board in Baltimore.[32]

On February 9, 1939, 1643 individuals were employed in the administration of old age insurance, of whom 309 were managers, 152 were assistant managers, and 1182 were classified as "other employees," including claims interviewer, personnel clerk, junior typists, and senior typists (Appendix B, Table I). As the recent amend-

28. Since January, 1937, lump sum payments have been made to covered workers at 65 and to heirs or estates of deceased workers. On August 10, 1939, lump sum payments to covered workers who have reached their sixty-fifth year were discontinued. Such payment on behalf of workers who die after 1939 will be made when the worker meets certain qualifications and leaves no survivor entitled to benefit for the month in which the death occurred. Fourth Annual Report of the Social Security Board, 1939, p. 29.

29. 53 *Stat* 1360, August 10, 1939.

30. Based on reports of 1937 wages. Fourth Annual Report of the Social Security Board, 1939, p. 24. The Social Security Board estimates that the cumulative total of employees for whom taxable wages have been reported for one or more of the calendar years 1937, 1938, and 1939 is some 41,500,000. Fifth Annual Report of the Social Security Board, 1940, p. 30.

31. On June 30, 1940, the number of field offices was 469 not including 13 branch offices and itinerant service for 1,705 localities. *Ibid.*, p. 121.

32. Eventually to be located in Washington.

ments to the Social Security Act are implemented,[33] it is anticipated that the number of field offices will be increased from 327 to over 600, with a corresponding increase in personnel.

Unemployment Compensation and Employment Service.—The organic relationship of unemployment compensation and employment service and the administrative integration which has been effected justify the discussion of the two services as one in the present study.

Unemployment compensation is dependent upon legislation in the states. The Social Security Act provides a payroll tax on covered industries, 90 per cent of which is returned to those states enacting unemployment compensation laws which include certain minimum standards.[34] By federal statute in 1933 a system of grants-in-aid to the states was established for the development of state employment services.[35] The two services have been integrated administratively in Washington since March 30, 1937, and are now parts of a single federal bureau.[36]

33. Advancing the date of payment of continuing benefits, and the change to Old Age and Survivors' Insurance.

34. Social Security Act, Title III and Title IX, 49 *Stat* 620, August 10, 1935.

35. The Wagner-Peyser Act in 1933 established the United States Employment Service in the Department of Labor and with the coöperation and financial assistance of the federal government made available for the establishment of state services. Wagner-Peyser Act; 48 *Stat* 113, June 6, 1933.

36. "That in order to achieve integrated federal action in rendering assistance to the states in the administration of state employment services, the Social Security Board, through the Bureau of Unemployment Compensation, and the Department of Labor, through the United States Employment Service shall act as if they were a single agency, jointly and concurrently, with respect to all matters affecting a state employment service including detailed plans of such employment service financed under the Wagner-Peyser and the Social Security Act. Resolution No. 1, under the agreement of March 30, 1937, between the Secretary of

Logically the functioning of unemployment compensation and employment service are linked together. While under such a plan of federal-state coöperation, the standards of unemployment compensation will vary from state to state, the systems provide in general for eligibility based on the industry in which the worker is employed, the period of employment, wages earned, availability for employment and a waiting period prior to benefit payment and a limited number of weeks during which benefits are paid.[37] In unemployment compensation administration, regardless of the type of law, the state agency will carry the following responsibilities: (a) determination of employer coverage; (b) collection of contributions; (c) payment of benefits, including contacts with claimants through the employment office, proof of eligibility to benefit, determination of amount and duration of benefit, and placement work; (d) adjudication of disputed claims; (e) financial controls and records, including employer's ledger and employee records; (f) research and statistics, including statistics for merit rating if the law so provides.[38]

The efficient operation of unemployment compensation calls for the application of a work test to check malingering and the greatest possible reduction of time lost by idle workers in order that insurance reserves may be conserved.[39] The employment service has become the agency through which continued unemployment is es-

---

Labor and the Social Security Board." Atkinson, Odencrantz and Deming, *op. cit.*, p. 80.

37. Comparison of State Unemployment Compensation Laws as of March 1, 1940, Bureau of Employment Security, May 1940.

38. Social Security Board, "A Plan of Personnel Procedure for a State Unemployment Compensation Agency," November, 1936, p. 4.

39. Atkinson, Odencrantz and Deming, *op. cit.*, p. 39.

tablished by periodical reporting and through which efforts are made to return the individual to gainful employment.

In June, 1939, the estimated number of covered workers with wage credits under state unemployment compensation acts was 27,980,000, and the number of subject employers was 719,600. Forty-eight states, Alaska, Hawaii, and the District of Columbia are now covered by such legislation.[40] The systems are administered by the states through local offices established at suitable points and are subject to federal supervision under the terms of the Social Security Act.

The total number of persons employed in the administration of unemployment compensation and the employment service on May 1, 1939, was 36,246, of whom 57.1 per cent were in unemployment compensation, and 42.9 per cent in the employment service (Appendix B, Table II). Data from the employment service covering principally the third quarter of 1939 (although a few are for other quarters) indicate that 276 were classified as state administrative, 934 as local administrative, 2531 as senior interviewers, and 4534 as junior interviewers (Appendix B, Table III). It was not possible to obtain figures for the classification of state unemployment compensation services, but it is estimated that between 5 and 15 per cent would fall in the operating, supervisory, or administrative levels and the balance in clerical personnel. The fact that the personnel in the two services is interchangeable in many administrations and payrolls arbitrarily charged to one or the other in many instances minimizes the usefulness of these estimates. No attempt can be made to present the number

40. Fourth Annual Report of the Social Security Board, 1939, p. 237.

of federal positions until the integration of the Bureau of Unemployment Compensation and the United States Employment Service is complete.[41]

Public Assistance.—Public assistance includes state and local services providing aid to the blind, aid to dependent children, and old age assistance under the Social Security Act.[42] General relief, which since 1936 has been a state or local function, is a fourth category of "public assistance" but is designated as "general assistance" to distinguish it from the forms of assistance within the scope of the Social Security Act. The system of grants-in-aid to the states instituted by the federal statute has made possible the establishment or development of programs of assistance to the aged in 48 states, the District of Columbia, Hawaii and Alaska, to the blind, and to dependent children in 42 of these jurisdictions. In June, 1939, jurisdictions coöperating in these programs made payments to 1,800,000 aged, to 298,000 families on behalf of 718,000 dependent children, and to 44,000 blind persons.[43] These forms of aid are administratively integrated in many of the states and are known as "public assistance." [44] The amount of assistance payment in relation to established need varies from category to category

41. The functions of the United States Employment Service, formerly a part of the Department of Labor, were consolidated with the unemployment compensation functions of the Social Security Board as the Bureau of Unemployment Compensation by the President's Reorganization Plan No. 1, April 25, 1939, in accordance with the Reorganization Act of 1939.

42. Social Security Act, *op. cit.*, Titles I, IV, and X.

43. Fourth Annual Report of the Social Security Board, 1939, p. 79.

44. During 1939-1940, the number of needy aged who received assistance approximated 2,200,000 in 51 jurisdictions; the number of dependent children who received aid was approximately 1,000,000 in 42 jurisdictions, and the number of blind granted assistance was approximately 55,000 in 43 jurisdictions. Fifth Annual Report of the Social Security Board, 1940, p. 8.

58   Education for the Public Social Services

and from state to state, inasmuch as the Federal Act leaves with the states the responsibility for determination of need.

The functions of a public assistance agency generally include the following: (a) to determine eligibility of those applying for assistance according to statute, regulation, and established policy; (b) to explore the nature and degree of need of those found eligible; (c) to administer assistance to those found eligible, including the use of constructive services for the care and rehabilitation of individuals requiring such services and for the prevention of future social dependency; (d) to study the social and economic problems indicated by the situations of recipients of aid, and to make recommendations to the proper authorities as to possible means of amelioration; (e) to coöperate with other agencies in the community in the development of more adequate planning for the care of those in need, who are not eligible for assistance under the existing statutes; to develop better public understanding of problems relating to the administration of public assistance and of methods of meeting such problems.[45]

Data concerning the number of persons employed in the administration of public assistance are not centrally available, but in an effort to secure this information for the purpose of the study a special questionnaire was sent to all the states, asking the total number of public assistance personnel employed. Only thirty states replied to the questionnaire. Yet a few general figures may be drawn from these replies. In fifteen states where the agencies administering public assistance (in a few cases,

45. "School-Agency Relationships," Bureau of Public Assistance, Social Security Board, Division of Technical Training, January 25, 1939, p. 3.

old age assistance alone) do not administer general relief, there was an average of one visitor (investigator or case worker) to every 7100 in the general population. In fifteen states where the public assistance agency does administer general relief there was an average of one visitor to every 4300 in the general population. If the latter figure is projected to cover a population of 125,000,000 it would indicate that there are approximately 25,000 visitors employed in public assistance in the United States. Returns also indicated that in the thirty states there was an average of one case work supervisor to every thirteen visitors, and of one county director to every seven visitors.

Child Welfare Services.—The services to children included in the present study are one group of those provided by the Social Security Act which has established grants-in-aid to the states to assist in meeting the cost of child welfare services, of services for crippled children, and of maternal and child health services. The child welfare services extend to the protection and care of homeless, dependent, and neglected children and children in danger of becoming delinquent, and for development in areas predominantly rural and for the encouragement and assistance of adequate methods of community child welfare organization in areas predominantly rural and other areas of special need. The services for crippled children include medical and "other services." The administration of these grants is within the jurisdiction of the United States Children's Bureau.[46]

Programs of direct care for children by the states or of supervision of programs locally administered by juvenile courts, child welfare, or local welfare authorities

46. Social Security Act, *op. cit.*, Title V.

are likewise focused to the concept of specialized service to children in their own homes or in foster homes. These programs must be considered along with the child welfare services under the Social Security Act to give a picture of the public services to children. Their omission from the present study was determined by reason of necessity to limit the scope and by reason of the belief that the program of services made possible under the Social Security Act has so stimulated and supplemented existing child welfare programs in areas not previously served as to constitute a new and almost unique contribution to the whole field.

By June, 1938, the programs of child welfare services were functioning in 47 jurisdictions reaching 43,000 individual children, and the programs of service to crippled children were functioning in 49 jurisdictions where the number of such children on the state registers was 164,798.[47] The number of persons employed in child welfare services on January 3, 1939, was 686, of whom 266 were employed on state and 420 on local staffs (Appendix B, Table IV).[48] The wide variety of practice possible under the plan is shown in the distribution of the personnel in the various states. On July 1, 1939, the number of social workers employed in the crippled children's services was 70, including 44 medical social workers.[49]

47. Annual Report, Secretary of Labor, 1939.

48. By July 1, 1940, the number increased to 735 of whom 240 were members of state staffs and 495 of local staffs. Twenty-eighth Annual Report of the Secretary of Labor for the Fiscal Year ended June 30, 1940, p. 177.

49. *Ibid.*, 1939, p. 132. By July 1, 1940, the number had increased to 77, of whom 49 were medical social workers. *Ibid.*, 1940, p. 173.

THE RELATIONSHIP OF THE SCHOOLS TO THE SERVICES

Professional practice provides a content which is studied and clarified by the professional schools until elements are discovered which have a general application and can therefore be incorporated into the educational program. A close inter-play between school and field is therefore essential if the educational program is to be kept vital and effective in relation to the area for which it is preparing students.

The nature of this relationship is not easy to develop. As indicated in a previous paragraph, the first schools grew out of the interest of social agencies in securing personnel better equipped for agency responsibilities. Thus the focus of agency objectives emerged in these programs. As the schools were affiliated with universities, the more general character of the educational process was established. Yet, at intervals, pressure from the agencies for greater and greater attention to their specific needs has been intensified.

The expansion of the social services under governmental auspices has heightened this influence. Programs quickly extended throughout the 3,000 counties of the United States and administered by personnel hastily recruited have focused particular needs within the agency setting which have been urged upon the schools as essentials. Efforts to clarify common content were complicated by this sudden expansion of agencies with function undefined, dominated by inexperienced and sometimes "partisan" leadership, confronted by mass loads, and staffed with personnel selected without a background of similar experience. Schools of social work with a long tradition and a rich experience behind them have been able to study and evaluate these pressures. Some institutions, however, have developed special "training programs for this and that," as for example, one university which has offered a complete curriculum in "social security administration." At best there has been confusion and doubt.

Schools of medicine, public health, law, and engineering are similarly related to practice in their respective fields and have felt like pressures from time to time. When 'the White House Conference of 1930 stimulated the interest in maternal health and infant care, a more adequate preparation in the field of obstetrics became a necessity for medical practitioners. Yet this was not advocated as a substitute for the general well-rounded training in the medical schools, but as a complement to such preparation. The development of administrative agencies with quasi-judicial functions has stimulated the interest in administrative law, but the general preparation for legal practice which is inherent in the philosophy of the law schools has not been crippled in favor of specific preparation for a particular field of practice. In social work, new foci of interest are not as easy to evaluate for several reasons. In the development of the profession, the common or general content in the field has received too little attention; the special content leading to agency placements has received too much. An example of this is the still frequent scrutiny by employing executives of the particular circumstances under which the student's field practice has been completed. Recognition of common content in classroom theory has not been easily followed by recognition of common content in field work practice. Another reason for difficulty in evaluating pressure is the rapidly changing character of social work programs, which are greatly influenced by economic and social forces of the time. Furthermore, professional education for the field has a short history of forty years, at least ten years of which have been developed in a period of profound social change. Perhaps these reasons account for the fact that schools of social work are more directly influenced than other professional schools by practitioner groups.

The school curriculums are to an extent an expression of the field, and as the field broadens the school curriculums will broaden. The relationship is dynamic, developed around a central core of method which is inherent in the practice of social work. It cannot be the dynamic which shifts with the wind. In some instances, the schools have been ahead of the field of practice and have prepared students in advance of present practice as developments have been predicted by the nature of the need for which a provision was made. The level of any service is dependent upon available personnel, protection from the influence of partisan politics, and the support of public opinion. And where these or one of these forces has seemed to fasten a limited concept of practice upon a given program, the profession and the professional schools cannot but keep the ultimate objectives of the service in mind.

The inter-relationship of field and school has occasioned the present examination of the needs of the field and the resources of the schools. As indicated in previous paragraphs, the selection of services for special study depended upon the necessity to limit scope to those of immediate significance to the problem of personnel needs in the total span of public social services. Services to delinquents and adult offenders, to the mentally ill and to the physically handicapped, and services of a supervisory and administrative nature long associated with public welfare programs constitutes an area for which the states and the local authorities carry responsibility at the present time. Their inclusion here would greatly expand the number of individuals served and the number of persons employed in the administration. It is important for the reader to keep in mind that data presented in the following chapters are selective rather than inclusive, so far as the entire field of public social services is concerned.

Within the services selected for study, there is a variety in scope and function; yet there are also common elements. In each can be identified the job by which the service is implemented and the job by which the service is directed. The first was designated by the study staff as the "operating level" and the second as the "supervisory and administrative level." The designation of these "levels," however, should not obscure the basic content of performance in the services, which is the primary focus of the study.

In turning attention to the content of practice and the skills and knowledge needed, it is important to bear in mind that some of the services are too new to permit descriptions of the jobs that tell more than a routine story. Present practices throw light on future trends and suggest the direction in which the services are developing. The chapters which follow emphasize the service rendered within a particular setting. Specialists and consultants attached to the services are not considered, in the interest of focusing attention upon the general content for which the personnel is responsible. Because the "operating level" is closely linked with the function of the administering agency, it is first to be presented in that relationship. Subsequently the training needs, the content of the supervisory and administrative job, and the training needs indicated are discussed.

The subsequent sections concerned with the offering of the schools will suggest the present trends in curriculum development. And in relating these trends the reader will be able to determine something of the contribution to the public social services to be anticipated from the professional schools of social work.

Chapter Five

PUBLIC SOCIAL SERVICES:
THE OPERATING LEVEL

THE CONTENT OF THE JOB

SERVICES IN AN EARLY developmental stage do not lend themselves to a study process in which job descriptions are stated in specific terms and paralleled by requisite skills and knowledge for each function. When organic change is made in a program, the concept of the service is subject to review. Changes which agencies believe to be inherent in the development of adequate service but yet not identified in the job performed can not be similarly observed. A fair analysis under such circumstances focuses attention on the direction in which the services are moving and thus the direction which the concept of the "job to be done" is taking.

The material which follows relates both to job descriptions and to the skills and knowledge believed by the personnel interviewed to be essential and desirable for satisfactory job performance. Necessarily the group interviewed covered a wide range of educational and professional preparation and it was not possible to classify material according to the experience or educational background or performance of the persons from whom the information was obtained. The nature of the group interviewed should be kept in mind as the following summary is considered.

Old Age Insurance.—Stated very simply, the establishment of eligibility to coverage, the maintenance of the worker's identity throughout his years of employment, and the establishment and payment of claims constitute the essential processes in the administration of old age insurance. In each local office through which the individual beneficiaries are served, the responsibility for these processes is in the hands of interviewers known variously as "claims interviewer," "personnel clerk," "junior typists," "senior typists," "assistant manager," or in a small office the manager himself.[1]

The assignment of a "Social Security Number" to the applicant is effected in the initial interview. For this purpose, information concerning his family composition, his age, and his employment and wages is secured. The system is interpreted and his rights and responsibilities explained. The importance of the educational process from the initial stage of application to the filing of claims is great and has been frequently stressed by the Social Security Board.[2] According to the study findings, however,

1. "Since January 1, 1940, claims interviewing in field offices has been carried by claims interviewers."—Letter from John J. Corson, Director of Old Age and Survivors' Insurance, December 31, 1940.

2. For example, note the following quotation from the Second Annual Report, Social Security Board, p. 48: "Education also must be continued to impress upon workers the uses and importance of their account numbers. In some cases a worker doubtless has applied for and received more than one number. It is possible that in other cases numbers have been shifted from one employee to another. To avoid confusion in the records, with a chance that the full wage credit due a worker may not be attributed to him, it is essential that a worker holds only one number and reports it accurately to his employer. Education of employees in the procedures to be used in filing claims also constitutes an area in which experience should promote efficient service."

the issuance of Social Security numbers has to date been regarded as a simple clerical task.[3]

Claims-taking is a further function to be administered. It is the function of the claims-taker to see that the claimant gets his full due, and this depends in large part upon effective interpretation to the individual. Although claims are finally determined in the Washington and Baltimore offices, the local staff must make all the necessary contacts and assume responsibility for adequate preparation of the claims before they are sent to Washington and Baltimore. A mass of documentary data must be checked and incorporated. Proof of identity and of age must be secured, as must proof of death in case of lump sum payments and of survivors' benefits under the revised act. In the case of a widow, it must be established that she has been living with the insured individual; and in the case of children or parents, both the fact of dependency and the fact of relationship must be proved. The remarriage of widows must be reported. Whether the claims personnel is responsible for these data is not yet determined.

The claims interviewer must be thoroughly aware of the legal rights of the applicant and those of the applicant's relatives. He must be alert to all means by which necessary proofs of the facts governing eligibility may be secured. He must be able to discourage useless claims, but also to see that all valid claims are explored.

Wherever necessary, the office staff assists the applicant

3. "It has been standard practice in all field offices for more than a year for the account number personnel to instruct applicants carefully as to the purpose, value, and use of the account number. The applicant's attention is directed to a poster chart found in each field office showing graphically the relationship between the account number and the all-important wage record." Letter from John J. Corson, *op. cit.*

to complete his claim. Thus the claims personnel obtains all the relevant details from the applicants and may suggest the sources of documentary proof. Home visiting is sometimes involved in this process. Meticulous care in preparing claims minimizes the number of rejections and will obviate appeals in many instances, although of course, appeals from administrative decision are provided. In some instances, the claims personnel is asked to advise concerning expenditure of benefits. Some such requests are referred to managers, but the claims personnel is expected to meet many of these requests. After benefit payments begin, beneficiaries will undoubtedly seek advice concerning the wisdom of ceasing work in order to claim annuities. A combination of interviewing and clerical duties constitutes one of the chief characteristics of the service at the present time.

The nature of the work load of the service is changing rapidly as the amendment to the act providing for survivors' benefits goes into effect.[4] Problems concerning the care of dependent children, foster care and guardianship, may confront the service with the need to provide for a function not originally anticipated. This has important bearing on personnel selection in the future. It also suggests that the present study might well be followed by similar inquiry which would reveal the impact of these changes upon training needs.

Typical of the job as observed during the study are the following two descriptions given by individuals interviewed during the study:

1. An interviewer in the office of a large city distributes work for other interviewers, maintains folders on each claim, and interviews claimants who come to the office. Many claims

4. Public No. 379, 76 Congress, August 10, 1939.

are handled by mail. The interviewer writes letters to secure proofs of age, distributes forms to claimants as needed, and gives instructions as to the filling out of the forms. She handles telephone inquiries concerning the Act and often talks to lawyers about claims of estates which they are handling. She checks over birth certificates or other public records, and looks up letters of administration issued on estates. If claims fail to materialize, she analyzes vital statistics records and follows up possible claims by telephone or letter according to circumstances. She visits the homes of claimants if necessary to avoid having claims remain incomplete in the office. She maintains a tickler on account number files in order to send notices to those persons who have reached the age of 65. Workers in her group average between 15 and 20 desk interviews a week and about ten telephone calls a day.

2. A "personnel clerk" (who is also assistant manager) in a small office in a thinly populated area averages about two to three days a week in the field. In the office he rechecks and reviews account number applications to see that they are kept up to date; checks claims which have been prepared for transmittal to Washington; interviews employers and employees who call at the office for any purpose other than obtaining account numbers; keeps a file of carbon copies of letters which the collector of internal revenue has written concerning employees' account numbers which were missing from employers' reports; keeps a file of unidentified names referred by the Records Division for additional information; corresponds regarding all phases of the work; and in addition, assumes the manager's responsibilities during his absence two days each week. When out of the office he travels through the eighteen counties in the district, visits employers and employees for the purpose of collecting additional information concerning unidentified accounts, and for the purpose of general educational work. He also visits claimants and assists in filing claims, sometimes arranges speaking dates for the manager, visits the newspapers, speaks on broadcasts concerning the program, and in general conducts a traveling office of the board.

In a few cases, the problems presented involve human adjustments which require a staff skilled in social treatment as well as in social investigation. One manager cited the instance of a widow whose situation made her the logical beneficiary for the entire lump sum payment. The claims of her parents-in-law to their portion versus the needs of her unborn child produced a set of circumstances requiring professional skill and understanding on the part of the worker. Likewise a knowledge of the physical and emotional disabilities of aged persons was believed to be desirable. The importance of adequate medical care for this group was also stressed. Understanding as far as possible the effect of major crises of bereavement was also cited as helpful.

Social problems appearing in the applicant group already constitute a considerable responsibility for referral to other social and medical agencies. This task will be more significant as the payment of a number of small annuities begins and as survivors' benefits are administered. No clear-cut administrative policy with reference to these problems has as yet been defined.[5]

5. "Administrative policies with reference to the social problems in the applicant group have been the subject of detailed study for well over a year. This study has included extended conferences with the Bureau of Public Assistance, the Children's Bureau, and representative State Public Welfare administrators.

The intention of the Bureau of Old Age and Survivors' Insurance is to refer many of these social problems to agencies prepared to deal with them, rather than to attempt to equip itself to treat them. Cases giving rise to such problems constitute a relatively small proportion of the total cases handled by the staff of this bureau; the referral of these cases should assist in developing the already existing welfare agencies in the community. Such problems arise most often in claims involving the guardianship of minor children and incompetent adults. Such cases are referred to social agencies in accordance with plans being worked out state by state with State Welfare Departments in consultation with the Bureau of Public Assistance. Some cases are dealt with by members of the State Welfare Department's staff; others are referred to local units of these

Unemployment Compensation and Employment Service.—Although unemployment compensation and employment service are treated jointly in this study, it seems appropriate to clarify the function of each service. In some jurisdictions, however, a separate emphasis will hardly be distinguishable. For example, in one state visited, employee classifications were made for budget purposes only and the personnel in the services was largely interchangeable.

In the employment service the duties of the junior and senior interviewers include the following: the registration of "applicants" for positions always involves the classification of the applicant's job possibility and may involve some vocational guidance. Each applicant must be given a primary and often a secondary classification under one of the 7,000 occupations listed in the United States Employment Service Code.[6] Atkinson, Odencrantz, and Deming have stressed the importance of this job.[7] Fairly complete information is recorded on the registration form. To prepare an adequate record it may

---

departments, or to local agencies. When the local office of the Bureau of Old Age and Survivors' Insurance learns that a local social agency knows a family from which an insurance claim has been received, and that claim presents a social problem, the local manager of the Bureau of Old Age and Survivors' Insurance is expected to call upon the executive of the social agency for such pertinent information as may be readily available to that agency. All requests involving independent inquiries by a social agency for the Bureau of Old Age and Survivors' Insurance are referred through Washington and the State Welfare Department for the present. It is the plan that such referrals may be made on the local level in the future in localities where there are agencies which can be recommended by the State Welfare Department as prepared to render this service."
—Letter from John J. Corson, *op. cit.*

6. "Occupational Titles and Codes for use in Public Employment Offices," *Employment Service Manual,* Series B and C. United States Employment Service, 1936.

7. Atkinson, Odencrantz, and Deming, *op. cit.,* pp. 297-298.

be necessary for the interviewer to check the applicant's references.

Receiving employers' orders for workers involves securing and recording detailed information. Applicants selected for recommendation to employers on the basis of their qualifications must then be reached either by telephone or mail. To verify placement, the employer is generally called in order to learn whether or not the applicant was accepted. This information may also be received from the applicant. After a given period of time, the interviewer telephones or writes to the employer to learn whether the worker is satisfactory. Field visiting stimulates the use of the Employment Service by employers and is also used to follow up placements or verify references or to obtain other information.

Although these duties are general and basic to Employment Service, considerable variation was observed. Most frequently, all functions were carried by the individual interviewer. In large offices where specialization exists, certain departments, especially the Junior Division or the Hard-To-Place Division carry definite responsibilities for vocational guidance. Trade tests are being used increasingly and are generally administered by interviewers. Data concerning employment trends and local working conditions are often gathered by the interviewer. In less well organized or in smaller offices, a large amount of clerical work also falls on the interviewer.

The following description of a typical task was furnished by one such interviewer:

"This interviewer is asked to supply 'a chemical engineer between 25 and 30, a college graduate of good moral character, pleasing personality, and supervisory caliber who does

not wear glasses and will work for $50 a week.' The inter-
viewer looks through his files for such an engineer; calls up
ten possibilities; finds that six are either working or cannot
be traced; interviews the four others, questions them about
their qualifications and sizes them up, keeping in his mind
the requirements. Three of these persons are then referred
to the employer to see if they are satisfactory, notes being
made as to the reasons for rejection of any of them. Annota-
tion is then made on the card of the man hired."

In most of the states visited, the interviewer may spend
a considerable portion of his time accepting claims for
unemployment compensation benefits. In fact, judging
from a few time studies, slightly less than one-fourth of
the interviewer's time is devoted to activities connected
with unemployment compensation. He secures from the
applicant the necessary information concerning his
claim, enters this information on appropriate forms, and
either sends it in to the state office or turns it over to the
local unemployment compensation official. Moreover,
time is consumed in interpreting unemployment compensation laws and rules to claimants and employers.
The function of preparing statements for the central
office in disputed or uncertain cases is usually the responsibility of the claims examiner, although in rare
cases it is assumed by the interviewer.

The work of the "claims examiner" in unemployment
compensation varies considerably from state to state.
The claim may be disputed either by the examiner or
by the employer. In states with employer-reserve laws or
significant merit-rating statutory provisions, the claims
review function is especially important, yet it exists
everywhere. Usually the major function of the claims
examiner is to conduct the first investigation into con-
tested cases by interviewing employers and workers, and

by attempting to secure additional information. The typical task includes reviewing claims cases to determine completeness of the record, establishing and verifying facts by telephone calls and interviews with employees and others, effecting adjustments, conducting hearings, informing attendants and witnesses of necessary documents, conferring with and advising employers and workers with reference to the unemployment compensation act; correcting, assembling, compiling and analyzing data concerning unemployment compensation; and checking claims for conformity with regulations and legal requirements.

After attempting to arrive at an agreement between employer and employee concerning the facts, the examiner forwards the claim, with a finding of facts and his recommendations, to the state central office for decision. The claims examiner considers general problems of eligibility, labor disputes and availability, refusal of suitable employment, termination of employment without sufficient cause, and misconduct in the course of employment. "Processing" of claims to determine whether necessary information is included before sending the claims to the central office is a function frequently assigned to claims examiners.

Decisions may be appealed by employer or employee to a referee or to a state appeal board. It is the examiner's function to prepare appeals for the claimant or any interested party who is dissatisfied with the decision. Infrequently, the legal process of prosecuting fraudulent claimants or delinquent taxpayers becomes the task of the examiners. Claims examiners in central offices usually specialize in different types of cases and carefully check field reports to determine whether the applicant is eligible on these points. Referrals to other agencies involved and a close relationship to other social services in the community are implied.

It is noteworthy that among the interviewers described by their superiors as the most promising, practically all stressed the occupational classification function in relation to a good placement job and subordinated the factual part of claims-taking to the interpretation of the law and to the assistance needed by many clients in determining their eligiblity under the law.

Public Assistance.—The administration of assistance may include general relief or a single one of the assistance "categories"—aid to the blind, aid to dependent children, old age assistance—or combinations of any or all of these services, in accordance with the law and administrative policy of the state and local agencies concerned. The duties involved in the administration at the operating level are carried by workers variously described as "junior visitor" or "senior visitor," "case worker" or "case investigator."

Junior and senior visitors are expected "to accept applications for public assistance, to make investigations and establish eligibility for public assistance, to maintain continuing contacts with recipients of public assistance, to accept complaints and where possible to effect adjustments on complaints and to assist applicants in applying for fair hearing when this service is desired; to render simple services to applicants and to call to the attention of the proper authority the need for specialized services to applicants; to keep accurate and current records and prepare reports; to modify and adjust provision made for recipients to changing circumstances; and to interpret the provisions of the plan to applicants for public assistance and to persons and agencies in the course of collateral contacts, reporting to the proper authority any need for special attention in relation to this aspect of the work of the agency." [8]

The range of activities carried by a visitor is thus very great. Eligibility to assistance according to agency policy must be determined, and recommendations concerning assistance grants and subsequent changes must also be prepared. The visitor has responsibility for developing a plan for the rehabilitation of the families under his care, for the recognition of causes other than financial need such as health needs, and for referral to other agencies offering special services not provided in the public assistance program, or in the absence of such agencies to develop the best possible plan for the families.

Eligibility is determined through social study or investigation which is "a careful inquiry into the circumstances of the applicant as they relate to the conditions of eligibility established by the state department, the accumulation of the best information available to substantiate his claim, the weighing and evaluation of this information as a reasonable basis for the determination of eligibility, and the decision to accept or refuse the application." [9] This process cannot be reduced to routine procedures, but involves the application of the essential skills of social case work and the use of discrimination which is required at every point.

The selection of candidates for CCC, certification to WPA, and referral to surplus commodities are frequently included among the visitor's responsibilities. There is

8. Guide to Public Assistance Administration, Bureau Circular No. 9, Bureau of Public Assistance, Social Security Board. September, 1940, Section 114, p. 1.

9. *Ibid.*, Section 300, p. 1.

also a great variety of activities connected with securing special information needed from time to time, such as occupational classification of beneficiaries, their health needs, and description of their housing and housekeeping habits incident to selecting tenants for public housing projects. The visitor also assists individual applicants in utilizing available resources for health, medical care, recreation, education, vocational adjustment, and employment to aid in the process of rehabilitation.

Referral to other agencies is accepted by administrative policy as an important part of the assistance program. In order to accomplish this satisfactorily, the worker needs a thorough knowledge of the social resources of the community; an ability to ascertain the needs of individuals and to make helpful suggestions to them; and an ability to interpret the pertinent facts known to the public assistance agency.

The number of cases carried by each visitor varies. In general it is agreed that even minimum standards cannot be maintained if the visitor is asked to carry more than 100 cases in an undifferentiated load. Continuing responsibility for 50 cases and investigation of 10 new cases per month constitute a maximum load if adequate standards are to be maintained. Beginning workers or those giving special services carry fewer cases.

The emphasis upon case work services varies greatly from agency to agency because of differences in administrative policy, in competence of the staff, in the attitude and equipment of the supervisors, and in resources to cover administrative costs in the agency.

Child Welfare Services.—The content of child welfare services must be considered from the standpoint of the emphasis in the federal program upon the rural or distressed areas in which these services function. Visitors who perform the operating functions in the services are usually assigned to county child welfare or public welfare departments. They may be asked to devote themselves to problems of neglected, defective, and delinquent children, to investigation of juvenile court cases, to improvement of undesirable home conditions, to the organization of community activities for the prevention of juvenile delinquency or for the care of dependent children, or to any combination of the above tasks.[10]

Social case work with children involves the process of social study with particular emphasis upon the special needs of children for adequate social, educational, and health supervision which is conducive to sound growth and development. The treatment process in case work is based on sound social study and is pointed toward the provisions of special health and social services which will increase the capacity of the child for normal development and which will secure for him the environment which permits this development.

To the child welfare worker, public relations is an important responsibility. Initially, she must interpret her case work services to county board, county director, and county judges who may be uninformed. Subsequently, she must engage in extensive planning for child welfare with private agencies, service clubs, or any other groups which can be interested. She will need to work with local physicians, public health nurses, the county medical society, and local and state health authorities

10. Child welfare services as discussed in this section constitute one of the three sub-sections of Title V, Social Security Act, which is administered by the United States Children's Bureau. Crippled children's services and maternal and child health service have special personnel needs which were not reviewed in the study.

and agencies. Moreover, most workers covered by this study function in rural areas and frequently on their own resources much of the time. The responsible nature of the job is clearly indicated.

Description of their activities by certain of the visitors interviewed during the study will illustrate the variety of tasks. One worker served primarily as consultant in a department of child welfare which was concerned with aid to dependent children, families without resources for care of children, transient families with children, and placement and supervision of children under foster care. She worked coöperatively with all the county staff members who were serving a medium-sized city area and, in addition, presented the program to service clubs and other organizations interested in child welfare problems in the community.

Another child welfare worker in an administration concerned both with assistance to families without financial resources and aid to dependent children and child welfare services was carrying 83 cases and working in an area as large as the state of Massachusetts. One of her major tasks was to plan for the care of children living at home but with parents at work and unable to provide suitable supervision. In cases involving aid to dependent children she was chiefly concerned with family rehabilitation and with special reference to health education and vocational guidance for the children.

Another worker described her responsibilities as including a limited "demonstration" case load of 25 problem cases and the coördination of existing social and health facilities in the county, since social workers in both the county welfare department and the relief administration, the parent-teachers' associations, the probation officers, and the school principals referred problems to her. She was also concerned with the development of new facilities, a general child welfare service in the community, a camp program, and a nursery project to care for children in a section where mothers were at work outside the home. In addition, she was chairman of the child welfare division of the local parent-teacher association. Another worker believed her major tasks to be the encouragement of the schools to refer problem cases to her and the follow-up work for crippled children, especially where behavior disorders were involved.

The job of the worker who serves a district including several counties is similar to that of the worker in the county except that she must deal with officials of several counties and probably has less opportunity to work closely with organizations in the various communities in her area.

These descriptions of job content, although necessarily brief, summarize the responsibilities inherent in the jobs of workers at the service or "operating level" in the four programs, and they present material for the analysis of common and special training needs.

REQUISITE SKILLS AND KNOWLEDGE FOR THE OPERATING JOB

Common Skills and Knowledge.—It is clear from the findings of the study that the personnel in the services identify certain skills and knowledge which are common to all the services and certain skills and knowledge which are specific to each particular service. These have been presented in their direct relationship to job descriptions, without thought to the educational methods or to specific experience through which they may be developed. It will remain for a later chapter to discuss these aspects of the problem. The following paragraphs present first the common needs in the services and later the special needs which have been described in terms of specific agency function.

Knowledge of the Organization of the Social Services: In each of the services, an understanding of the structure and organization of the service and of related social and health services in the community is essential. This understanding begins with the knowledge of the statute establishing the program. As the responsibility of the public agency is defined by law, its statutory basis is fundamental. The findings of the present study emphasized again and again the importance of knowing the law under which the agency operates.

Some of the workers interviewed expressed only the need to know the particular statutes covering the agency in which he was employed, such as "public assistance" or "unemployment compensation." Others recognized the larger scope of the Social Security Act and its relationship to state acts required for implementation. Be that as it may, the study material indicates that the "broader perspective" which is desired by many is in part related to the meaning and significance of the statute in relation to other statutes, both federal and state, which may affect the service.

The recognition of the place of the social services in modern society and of the place of the particular service in which the employee is functioning seems to be a need common to all the services studied. This involves a knowledge of the structure of government, the development of the public social services over a period of time, and the responsibilities they carry at the present time. It also involves an understanding of the extent of development prior to the passage of the Social Security Act, the limitations experienced by states and local communities in attempting to meet expanding needs, and the mosaic into which the provisions of the act were fitted in order to provide a minimum of economic security to specific groups within the accepted framework of federal, state, and local relationships.

Furthermore, in all services, workers should possess a general acquaintance with the program of the social and health agencies functioning in the community if referrals to other agencies are to be made properly. They must possess some knowledge of the principles on which eligibility in other agencies is based. Some of this information is obtainable on the job, but to acquire all of it in this way is very difficult. A lack of information on this point may lead to confusion and misunderstanding on the part of applicants.

Acceptance of Agency Function: Acceptance of function is not limited to knowledge of the statute alone. It suggests the importance of knowing the relation of one service to others and the acceptance of these relationships by the workers. As one worker in public assistance expressed the need, it is fundamental to know "what the agency is for" and "what it is trying to do" and "where it relates to other services." This is in contrast to a philosophy of administration which subscribes to meeting all needs, "whoever comes, whatever the request."

The personnel clerk or field assistant in old age insurance, the interviewer or claims examiner in unemployment compensation and employment service, and the visitor in public assistance and child welfare carry important responsibilities in meeting applicants who request service. Applicants must be received in a way that conveys respect for them and interest in them so that they will feel the worker's understanding of their situation. The needs must be met so far as possible through the resources of the service or referrals to other services. The worker must avoid an intimate relationship, must refrain from criticizing any personal shortcomings of the applicant and from identifying the applicant with his dependence or unemployment; he must also avoid an emotional identification of himself with the problems of each individual applicant. During the course of the study the "inquiry and information-giving" function which has been the sole characteristic of much of the old age insurance administration was challenged by many alert and critical officials. But even in its simplest form, this task involves an objective and unbiased attitude on the part of the worker and the recognition of budget limitation and eligibility rules in the service and the acceptance of the client with whom he works.

Again, in the unemployment compensation administration the worker's own attitude toward unionism, toward sub-standard employment, toward what is "suitable employment" is beside the question as he meets the unemployed worker. It is his function to establish beyond all reasonable doubt the right of the worker to claim compensation and to appraise objectively his capacities for future employment so that a satisfactory placement can be made. The element of self-discipline which enters into any job is great, but it is believed to be especially important on the part of a worker who is serving the public as an agent of the governmental authority. Differentiation in clientele cannot be made, and all who come must be served.

Fundamental in the process in public assistance is the meeting of individual needs; the recognition of environmental factors and individual capacity; and assistance given in a way to conserve rather than to diminish the client's ability for self-help. The acceptance of behavior and the limits placed upon the agency to meet need require a disciplined approach which is very important. A capacity for sound judgment is also involved in the service, and a sense of responsibility is inherent.

The data collected from the interviews indicated that no one of the services can function in relation to the beneficiary unless skill is exercised in recognizing situations with which the agency cannot deal and in an intelligent referral to agencies able to serve him. The body of knowledge relating to this subject is common to all the services and transferable from the one to the other.

Agency Organization and Procedure: A knowledge of office and administrative practices is definitely required in all the services. Office deportment, methods of writing and filing information, clearance of letters and policy questions through supervisory or administrative personnel, and the plan of receiving applicants and visitors are important. Effective use of written English is necessary for the preparation of case records by the visitor in public assistance and child welfare, for disputed claims statements by the unemployment compensation claims examiners, for notes on registrants by the employment office interviewers, and for letters by the old age insurance office staff. In addition, workers at each level in the services need to be able to write letters which are clear and cogent.

Some ability to classify and analyze administrative data of various types is essential. By this is not meant an acquaintance with the specialized techniques taught in courses in social or economic statistics; but rather an ability to determine under what categories data should be placed in order to achieve a workmanlike report of office activities. For instance, there is a frequent call for reports on numbers and types of placements, on classification within various categories of public assistance, and on claims in old age insurance and unemployment compensation. Adeptness in making simple arithmetical calculations is closely connected with analytical skill, and is much to be desired.

These requirements relate to the acceptance of office discipline and routine and to the ability of the worker to master rules of office procedure in order to carry out his own function adequately. It is not suggested here that such a quality is peculiar to functioning in the social services, since large-scale operations in private business present many of the same demands. One factor perhaps differentiates the worker in the public social services. The responsibility to the body politic, which is inherent in the function of the agency, imposes the obligation to accept procedure which is necessary to this relationship. For individuals trained or experienced in agencies not answerable to the body politic, the adjustment has often been difficult. "The field needs professional workers who have something better than the usual impatience with tasks and burdens imposed by administration." [11]

Related to the acceptance of office routine is the worker's need to understand his own opportunities and obli-

11. Fred K. Hoehler, American Public Welfare Association, at Annual Meeting, American Association of Schools of Social Work, January, 1939.

gations as defined in the personnel procedures. This is important in many respects because of the close relationship between his role as a worker and his role as a citizen. Here it is interesting to call attention to the passage of the Hatch Act prohibiting political activity on the part of federal employees and the widespread implications for personnel in the public social services.[12]

Professional Attitude: Whether or not at the present time the public social services constitute an area of professional practice, it is possible to identify a professional attitude as a requisite for satisfactory performance on the job. This includes the recognition on the part of the employee that he is administering a service which the body politic has determined to be socially desirable. It embodies also the recognition on the part of the employee that to be effective in such administration, he must approach the problems of the service objectively and without economic or social bias. He must also accept certain limitations of the framework in which he operates, in terms of the statute which sets up the agency, in terms of budget and in terms of clientele eligible for service.

The findings of the study staff have revealed convincing material on this point, and although expressed differently by those interviewed in the various services, the common denominator seems to be adequately stated as a "professional attitude." In old age insurance administration, the recruitment of personnel from the field of commercial insurance [13] has provided an opportunity to

12. Hatch Political Activity Act; 53 *Stat* 1147; August 2, 1939.

13. Since January, 1940, the major recruitment is from the Junior Professional Assistant Register at grade CAF–3 level, with vacancies in the higher grades being filled by promotion from the next lower levels. Thus the general picture is that of replenishment of our administrative

evaluate the worker's attitude as a factor. The utility of skills carried over from private insurance experience is not to be underestimated, but the necessary adjustment from an operation which is linked up with private gain and therefore has inherent qualities of persuasion or "salesmanship" in it, to one which has no rewards except the social good is not without its problems. As one manager commented, it is important to realize that the workers are serving the public and the people; to distinguish this concept from the "public relations attitude" such as "the customer is always right." The in-service training program for the Old Age Insurance Division of the Social Security Board which has placed great emphasis upon the public service aspect of the job is evidence of the need to meet the problem.[14]

A professional attitude is also recognized as a necessity in unemployment compensation. The findings of the study point to the ease with which this attitude has been developed, due in large part to the fact that benefits are administered by the employment service. For the objective of the Employment Service has always been the return of unemployed persons to jobs for which they are suitably equipped, without any regard to fee for service. Support of this concept is contained in the emphasis upon the "larger responsibilities" which the Bureau of Unemployment Compensation of the Social Security Board has stressed.[15]

In the public assistance and child welfare services, the recognition of a professional attitude is inherent. The

---

material at a low grade and dependency on in-service training and natural development for the higher administrative jobs.—Letter from John J. Corson, *op. cit.*

14. This program is discussed in Chapter VII.

15. First Annual Report, Social Security Board, 1936, p. 45.

traditions of social work practice characteristic of earlier programs of assistance administered by the states, and characteristic of existing programs of assistance under private auspices, have been carried over into the present program of aid to families and individuals stimulated or developed under the Social Security Act. The influence of these traditions was reflected throughout the interviews with workers in public assistance and child welfare. As will be indicated later, it is also shown through the keen awareness for the possibilities of formal training as well as through criticism more sharply focused upon the existing educational facilities.

Understanding of Behavior: During the interviews with the personnel in the services the need to know something about human behavior was variously described. "Knowing how to handle people," "human adjustment," and other phrases gleaned from the interviews relate to the subject of behavior. The nature of this understanding was described by some of the persons interviewed as "the sales psychology," "sales talk," "how to win friends and influence people," or as "constructive salesmanship."

Some appreciation of the practical values of this knowledge is indicated in the comments made by workers in the various services, as follows: one interviewer in the employment service, carrying the receptionist function, suggested that "understanding human relations was most important, for without this, the interviewer could not be free as one man to another, or be able to put himself in the other man's place." A manager in a rural office commented that "applied psychology would be helpful provided it would be interpreted to include diplomacy and tact." A senior interviewer believed that "it was an innate characteristic if the person was qualified for the job. The people have to be handled with soft kid gloves." An interviewer who was specializing in work with young people believed understanding behavior was especially important in her department because "the young people who were coming for jobs are so frightened." Another, specializing in professional and commercial referrals commented that the greatest problem of adjustment is with women over forty and men over fifty. Another observed that "some people think they are things they are not, and the interviewer must know how to handle them." A fourth interviewer commented that "one cannot help other persons unless one understands human problems." He did not think that "the employment services should be put on the basis of social services, however, because it should fill in the gap between the employer and the worker. In other words, social service gives an idea of what to do about people in need even though one does not follow this concept rigidly." Another interviewer emphasized the need "for rigorous elimination of workers whose social attitudes are demonstrated to be such as to produce ineffective or unfortunate individual contacts or the familiar bureaucratic attitudes or procedures which endanger this type of government."

At the employment office apply individuals for whom society has provided a system of limited security during periods of involuntary unemployment so that they may function normally while they are seeking entrance to the labor market. Determining eligibility involves far more than a routine process of checking the employment record. The organic relationship to employment service, which is now a part of the unemployment compensation administration, in itself shows the ultimate objective of this system. The individual anticipates return to normal employment in a suitable occupation under conditions which are socially acceptable. As a person, he represents a constellation of capacities and handicaps which cannot be classified routinely. It is the understanding and use of this constellation of individual aptitudes which will establish the service as professional. And its justification lies not so much in the necessity of use in every situation which is presented, as in the confidence that a background of skill and information exists and may be called upon when needed. The way in which it is used becomes a part of the professional practice.

The workers in public assistance discussed the understanding of behavior as an element of the case work process in the service. One worker defined this as the ability "to see individual needs and take care of them"; another defined it as "the individual approach to people." Understanding the behavior of the special groups served was also indicated. For example, the desire of the older person to cling to the known way of living, however difficult, frequently complicated the treatment of health problems. Workers serving aged persons recognize the need for slower tempo in the interview; greater assistance in establishing eligibility; greater willingness to accept the client's present standard of living and his own choice of medical facilities; development of interests which may prove to be a substitute for work.[16]

The instances cited seem to center around the understanding of fundamental drives within every human being. A recognition of these drives helps to understand the individual's method of expressing his need. Inherent

16. Ruth Hill, "Understanding Old People," *The Family*, January, 1938.

in this understanding is a respect for human personality, whatever its manifestations appear to be. Respect makes it possible to accept the differences in individuals and to maintain in the relationship the constructive attitude which must be a part of every social service.

Knowledge of the Community: Information about the community and the community life is necessary for workers in all the services. Such knowledge includes the types of occupations in the community, wage levels, standards of living, health standards and contemporary economic and social conditions. It is useful to visitors in the social study of applicants for assistance, to claims examiners in judging suitability of work, and to employment interviewers in counselling employers and employees. Thorough and systematic knowledge of employment conditions in the community was considered necessary in every office of unemployment compensation and employment service visited. Few workers know where to turn for information concerning occupational classification and population trends, either in federal reports or in state and local reports. The occupational research studies now being conducted by the United States Employment Service are an example of such a source of data. Health needs and the place of health service in the community are important, and the reports of the State Departments of Health and the United States Public Health Service are valuable for this purpose.

In old age insurance administration, the knowledge of local conditions involving occupation, employment and business conditions, housing conditions, trade union and labor activities, and wage levels were regarded as only "moderately desirable," and it was frequently stated that much of this information could be acquired on the job.

Up to the present time, the fact that the program is federal and operation is to a great extent routinely prescribed substantiates these comments. But with the payment of claims and with the changing function of the service, new factors enter in and suggest a closer relationship to other services in the community.

More important than many of these factual fields is a knowledge of community attitudes and culture patterns which have bearing upon the development of social and health services. The employment service interviewer must know any racial and religious bias which exists in placement. The child welfare worker must be equally sensitive to these prejudices in developing plans for children under care. The old age insurance office needs to know something of the attitudes of the community towards old age and retirement from employment. Differences between urban and rural community culture patterns also have a bearing here. The complex mosaic of attitudes in which the service operates must be understood and utilized.

Related to the knowledge of the community is the broader social setting in which the community itself is functioning. Interviews with workers in all the services stressed the need for this material as a background for the particular operation in which they were engaged. The In-Service Training Program of Old Age Insurance is likewise evidence of recognition in that service.

The need of such knowledge was expressed in an interesting way by the director of one of the employment services who deplored the fact that "so many people were working who have never heard of the Unemployment Compensation Law, not to mention the other parts of the Social Security Act and the Wagner Labor Relations

Act." He believed that a "broad training in economics with a general picture of the job to be done should be required, the details to be acquired through in-service training." He pointed out that the department has had to do a great deal of training itself in spite of the fact that the state agricultural college has a course on the Social Security Act. He underscored the importance of the "history of economics and of all this social legislation and the importance of understanding unemployment," because of the fact that "the whole democratic form of government in his opinion is to depend on the handling of unemployment within the next few years . . . the university is not giving any common-sense training in attitudes toward it, and people come into the service in as great number as they are found in the general population believing that they are all able to get jobs if they only tried." One person believed it essential to know what industries would be declining in the community in the future; another said that the responsibility to the young persons just entering the labor market demands widespread knowledge of economic trends.

The need for this general knowledge was emphasized more strongly by workers in public assistance than by those in the other services. Background information was also stressed by this group. One visitor said, "We need to know the interplay of life upon the individual"; another one needs, "to see the client in his social setting"; a third commented, "if the client tells you that President Roosevelt says such and such in his speech, you have to keep up with what is going on in Congress in order to keep your respect." These comments, although variously expressed, point to the same body of information. From the interviews with workers in these services it is possible to conclude that a background of understanding of the social and economic framework of society is fundamental, although difficult to relate specifically to the demands of the job.

These skills or needs are common to all the services studied. Some have been emphasized more than others in the interviews through which the data were gathered. All have given testimony to a common denominator of skills discussed and have suggested the *sine qua non* of successful operations of any of the services.

Special Skills and Knowledge.—An examination of each service in turn will reveal the extent to which an additional set of skills or knowledge enters into the successful performance of the specific functions. The data summarized from the findings of the study and presented in the following paragraphs indicate that such special knowledge is required because of the function or the setting in which the service operates or because traditions of standards in service have been developed over a period of time and are accepted as the new framework is established.

Old Age Insurance: As old age insurance is administered at present, the emphasis upon the clerical content of the job is apparent. Clerical operations are performed with a sense of the responsibility of service to individuals which requires understanding. The emphasis on clerical functions and mechanical accuracy was necessary in the organization of a vast accounting and record keeping system. The lump-sum payment claims of 1938 were ordinarily insurance transactions in which accuracy and adherence to mathematical formula seemed more important than an understanding of human relationships. As the number of claims for monthly benefit payments upon which individuals depend for their subsistence grows, there will be an increasing emphasis upon human relationships.

Unemployment Compensation and Employment Service: The employment service and the unemployment compensation administration deal constantly with employer-employee relationships. The special knowledge in this area, it was agreed, is needed alike by interviewers in the employment service and by claims-takers in unemployment compensation. The interviewer needs to know the frame of reference in which the individual is served and in this instance it is the employer-employee relationship. The emphasis is essentially upon the qualifications of an individual in this relationship rather than upon his right or his need.

The adjustment of the individual to employment or to unemployment is the central focus around which the understanding of the individual is applied. The short-time contact nature of the interviews in these services is suggested in two studies of local offices which indicate that most registration interviews took slightly less than twenty minutes, and subsequent interviews less than ten minutes. These limitations imply the need for a high degree of skill on the part of the interviewers.

Next in importance is the ability to use the method of occupational analysis. A considerable group in the Employment Service believed that the necessary knowledge of trades or occupations can be obtained only through experience in actual employment. A larger group, however, stressed the impossibility of gaining personal experience in even a fraction of the types of positions which clear through a normally active employment office, and contended that the nature of the various occupations may be learned by the interviewer from field visits, from the applicants, and from the detailed job descriptions issued by the United States Employment Service. The fact that elaborate in-service training programs in occupational classifications are now in use indicates that previous working experience is not deemed the only means of satisfying this training need. The findings suggest that any effort to cover even the major aspects of all occupations in pre-entry education would be unwieldy. The theory of occupational classification can be taught fairly successfully in professional courses which include job analysis methods and field trips to plants, followed by the analysis of sample positions.

A considerable majority of employment service workers believed some knowledge of vocational guidance to be essential. Most registrations where occupational classification is based entirely on work experience involve little vocational guidance. Tool and die makers usually remain tool and die makers. Although other interviewers will have occasion to use guidance techniques from time to time, most work of this kind is confined to interviewers specializing in junior placements or to those concerned with the vocationally maladjusted or physically handicapped workers. Such interviewers need special training in counselling procedures, in the vocational importance of the more common disabilities, and in jobs suitable for persons with such handicaps.

Since state unemployment compensation acts generally permit the state agency to require vocational retraining or readjustment of persons receiving unemployment compensation benefits, the demand for equipment in these fields may increase. Yet from the evidence of the study, vocational guidance, as taught and practiced in most schools and colleges, does not meet the particular needs of these services. First of all, basic to the success of this program in the employment service is an extensive knowledge of the type of occupational research described above. Plans for occupational orientation or reorientation should take into consideration the number of positions available in any given field and the number of applicants for these positions. Educational programs may well be based on such practical data. In the second place, the type of counselling which advises preparation for certain kinds of work on the basis of certain aptitudes is outside the scope of the employment service in most instances, and further training is temporarily impracticable for most applicants. Even were this possible, satisfactory training for guidance work in the employment service cannot be secured from the traditional academic courses in vocational guidance if the findings of the study are to be relied upon.

Some knowledge of testing methods must be indicated as a separate technique connected with guidance work. Tests are increasingly used in connection with clerical and a few industrial positions, and an interviewer should be capable of handling this aspect of placement. This does not involve the construction of tests but simply their administration and interpretation.

A study of labor relations was emphasized in almost every instance. Since the interviewer often serves as a middle-man between employer and employee, he must be equipped with a knowledge of employer-employee relations. He must have an understanding of the points of view of capital and labor and must be disciplined in the maintenance of an objective attitude. Major policy questions, including whether or not to refer workers to a plant where there is an industrial dispute, whether to refer union or non-union employees to particular employers, what arrangements to make in connection with union seniority lists are, of course, determined by state or local administrators. But to carry out such policies and to interpret them satisfactorily to the public, the interviewer needs a grounding in labor relations which has made him objectively and unemotionally alert to the strong and weak points of each side in any dispute. The re-classifying and shifting of labor from one industry to another requiring the same skills has emphasized the importance of this area of information.

Public Assistance: The administration of public assistance to the aged, to the blind, and to dependent children introduces processes involved in "giving service and financial assistance or personal counsel to individuals by representatives of social agencies, according to policies established and with consideration of individual need." [17] There is one contrast only to the administration of the other social services included in the study. The determination of eligibility for the assistance is based not on a simple right to assistance but upon the right to assistance in relation to need. This individualized service, known as social case work, has official sanction in the program.[18] In the determination of eligibility

17. Elizabeth McCord De Schweinitz, "Can We Define Social Case Work?" *The Survey*, February, 1939.

18. "Decisions of this type (financial eligibility) and many others which affect the lives of persons who are living on the margin of subsistence require capacity to observe, evaluate, and to the greatest possible extent, to harmonize the often tangled and apparently conflicting interests of public policy and personal relationships. They underscore the need of permanent experienced personnel in the staffs of the State and local public assistance agencies and for a level of education and training which will ensure that these staffs have both a mastery of necessary professional skills and a broad and unbiased understanding of the purposes of the

there is first the establishment of a relationship of confidence between the client and the agency as represented by the visitor, which leads to the sharing of information with the visitor and the acceptance by the visitor of the attitude towards this sharing, involving as it does the need of the client to maintain his self-respect and dignity. It also involves the exercise of sound judgment in evaluating data and attitudes or behavior manifestations and discretion in noting signs of social and medical need which require special attention. Referral may here constitute a peculiarly difficult problem. The development of a plan for the use of assistance and other resources is likewise a requisite skill involving as it does the essential need to administer assistance without jeopardizing the independence or the self-respect of the client. The complexity of this process is suggested by one experienced writer as follows:

> The public worker must have at his fingertips the understanding of insurance and property problems, budgeting, diets, and of community resources and deal with them with speed and accuracy, sound judgment, must understand community attitude and be able to interpret philosophy as well as practice. Must have the individual approach in establishing eligibility and yet within the agency limits. Must know when to make referrals and where.[19]

The material gathered in the interviews in the present study substantiates this statement. The complexity of the picture of need makes the diagnostic skill of great importance. To differentiate between the individual who

---

program and of the individuals with whom they are dealing."—Third Annual Report, Social Security Board, 1938, p. 106.

19. Eda Houwink, "Case Work in Public Relief," *The Survey*, January, 1939.

can successfully work out his own plan and the one who needs counselling in the administering of his budget and the one who can carry little other responsibility requires discretion.

Sufficient knowledge of medical diagnoses to permit an intelligent referral and thorough knowledge of medical resources in the community was emphasized by many of the persons interviewed. It is important also to know the implication of these conditions in relation to agency function and to be able to work effectively with physicians and public health nurses in the treatment and prevention of disease. Knowledge of the laws concerning domestic relations, real property, and inheritance, and of laws protecting the individual in society was stressed as important.

Because of the relationship of public assistance programs to governmental finance, it was believed by many that the visitor in public assistance needs to have information concerning taxation, governmental organization, and finance so that he can discuss his program effectively with taxpayer's groups and officials otherwise unacquainted with the need for such provisions.

Knowledge of vocational guidance and occupational opportunities especially for young persons is useful in service to mothers of dependent children. Questions of home management, especially budgeting and diets, call for understanding on the part of the workers. Opinion as to the utility of such information, however, differed widely among the individuals interviewed.

Child Welfare: The special needs of child welfare services are basically the same as in public assistance. Case loads, however, are lower in child welfare services, and specialization is more intensive. The child welfare worker is frequently a case consultant for workers in public assistance or other agencies. Although a number of individuals interviewed questioned the necessity of extensive knowledge of case work methods in public assistance, none questioned such a need in the child welfare services. The emphasis upon a demonstration of service in the program is very important to the understanding of personnel needs and to the selection of trained personnel.

The degree of specialized preparation which is necessary for positions in child welfare aroused some controversy. A few persons observed that desirable preparation embodies general family case work procedure with emphasis on the public assistance administration. The visitor in child welfare services works closely with the public assistance agency in most cases, and her comprehension of the problems on which she is consulted by public assistance workers will be considerably greater if she has a full knowledge of their work. Frequently, too, cases of aid to dependent children or cases involving other types of assistance are referred to the child welfare worker on account of some special problems, and she is expected to assume the total responsibility for case work service. The fact that the entire program provided by the Social Security Act is one of demonstrating child welfare services in rural communities places the emphasis upon the orientation of the worker to the rural community and upon her skill in working in a position of leadership with social and health groups.

Knowledge of child health standards and ability to work with medical and other groups to develop resources for medical care for children are also important. Because of the extensive responsibilities for child placement in this service, a knowledge of the laws of adoption, illegitimacy, school attendance, and court procedure is essential for child welfare workers. Many desired greater experience and training in child placement and in home-finding.

With both public assistance and child welfare, however, it is clear that the tradition of general education and professional preparation at the graduate level which have stimulated standards of personnel in the agencies have made it possible to impose tasks involving a high degree of maturity and leadership upon the representatives of these agencies.

Summary.—It is clear that the personnel interviewed has indicated certain skills and knowledge which are common to all the services and certain skills and knowledge which are specific to each of the services. A common content is apparent, and its existence will raise immediately in the mind of the reader this question: Is it possible to devise an educational program which will prepare personnel for the social services administering various types of benefits? If so, what should its content be? Such a proposal would today be variously discussed by the services. The interviews summarized have revealed a "fear of the academic" on the part of workers in some of the services. In the employment service particularly there is the widespread impression that the service does not require a substantial academic content. In this service there is the tendency to place high value on experience and a low value on education. The conflict between the two is very real, and the result is the loss of value of educational background. To what extent this is due to the lack of any educational programs recognized by the field is not known. Whatever the reason, this factor must be faced in any attempt to arrive at the educational base for these services.

Chapter Six

PUBLIC SOCIAL SERVICES:
SUPERVISION AND ADMINISTRATION

THE CONTENT OF THE JOB

As THE FUNCTIONS of supervision and administration are examined, important differences are apparent within the services studied.[1] These relate not so much to the training needs within the various services as to the degree of differentiation which is made between supervision and administration. In old age insurance, for example, considerable difficulty was encountered in distinguishing the supervisory from the administrative function. The work of the assistant managers and the managers is so often interchangeable that separate treatment would be extremely difficult. In unemployment compensation and the employment service, a somewhat clearer differentiation is observable, and the positions of director, assistant director, office manager, field supervisor and referee are easily identified at the present time. Yet the distinction cannot be said to be clear. In public assistance, a very clear differentiation is made, and it is

---

1. It should be noted here that this discussion of administrative positions excludes the specialists such as accountants, consultants, research directors, personnel directors, and referees.

necessary to consider separately the position of the supervisor and of the administrator, including the directors at the local, state, and federal level. The brief job descriptions which follow will indicate these differences.

Old Age Insurance.—The duties of the manager vary with the size of the office. In the smaller offices the manager sometimes interviews all claimants who arrive when he is in the office, and even in the largest offices he occasionally interviews applicants for lump sum payments. More frequently, however, only the unusual cases receive his attention. The manager is responsible for the supervision of production and review of claims applications, for interpreting policy changes to the staff, for preparing a weekly report of activities, and for making studies of office preparations.

The strictly administrative duties of managers are relatively limited. The managers are not responsible for their own office budgets nor do they have final power to hire or discharge personnel. The only expenditures which they can authorize are payments for such emergency work as repairs. The control of finance, to an increasing extent of personnel, and the devising of new procedures and supervision of work is chiefly the function of the Regional Office of the Social Security Board.

The principal responsibilities of the manager are in the area of assignment of work, supervision of performance, training on the job, and the important task of public relations. The coöperation of employers and executives of large corporations is important, and the interpretation of the program through public speeches and radio broadcasts becomes a sizable demand upon his time.

Unemployment Compensation and Employment Service.—It seems appropriate to consider the several positions of a supervisory and administrative nature in order to give an adequate picture of the functions at a level higher than that of claims examiner or interviewer. Within the group are included the office manager, the referee, and the director and assistant director. Their duties are briefly indicated as follows: The office manager is directly in charge of all the activities of the interviewing and clerical staff for both unemployment compensation and employment service. He is often nominally in charge of any claims examiners in the office. He has responsibility for public relations and numerous functions involving community contacts. Especially must he maintain cordial relationships with employers and with labor unions.

Directors and assistant directors are regularly found in both services. For the obvious reason that unemployment compensation utilizes more clerical workers who must be supervised, there are a greater number of division and section chiefs in this service. In the better managed employment services, however, there is an increasing tendency to establish specialized divisions in the central offices. The responsibilities of division chiefs are related to the type of service rendered by the division.

Public Assistance.—In the administration of public assistance, the line of promotion is very likely to be from visitor to supervisor and then to executive director. The responsibilities assigned to each one, however, vary from urban to rural communities.

The case supervisor is responsible for establishing and maintaining acceptable standards of social work practice in the local unit; supervising the work of individual visitors; making sure that the methods prescribed by the state agency and those established in the county are carried into effect; assigning applications to individual visitors for investigation; promoting a steady growth and development of staff capacities by individual and group conferences, by use of facilities offered by the state agency and by stimulating an interest in professional training; assisting the county director; reviewing action of the local unit in relation to complaints, appeals, or fair hearing; directing and making such additional investigations as seem advisable; and referring to the appropriate authority recommendations concerning the adjustment of complaints and fair hearing provisions of the state plan.[2]

The case supervisor is a key person in the administration of public assistance, as he carries certain responsibilities for supervision, for administration, and for public relations. Supervision of staff, however, constitutes the important focus of these activities, and as such includes determination of case load assignments, consultation on individual cases, and case work policies. Usually he assists the director in the determination of the agency budget and then undertakes its interpretation. Frequently he shares some of the director's public relations responsibilities. In many cases, he is in charge of inservice training, especially in those agencies where the emphasis of in-service training is on developmental supervision.

The duties of these supervisors vary considerably, but in general their major responsibility is to supervise a

2. Guide to Public Assistance Administration. Bureau Circular No. 9, Bureau of Public Assistance, Social Security Board. September, 1940, Section 113, p. 1.

number of workers who carry direct case loads. In some
situations, especially where the number of workers supervised is small, the supervisor may carry cases directly
or spend time at the intake desk. But whatever the arrangement, the degree of responsibility for service to individuals is very great.

The administrative positions included in the study
cover a range of local, state, and federal units. Those to
be discussed here are the county director and the state
administrative officer.

Subject to the general directions of the state department and the authority of the county board, the director
carries responsibility for administering the work of the
local unit and for selecting his staff according to established procedure and participating in periodic evaluation; establishing a suitable office equipment to meet the
requirements; participating in development, directing
application, and interpreting to staff and local community the rules and regulations of the state agency; preparing and submitting the county budget and other
reports to the state agency and maintaining an effective
working relationship with the agency; establishing and
maintaining acceptable standards of administration in
the local unit; and for initiating and carrying out experimental projects and coöperative agreements with local
agencies, subject to the approval of the state agency and
in general coördinating the work of the local unit with
that of other agencies in the community. He assumes the
responsibility of the case supervisor where other facilities have not been provided, he assumes responsibility
for interpreting to the state agency the needs of recipients of public assistance and of adequacy of existing
provisions to meet these needs, and interprets to the

recipient and the community facilities available for their
use.[3]

The county director carries major responsibility for
directing the organization and operation of the program, and for interpreting the place of the public assistance agency in the community. This involves the
organization and coördination of district offices; the interpretation and application of rules and regulations of
the state agency; the preparation of the budget and other
statistical reports; the application of personnel policies
in accordance with the rulings of the state agency, general responsibility for staff development and for effecting
good relations with other public officials, representatives
of other agencies, the public, and the press.

In smaller counties the director acts as the case work
supervisor, and in the smallest counties he carries responsibility for direct case work with families and individuals.

Administrative positions in the state and federal
agency vary considerably, and generalization is difficult.
They include the executive director, primarily concerned with the administration of public assistance and
its coördination with related welfare activities of the
state, and staff members of administrative rank, such as
the director of personnel, the director of research, and
the director of social work, sometimes with two or three
assistants; and sometimes a director for each of the
various forms of assistance, such as old age assistance, aid
to the blind, aid to dependent children, and general assistance.

3. Guide to Public Assistance Administration. Bureau Circular No. 9,
Bureau of Public Assistance, Social Security Board. September, 1940,
Section 112, p. 1.

Child Welfare Services.—The state director of child
welfare services carries general responsibility for the program, which may be organized as a separate department
or as a division in the public welfare department. The
development of the plan, the selection of personnel,
the determination of budget, and actual supervision of
the program are inherent in these responsibilities.

The supervisor in child welfare services is usually an
itinerant field supervisor who meets once or twice a
month with county and district workers, reviews cases,
advises on new policies, and in general carries the responsibilities of a case work supervisor. If the licensing
of institutions is assigned to the department, it frequently becomes the task of one of these field supervisors.

Liaison between Local, State, and Regional Units.—
Although the primary focus of the study is the administration of the service at the local level, a brief word
should be said about the relationship between the local
unit and the state, or between the local unit and the
regional office. This relationship is the responsibility of
a field representative, and, although the duties of such a
staff member will vary from service to service, the function is very much the same.

In old age insurance, local offices are governed by the
regional offices, which carry major responsibility for the
control of finance, increasing control over personnel in
local offices, the devising of new procedures, and supervision of work loads. The relationship of the local office
to state and federal offices is administrative.

In unemployment compensation and the employment
service, field supervisors attached to the state service
assist in the oversight of the work of the local offices.

Previously each service had its own field supervisor, but a combination position is rapidly becoming the rule. The field supervisor is the liaison officer whose duty it is to develop *esprit* within the local office staff, to inspect and criticize, to explain new rules and regulations, and to keep the central office informed as to the attitude of the local offices toward state rulings. The supervisor is concerned with problems of office management and problems of procedure in the local offices and with the development of policies or programs designed to carry on the function of the local offices.

In public assistance, the field representative is the liaison officer between the local unit and the state. He interprets federal and state requirements relating to local practice; makes available guidance and consultation on community problems; shares with local communities experiences of other communities; establishes effective working relationships between the state agency and the local community; reviews periodically a sampling of case records in the local unit; participates in periodic evaluation of staff performance; provides the state agency with reports on local progress and development; and interprets to the state agency the circumstances within the local unit which warrant adoptions of policy.[4]

In some states visited, the field representative is restricted to consultation concerning the service program, and state auditors are responsible for advising the counties on all fiscal questions. Usually, however, this separation of functions has led to confusion, since it has proved impossible to isolate service questions from administrative and fiscal questions.

4. *Ibid.,* Section 106, p. 4.

TRAINING NEEDS OF SUPERVISION AND
ADMINISTRATION

Data from the interviews concerning the needs at the
supervisory and administrative levels indicate first the
need for knowledge concerning the basic job in the
service; second, qualities and preparation for the role
of leadership; and third, capacity to develop public opinion in support of the program of the service through
the interpretation and understanding of pressures lev-
elled against the agency. The relative emphasis placed
upon these needs varies from service to service. It is
suggested here that in the service where the content of
practice has been more clearly defined, more emphasis
is placed upon the role of leadership in supervision and
administration within the agency, and that where the
job is poorly defined, tasks are interchangeable and the
emphasis of administration is upon interpretation and
development of opinion in support of the agency.

In general, in all the services certain needs are apparent for successful executive leadership. They include the
understanding of personnel policies; preparation of the
budget and the principles of budgeting, except where
the service is federally operated; the legal basis for the
operation of the agency; joint-planning with other social and health agencies in the community; the participation in committees and conference groups for this
purpose, and the handling of complaints; and the maintenance of public confidence and effective relationships
with the press. Understanding the group process is important in conferences with employers' and workers'
groups and in committee meetings with representatives
of other social agencies. Capacity to select and direct

staff is vital in the administration of an important service which is scrutinized by the public eye and yet not always favored by public opinion insofar as salary levels and working conditions are concerned. Devising office procedures, supervision of work loads, and responsibility for performance and fiscal control are all inherent in the process. The ability to analyze experience and project future plans for the agency is important in all administration. Knowledge of administration, organization, and public finance are also essential.

The qualities of leadership necessary for supervision and administration are shown by the following brief review of each of the services.

Old Age Insurance.—Administrative skills were not emphasized in old age insurance to as great an extent as in the other services. Budgetary procedure, for example, was properly omitted since it is handled by the regional office. Office practice, and procedures in accounting and in filing methods were stressed. The volume of clerical work of all types, which is characteristic of the old age insurance office, was accepted as inherent in administration, and there was general acceptance of the need for skill in operating with speed and accuracy. Procedures have in large measure been devised by the federal office, but the managers still have considerable initiative in devising ways of implementing these procedures skillfully.

The need to know about personnel management was indicated by the managers in old age insurance, who also stated that it was very expensive to learn this on the job.

In general, the managers emphasized the importance

of skill in public relations. A considerable amount of work with employers is involved, to secure their help in assisting employees with application forms, in notifying the office when employees become sixty-five years of age, in checking wage records, and in identifying names on tax receipts. These duties impose upon the manager the task of working effectively with the employers of the community. If similar services may be performed by labor unions for their members, a coöperative working relationship with the old age insurance office becomes desirable. Relationship with employee organizations will probably continue to be an important aspect of the managers' and assistant managers' duties. Knowledge of business trends is helpful in such contacts, as is the knowledge of community organization, especially of labor unions and business organizations.

These public contacts seem to the majority of managers the most important part of their work. This is logical, on account of the problem of employer and employee education in the basic principles and practices of old age benefits. Under the amended act, the complexity of claims work and the growing number of beneficiaries will draw heavily upon the manager's time. Also, as the general understanding of the program increases, such relations continue to be necessary, but less demanding of the manager's time.

Knowledge of economic and business organization seemed essential because of the manager's frequent contacts with employers. Political science, sociology, and psychology were viewed as desirable backgrounds for public relations in other aspects of the job, as were the history of public welfare and social insurance.

What the effect of the increase in claims payments and

the changing nature of the service will be upon the attitude of management is not known. The volume of claims
payment and the problems involved may require more
attention to the administrative process within the organization, and the need for educational and interpre-
tive work may become less absorbing as the program is
more thoroughly understood.

It is interesting also that the managers indicated little
concern over the need to relate the work of the agency
to that of other social services within the community.
This fact illustrates clearly that old age insurance does
not yet "tie in" with other social programs, even to the
extent of the joint analysis of common problems. Here
again the present stage of development in the administration of old age insurance may be cited in partial explanation.

A knowledge of the structure and nature of the community was regarded as essential. The existence of na-
tionality groups or religious differences in the community may have some bearing on the method developed
to carry out a specific policy. Knowledge of employment
conditions, social agencies, political conditions, housing
conditions, and wage levels are considered advantageous
as backgrounds. With the exception of employment conditions, this knowledge was deemed useful for referral
purposes. If, however, the manager's job is ever interpreted to include some community welfare planning,
such knowledge will become even more important.

In scrutinizing old age insurance, the study staff concluded that information should be elicited from and
advice given to applicants according to the same professional techniques as those employed in an assistance
office. This observation was not shared by the managers,

who were often not very conscious of the need of skill in understanding behavior except as it would be helpful in dealing with personnel in their offices.

Unemployment Compensation and Employment Service.—In unemployment compensation and in the employment service a close relationship exists between the needs of the various jobs within the service. The study staff found differences between job levels less marked here than in the other services, but also found that few administrators appreciated the breadth and depth of training needs at the beginning performance level.

All the equipment required of the interviewers and the claims examiners is necessary at the higher levels. Certain detailed knowledge is the exception, as for example, the extensive knowledge of vocational guidance necessary to the interviewer in the junior or in the commercial division, or the detailed knowledge of claims eligiblity necessary to the claims examiner. But, aside from this, it was indicated that the difference between the express needs for the service jobs and the administrative positions is less in this than in other services studied. The chief difference which is apparent is one of degree.

Especially important in this service is the knowledge of general business trends and a broad view of local occupations and employment conditions and the knowledge of the migration of labor on a state- and nationwide basis. The administration of laws providing for vocational retraining and the possibility of extension of the employment service into professional and new business areas are further indications of the need for a broad grasp of the employment trends and economic forces affecting community life. Important decisions in budget-planning, policy-making, and in-service training are inevitably based upon the administrator's judgment of business conditions, and it is important that he be fully conversant with the sources of information in this area.

Skill in employer-employee relations is a basic need. Public relation contacts in this area are very important. State-wide agreements between employer and employee organizations may be enforced by the administrator, and it is important that he understand their provision and significance.

The manager of one office stressed education in economics, emphasizing the fact that a college degree was not in itself sufficient, and that one should have at least executive ability and two years of experience in a supervisory capacity, along with sufficient courage to make policies and an ability to establish good relationships as well as a knowledge of the industries and the general organization of the community and of the state. He does not want what he calls "surplus of theory" but rather a knowledge of labor laws and trade unions, and a complete knowledge of the laws and workings of unemployment compensation and the public employment agency. He distinguished between the ability to supervise and instruct rather than to "boss."

The administrative techniques which were stressed included the principles of organization, especially the use of the group process with committees and delegations. Responsibilities for time and production studies frequently carried by administrators require some knowledge of job analysis and elementary statistics. It seems very clear that a substantial number of those interviewed desired special training in administration. The overwhelming evidence is that people at all levels, and the people at the higher levels on behalf of those under their supervision, want primarily training in basic subject matter such as that commonly termed "psychology" and "economics" plus the subject matter of the job itself. The administrative techniques were considered equally important with this basic knowledge or skill.

Public Assistance.—As indicated in a previous paragraph, there is a clearer differentiation between supervisor and administrator in public assistance than in the other services studied. It is recognized that within a small county unit where there is little division of labor in administration, the executive director may carry some responsibility for case work supervision. In large counties this is assigned to the case work supervisors.

The study reveals the importance of a broad background in addition to technical training if the supervisor is to be successful. In one interview a supervisor stressed the importance of knowing the laws, the fiscal and taxing basis of the agency; the industrial, agricultural and labor conditions, and a knowledge of agencies operating in the area. The fact that his major responsibility is that of case consultation necessitates competence in professional skill, yet desirable skills indicate the range of activity and the scope of knowledge and experience which is necessary to develop this competence. One group of supervisors interviewed indicated the following as basic to their job performance: bookkeeping, arithmetic, business administration, budget process, statistics, elementary mathematics, and accounting; capacity to read and understand legal documents; accuracy in case reporting; the ability to know what to include that is relevant to the function of the agency; treatment of family problems; knowledge of health problems—medical and psychiatric information; techniques of interviewing; practical psychology—why people behave as they do; study of the relationships of the individual to the community and the process of community organization; home economics—ability to help people get along on the "welfare budget"; letter-writing; ethics of relationships—between worker and client, worker and supervisor, workers and the other members of the community; case work; supervision; economics and labor problems.

The administrator in the field of public assistance should have, according to the study, adequate knowledge of the content of the entire program. He cannot depend upon the case work supervisor to supply this, but must have enough knowledge at his command to evaluate and interpret the professional services in the departments. It was generally accepted that executives should have had experience in social welfare programs as workers or supervisors. The administrator who does not know what the public welfare program demands and the social worker who does not know the principles of good organization and administration are both hazards to a public welfare service.

Whether the unit is large or small, a knowledge of economic trends and social conditions in the community in which the agency operates is important. Administrative and fiscal knowledge is practically indispensable. In a large unit the administrator requires a broader grasp of administrative organization and various specialized techniques which are not utilized in small agencies. The needed administrative content includes lines of administrative organization, allocation of function, job analysis, fiscal policies and procedures, accounting, personnel management, use of consultative services, board and committee work, political factors affecting public welfare programs, and the relation of the organization and its functioning to other government agencies. The increasing need for persons fully equipped to carry the problems of administration in rural areas was stressed.

The need for community interpretation and especially interpretation to tax-payers' groups, professional associations, and business organizations was emphasized in many interviews. Knowledge of allied fields, such as government and public finance, was deemed important. It was considered necessary to see the social work program in relation to the total social and economic structure.

Persons holding the position of county director in the states visited were almost invariably found to be college men or women with some additional professional training. Frequently they were graduates of schools of social work. Comments on training needs included the following: a reasonable time in government service in addition to technical courses in public administration, including public welfare administration, training in business administration and organization; current case work methods, employee training, and other related public work; general community social work, organization and methods, methods of supervision, public speaking, labor problems, labor relations, and social insurance. Greater understanding of economics and the biological sciences as related to medicine, the relation between health and dependency, standards of medical care, and ability to develop and coördinate medical facilities to meet needs of persons whom the agency serves were deemed necessary. A course in practical politics with attention to "who's who on the political horizon"; ability to secure and evaluate quantitative information, that is, the administrative use of research and statistical material, and further training in office methods were considered desirable. Most frequently mentioned in the foregoing group were more content in the field of economics and political science, more in the field of research and the handling of data, and a more thorough-going instruction in current case work and personnel management.

Child Welfare Services.—In child welfare services, administrative skills were not considered to be so important, because large-scale operations and administration of material benefits are not involved in the program. But the need for skill in interpretation and in public relations, on the other hand, and the need to work coöperatively with other social and health organizations in the development of a program were greatly emphasized. Specialized technical skills are essential, since the successful practice of case work with children is of primary importance. And there is also the need for capacity to supervise the case load carried by a worker, frequently in isolation from the state administration.

*   *   *   *   *

In all the services, the importance of the community setting in which the agency program is administered is apparent. This was stressed in many instances in connection with the rural field. In rural communities, as was pointed out in several interviews, the personal qualities of the supervisor or director are especially important. To direct a program effectively in a rural community, the leader must accept the difficulties of working alone, and of working in a group which has a close personal interest in government. The nature of the industrial background and of the social activities varies in these communities, but it is vitally important that the leader know and accept the importance of working within these limitations, for the attitude towards outsiders is to be reckoned with everywhere.

In addition to this community orientation, a knowledge of social, health, and economic trends was believed desirable in all the services studied. Ability to carry administrative responsibility, to interpret the program to various interested groups, and to coöperate with related groups, such as medical or health groups, was stressed on all sides. Especially important for the study was the widespread recognition of the need to know the fundamentals of the agency program either through professional training or experience, or both, before an adequate administrative job can be attempted.

Chapter Seven

PERSONNEL POLICIES

FROM A DESCRIPTION of the jobs and a summary of training needs it is logical to turn to a discussion of personnel policies which are vital factors in the recruitment of individuals to employment in the services studied. The policies, as presented in the following paragraphs, include the present basis for selection of personnel, merit systems, residence qualifications, salary levels, staff development programs, and promotion. The place of federal leadership in establishing these policies will also be discussed.

THE PRESENT BASIS FOR SELECTION OF PERSONNEL

Old Age Insurance.—Field assistants in old age insurance are recruited from the clerical staff[1] in the field offices and in the Baltimore office, and from the Junior Civil Service Examiner and Junior Professional Assistant[2] Registers. The register of Junior Civil Service Examiner was composed of lists of college graduates who had qualified on a mental test and on a general ex-

1. Clerical, Administrative, and Fiscal 1.
2. Later, Junior Technician.

amination "designed to test the competitors' information of a variety of subjects, including grammar, literature, spelling, history, geography, general science, civics
and current events." [3] The specifications for junior professional assistant included college graduation with major study prescribed under one of a series of optional
subjects. Two of these subjects and their specifications
are as follows: (1) for junior administrative technician,
twenty-four semester hours in public administration,
political science, or economics or in a combination of
these subjects, provided that at least twelve hours have
been in any one or a combination of the following: principles of public administration, public personnel administration, organization, management, and supervision,
public budgetary or fiscal administration, administrative
or constitutional law, and courses in the application of
public administration principles to functional activities
such as public welfare administration, public health administration, and public utilities regulation. (2) For
junior public welfare assistant, completion of a full four-
year course leading to a bachelor's degree, including or
supplemented by at least one full year of study (undergraduate or graduate) in social service in an accredited
school of social work with a minimum of 300 hours of
supervised field work. [4] It was the opinion of the study
staff that promotion from the clerical staff on the basis
of intelligence, general education, and service record

3. Duties—"under direct supervision, to perform tasks requiring training along definite lines and demanding intelligence, judgment and ability
to make independent decisions in matters of minor importance."—U. S.
Civil Service Commission Announcement No. 45, applications filed June
10, 1936.

4. U. S. Civil Service Commission Announcement No. 10. Application
filed February 8, 1940.

and recruitment of college students will continue to be in favor.[5]

Assistant managers have been recruited from the lower brackets of the Administrative Office Register,[6] transferred from other departments or more frequently selected from the Junior Civil Service Examiner Register.

Managers have also been selected from the Administrative Office Register. This register, which was established by the United States Civil Service Commission for the Social Security Board, included the basic requirement of one to three years' experience (varying with the level of the position applied for) in one of the following lines:

a. In a life insurance or workmen's compensation company, in actuarial, statistical, accounting, record keeping, or claims adjudication work, or in work dealing with group insurance, or salary saving plan.

b. In work dealing with administration of a retirement system, an unemployment insurance plan, private pension or

5. Here it is interesting to call attention to the basis of selecting claims interviewers from the present staff since January 1, 1940. The standards for selection are as follows:

"Individuals assigned to the position of claims interviewer (CAF–3, $1,620) meet the following requirements: (1) not less than two years' college and a minimum of six months' field office experience, or (2) Not less than a high school education and not less than two years' field office experience requiring not less than 25 per cent of the time in an interviewing capacity, and having an efficiency rating of 'Very Good,' or (3) Not less than four years' interviewing experience either with the Board, another government agency, or in private industry and having an efficiency rating of 'Very Good.'

"In placing individuals meeting the above requirements, extreme care is taken to insure that the individual is of good appearance and dress, possesses judgment, resourcefulness and tact."—Letter from John J. Corson, December 31, 1940.

6. U. S. Civil Service Commission, Announcement filed September 14, 1936, included Manager of District Office and Manager of Branch Office.

group annuity plan, workmen's compensation, or group insurance.

  c. In administration of labor legislation, or in labor relations work.

  d. In welfare administration or the administration of social legislation.

  e. In administration of insurance laws.

  f. In a department or establishment of the federal government.[7]

Competitors were "rated on their education and experience on a scale of 100, such ratings being based upon the competitors' sworn statements in their applications and upon a report" of 2,000 words describing the structure and problems of the organization in which they had been working. No written examinations were used.

It was generally agreed by the administrative staff that recruitments from this examination were not altogether satisfactory. Inter-departmental transfer was substituted when this method was found to be disappointing. As a matter of fact, the study staff found that the type of persons secured was very similar in both cases and that both groups of recruits were largely composed of (1) former employees of the Department of Commerce, often with brief experience in the National Recovery Administration; (2) former employees of the Veterans' Administration; and (3) former private insurance salesmen.

Since in the future the Bureau of Old Age Insurance can promote its own staff to higher positions, it seems unlikely that the method of recruiting general administrators from a register will be repeated to any great extent.

7. *Ibid.*

Unemployment Compensation and Employment Service.—For junior interviewer in the Employment Service and the claims examiner in Unemployment Compensation, entrance requirements vary from state to state, yet the pattern set by the sample class specifications of the United States Employment Service and the Bureau of Unemployment Compensation is most widely used. In both cases, almost no educational requirements are specified if there is a sufficient amount of experience. Substitution of education for experience on a year-for-year basis is possible with the qualification that at least one year of experience—for which no substitution may be made—is offered.

In the specifications most frequently used, "pertinent experience" for the junior interviewer is defined as work "definitely providing knowledge of occupational requirements and familiarity with employment problems and practices such as are entailed in agricultural, commercial, industrial, labor, and professional fields." The junior claims examiner or deputy must have had a year of "employment in a professional or other responsible capacity in at least one of the following fields: labor or industrial relations, public employment service, social work, law, accounting, enforcement of federal or state labor laws, or in related fields."[8]

The examinations for interviewers in the United

8. The sample qualification requirements are:

(1) *United States Employment Service: Junior Interviewer.*

Experience and Education—The following alternatives are permitted:
Five years of pertinent experience (as defined below); or
Three years of pertinent experience and graduation from a standard four-year high school or equivalent education; or
One year of pertinent experience and four years of college or university training; or
Any equivalent combination of experience and education.

States Employment Service have varied from state to state. A recent examination includes the following parts: objective questions (true-false and multiple choice) designed to test knowledge of employment and unemployment compensation laws and administration and related laws and administration, of business practice, and of many general aspects of economics and psychology; questions relating to the industries, the labor law, and the unemployment compensation law of the state; questions requiring the selection of the more grammatically correct of two words in specific sentences, and questions based on elementary arithmetic; multiple choice and

---

Pertinent experience is defined as full-time paid employment within the last 15 years in work definitely providing knowledge of occupational requirements and familiarity with employment problems and practices such as are entailed in agricultural, commercial, industrial, labor, and professional fields. United States Employment Service, Personnel Standards, Washington, 1938, p. 20.

(2) *Bureau of Unemployment Compensation: Junior Claims Examiner.*

Education equivalent to graduation from a standard four-year high school and at least five years of successful full-time paid employment in work related to the above duties, of which two years within the past five years must have been in the special experience defined below; or

Graduation from an accredited four-year college or university, and at least one year of full-time paid employment within the past five years in the special experience defined below; or

Any equivalent combination of education and experience, substituting one year of experience for one year of the required high school education and substituting one successfully completed year of college education for one year of the required general experience with a maximum substitution of three years.

Special experience:

Employment in a professional or other responsible capacity in at least one of the following fields: labor or industrial relations, public employment service, social work, law, accounting, enforcement of federal or state labor laws, or in related fields.

It should be noted that these specifications are widely used, but not universal. Many states have adopted somewhat different requirements. Personnel Standards, Bureau of Unemployment Compensation, Social Security Board.

true-false questions regarding employment service administration, and multiple choice questions requiring general knowledge concerning various occupations.

Examinations for higher positions include more detailed questions on administration, law, and local industrial and employment conditions, such as might be answered by an intelligent person with some experience in the service. A small number of free answer questions on employment office management were also included.. It was generally agreed by administrators in the states that a fairly acceptable personnel has been recruited by the United States Employment Service examinations. The same officials, however, are not in complete agreement as to the qualifications desired of employees.

Examinations for claims examiners in unemployment compensation cannot be described as fully since the Social Security Board has only recently received statutory power for as strict a control of procedure as that possessed by the United States Employment Service.[9] In the examinations reviewed by the study staff the questions asked of candidates for claims examiner positions are, on the whole, similar to those asked of candidates for interviewer positions. In the examination for claims examiner, however, more emphasis is placed on the legal aspects of administration than in the examination for interviewer. Procedure is less uniform than in the case of employment service examinations, but the weightings of the various parts of the examination are quite similar.

Public Assistance.—As evidence of sound administrative planning, the Social Security Board has requested the state public assistance agencies to establish control over the selection of personnel for local units. In the

9. 53 *Stat* 1360, Title III, August 10, 1939.

majority of states included in the present study, examinations in some form have been provided as a partial fulfillment of this requirement. In states where selection and appointment of personnel in public employment has been governed by civil service statute, the personnel in public assistance has been similarly recruited. In others, the state agency has established an examination system or has instituted a certification system with the same objective. The tendency within the states visited is towards the use of some form of competitive examination. The increased powers of the Social Security Board which became operative in January, 1940, will undoubtedly have profound effect upon this process, which at the time of the study varied considerably from state to state in standards and in effective control.[10]

In developing plans for recruiting personnel for the visitor, supervisory, and administrative levels, the states have been encouraged to attempt the selection of candidates for the lowest rank who have acquired the essential professional education which will make for continued development on the part of the worker and thus make him eligible for promotional examinations when positions at the higher levels are to be filled. Where this goal has been impossible of attainment, the states have been encouraged to require graduation from a four-year accredited university or college, so that individuals appointed to the staffs may be eligible later to attend schools of social work when plans for educational leave have been formulated.

In recruiting personnel for supervisory positions, qualifying experience is usually included and where this is

10. Amendment to the Social Security Act, Titles I, IV, and X, August 10, 1939. 53 *Stat* 1360.

specified refers to professional experience in social case work in a public or private agency. Frequently in states visited, college graduation and a degree or diploma from a two-year accredited school of social work may be substituted for such experience requirements. Thus recent graduates of schools of social work with little experience in the field may be eligible for appointment to supervisory positions.

In initial selection of personnel for administrative positions, qualifying experience is usually included. While preference is frequently given to individuals offering administrative or supervisory experience in the social work field, qualifying experience often includes public administration or business administration.

Child Welfare Services.—The personnel in the child welfare services has been selected by the state agencies in accordance with qualifications included in state plans for child welfare services developed jointly by the state agencies and the U. S. Children's Bureau. States having civil service laws select personnel in accordance with requirements of the statutes. In some non-civil service states, however, the state authority has established competitive examinations. No uniform examining program has been specified in these states.

According to recommendations of the United States Children's Bureau the basic requirements for child welfare workers include "specific training and experience in social welfare work as applied to individuals in need of assistance or service, preferably including experience in an agency giving case work service to children." [11]

11. United States Children's Bureau, "Standards for Personnel Employed in Maternal and Child Health Services, Services for Crippled Children and Child Welfare Services" (Washington, N.D.), p. 4.

Great value is placed on experience in child welfare agencies under private auspices. Experience in furthering development of community social resources, training experience, or executive experience are required for the more responsible positions. It is interesting to note that state directors of child welfare services are required to have "specialized experience in case work for children." [12]

The extent to which educational requirements have been utilized can be seen in the qualifications of the present personnel as of January 3, 1938. Of 478 workers and administrators concerning whom information was available, 391 were college graduates. Of these 391 workers, 358 had some preparation in schools of social work and 214 of the number had completed at least one full year of such education. It is to be expected that as more individuals meeting residence requirements of particular states are qualified, an even higher level of professional preparation will be possible. Concessions are made only when workers who have had neither agency experience nor professional education can be secured.

MERIT SYSTEMS

The preceding paragraphs have indicated the extent to which merit or civil service selection is used in the recruitment of personnel for the services included in the present study. It is beyond the scope of the present discussion to consider the theory of civil service and the

12. *Ibid.* Typical of the more adequate state civil service requirements are those of California. For a child welfare field worker the state requires a Master of Arts degree from an accredited school of social work or six quarters' and three semesters' work in a school of social work with emphasis on child welfare. An alternative is one year in school plus one semester of field work in child welfare. There is also an experience requirement of three years of successful employment in social work.

present methods used by those systems which are in operation at the local, the state, and the federal levels. The data gathered for the study, however, revealed certain problems reported as existing in civil service and merit selection systems.

Because the assembled examination is more frequently used for positions at the performance level, this discussion is mainly concerned with problems expressed concerning its use. The assembled examination, in addition to including or accompanying written, oral, and performance tests, sometimes included an evaluation of education and experience of the applicants. No uniformity in practice or opinion as to what weighting should be given for education and experience was found. Substitution of experience for education was often allowed without definitely stating how much or what kind of experience could be considered equivalent to the required education. There was no evidence in any of the services studied as to whether or not those in charge of examination programs considered lack of uniform standards or requirements as a handicap. There was no indication that concerted efforts were being made to consider the question of weighting and equivalents from the standpoint of valid examination. While the procedure of admitting as many potential eligibles as possible is desirable, attempts at setting up standards of selection for getting the best possible eligibles were rarely found.

In one state which prescribed no education qualification in eligibility for examination, the number of candidates was extremely large in relation to the number of positions to be filled.[13] In situations where a large number of eligibles had to be examined for a comparatively small

13. Pennsylvania.

number of positions, the use of the short answer or objective type of test was necessitated. In those situations the public assistance personnel interviewed found the selective process unsatisfactory. The objection was not based primarily on the short answer type of question. The chief difficulty seemed to be with the content of questions which had little relationship to the nature of the professional positions to be filled.

The problem of recruitment of qualified personnel in sufficient numbers for the services studied was made more difficult by the questions of weighting, substitutions of "equivalent" education and experience, and by the type of content of the examinations themselves. Even though some of the services had had longer experience than others in selecting personnel through a public central personnel agency, it was evident that they were all concerned essentially with the problem of establishing a valid method of selecting personnel.

The schools of social work have been concerned with the education of students who eventually seek employment in public assistance or child welfare services, and many of them have encouraged their students and graduates to take civil service examinations. Although 33 schools were included in the total study, comments in relation to the use of merit systems were received from only 16 schools. Their comments were related: (1) to some problems which antedated the establishment and use of merit systems and (2) to examinations used in selecting personnel. In the first group was included a comment in regard to racial discrimination which appointing officers may exercise regardless of legalistic attempts to make it impossible. Granting preference to veterans was also recognized as an example of giving advantage to a special group. The residence requirement established in many states was seen as a barrier to students who could accept employment anywhere. Some schools pointed to the fact that residence requirements prevented qualified students and graduates from seeking employment in states having such requirements. However, the fundamental difficulty in connection with residence requirements lies in the fact that they prevent some states from getting a sufficient supply of qualified eligibles while there may be an oversupply in adjacent states.

In the second group the comments indicated a general dissatisfaction with most of the aspects of the examinations. They indicated objections to the substitution of experience for education to the extent that professional education was minimized or obliterated. The content of the examinations in one state was said to be concerned with social sciences and current events rather than with professional principles and practices taught in professional schools. The season of the year in which an examination was held was considered to be significant, because students who had not completed the minimum curriculum could not take examinations given in the middle of an academic year. Comment was made upon the short time period between the date of publication of an announcement and the closing date for receipt of applications. The lack of established confidence in the integrity of the personnel agencies was another reason for resistance to the centralized method of selecting public personnel.

Any generalization with reference to civil service must take into consideration that this method of selection in the public social services has been extensively used for the first time during a period when these services have been rapidly changing and expanding. The amendment to the Social Security Act providing for merit selection [14] and its administration have been too recent to offer any basis for data to be used in this study.

RESIDENCE REQUIREMENTS

Old Age Insurance.—Since old age insurance is a federally operated service, no state residence requirements need to be considered. It has, however, been the practice to recruit local office personnel from the state of residence or to assign appointees to their "home" states. A departure from this tradition has been noticeable recently as some of the regional offices have been transferring personnel across state lines within their region. The distribution of the "personnel clerk" (field assistant) group has apparently been on the wider, regional basis, and no change in this policy has occurred. Inter-regional transfers remain exceedingly rare.

Initially, at least, these residence requirements were urged upon the Social Security Board by vigilant congressmen who coveted administrative appointments for their constituents. This pressure was undoubtedly facilitated by the use of the administrative register referred to in a preceding paragraph,[15] and may be less marked as a tradition of promotion through the service develops. At the present time, however, it must be admitted that the administrative practice of tacitly requiring state or regional residence constitutes a serious, though not insuperable, barrier to careers in old age insurance. Some of the study staff gained the impression that in certain

14. 53 *Stat* 1360, August 10, 1939.
15. *Supra*, p. 126.

places promotional possibilities for lower ranks of office personnel were deemed very limited and even more limited for managers who can only be promoted to a larger office in the same region.

Unemployment Compensation and Employment Service.—Both employment service and unemployment compensation are state-administered, and state residence is almost universally required, either formally in the class specifications or tacitly in administration of examinations and in appointments. On a few occasions, personnel has been transferred from one state to another, usually to satisfy a need for specific training or equipment. No policy of inter-state exchange of personnel, however, has been established.

Requirements of local residence within the state rarely exist, but for reasons of political allegiance, administrative necessity, or employee convenience, there is a definite tendency to assign individual workers to sections of the state where they reside. In California, a specific district residence is required, and in Texas, local residence is a fact if not an announced policy. In Michigan, it is customary to place individual workers near their home communities.

Obviously, state residence requirements hinder the development of a public service. A system under which an able, well-trained person may wait for years to obtain an administrative position in one state while less competent individuals secure such positions in other states does not present an alluring prospect. So far, there is little evidence to indicate, however, that the preference for local personnel will seriously affect promotional possibilities. While, undoubtedly, a promising senior interviewer has a slight advantage in the competition for a vacant managership in his own office, there have already been instances enough of inter-office shifts to indicate that able individuals will be transferred within the state according to the needs of the service. Residence requirements are, of course, no barrier at the present to promotion into the central state office or into the controlling federal services.

Public Assistance.—In the absence of any nation-wide standard it becomes difficult to generalize about residence requirements in public assistance administration. State residence is usually required by state laws, and it is probably safe to say that very few workers who are not residents of the state are appointed to county staffs. While county residence is not generally specified in state laws and regulations, it is tacitly understood to be a matter of county policy, and is usually required except where the program is state-operated. Occasionally, a state, as for example, Michigan, provides by statute that the county director shall have county residence, thus greatly limiting promotional possibilities for personnel. The Pennsylvania plan requires county residence of other agency staff members. On the other hand, a few state departments have succeeded in persuading county units to employ persons from outside their borders.

On the state staffs a little more flexibility has been possible, though state welfare authorities are far from enjoying the freedom accorded to some other departments in state government. A few states have been forced to abandon the practice of recruiting non-resident personnel. West Virginia, for example, has recently dismissed out-of-state personnel holding key positions. Nebraska, on the other hand, has thus far been successful in resisting pressure to adopt the same practice.

It is appropriate, however, to point out that as long as strong sentiment for such requirements exists, promotional possibilities in public assistance are limited. According to the Second Annual Report of the Social Security Board, some results of residence requirements are disadvantageous. While it may be assumed that the Bureau of Public Assistance is opposed to an extension of residence requirements, it has not attempted to forbid their inclusion in state plans.[16]

Child Welfare Services.—The fact that salaries for personnel in child welfare services are provided in part or in full through grants to the states from the federal government and that special qualifications are required by the federal authority make it possible to avoid state residence requirements more successfully than in any other of the services studied.

The absence of residence barriers in the child welfare services in the future, however, cannot be assumed. The United States Children's Bureau has been attempting to demonstrate special services to children in the hope that states and counties will soon assume responsibility for programs. Since most of the child welfare workers are employed in rural areas, there is some justification for rural residence requirements. In many cases, workers who have lived only in cities find difficulty in adjustment to rural living conditions.[17] Pressures for state and local residence undoubtedly exist. Even where sentiment for

16. Second Annual Report, Social Security Board, 1937, pp. 34-35.

17. It is interesting to note that for the job of county agent a farm background in addition to agricultural college training is usually demanded. It is also interesting to note, however, that most states refuse to appoint county agents to their home counties, although the appointment is usually made in the home state.

local residence is powerful, however, it seems to apply less in child welfare service than in public assistance.

*   *   *   *   *

In all the services studied, residence is a potent influence in the selection of personnel.[18] Whether officially provided by statute or unofficially by popular will, it is a factor to be reckoned with seriously if these services are to recruit and hold able employees.[19]

SALARY LEVELS

Basic to any effort to meet the needs of these services is a salary level which will attract competent personnel and through differentials for higher positions offer a reward for outstanding achievement. It is important, therefore, to turn to the analysis of salaries in the services studied.

Old Age Insurance.—Salary payments for employees in the clerical-interviewing group in old age insurance range from $1,260 to $1,620.[20] For most of the specially-trained interviewers, the salary range is $1,620 to $1,980.[21] Assistant managers are paid between $1,800 and $2,500, though a few receive more than this maximum or less than this minimum. The salary range of managers is from $2,000 to $6,000 with 75 per cent of the group receiving between $2,500 and $4,000.

18. State Residence Requirements for Personnel in Public Assistance Agencies, American Public Welfare Association, Chicago, 1941.

19. In this connection, note the following resolution passed by the American Association of Social Workers Delegate Conference, 1940: "That requirements of state and local residence, veterans' preference and other extra-professional considerations are inimical to selection of personnel on the basis of professional competence."—*The Compass,* June-July 1940, Vol. XXI, p. 13.

20. Grade 1 of the Federal "clerical, administrative, and fiscal service."

21. Grade A of the "clerical, administrative, and fiscal service."

Detailed data on administrative personnel in the central office are not given, since many of these are connected with the central records operation at Baltimore, with which this study has not been concerned. Regional representatives receive a minimum of $5,600, assistant regional representatives a minimum of $3,800, and senior assistant regional representatives in larger regions a minimum of $4,600. These positions represent opportunities for promotion from the local offices.

Unemployment Compensation and Employment Service.—Salary levels in the employment service are more or less adjusted to general state salary levels and thus vary widely, especially for the higher positions.

Junior interviewers receive between $1,320 and $1,800 a year. In the greater number of states studied, the range was between $1,500 and $1,800. Senior interviewers receive from $1,620 to $2,400, with the modal salaries between $1,800 and $2,280. In western states when the higher range is reached the senior interviewer frequently becomes the manager of a small office. Remuneration for field office managers varies from $1,920 to $3,000, with a modal salary range of $2,400 to $2,880. District managers and field supervisors usually receive from $3,000 to $3,600. Directors' salaries varied from $3,000 to $6,000 in the states studied, with $4,800 as a modal point.

On the whole, the salary range in unemployment compensation is comparable. Claims examiners (or claims deputies) are paid from $1,620 to $3,000. Usually, although not invariably, the salaries over $2,100 are reserved for "senior" examiners or others with administrative responsibilities. The remuneration of the deputy without such administrative responsibility is intermediate between a junior and senior interviewer. Salaries for administrative positions in the benefits sections range from $2,040 to $6,000. Chiefs of benefit sections receive between $2,700 and $6,000 with the dominant salary between $3,000 and $4,200.

Public Assistance.—Data concerning salary scales in public assistance, from the states studied, will give some idea of the range throughout the different sections of the country.

Generalization is difficult for many reasons. The number and descriptions of job specifications at the three levels vary from state to state, thus making salary schedules difficult of comparison. The degree of responsibility exercised by state and local units in the fixing of the salary schedules also varies from state to state, making generalization even in one area very uncertain.

Information obtained in the states studied indicates that the visitors received from $1,200 to $1,860 a year, the range including junior and senior grades. Supervisors receive from $1,500 to $4,200, the wide range determined in part by the variety of responsibilities carried by individuals so designated. Administrators at the county level received from $1,500 to $7,500, depending on the size and nature of the county administrative load. As previously indicated, in some counties, where the administrator is the only worker or one of two workers, his responsibilities and salary returns are in marked contrast to the situation where he is in charge of a sizeable staff and of administrative processes of a highly complex nature.

In the analysis of salary data, the study staff commented most frequently on the low salary level for staff positions in public assistance. Here, where there is definite recognition of the need for professional education at the graduate level and considerable effort expended in that direction, it is the opinion of the staff that salary levels are far from commensurate with the financial investment involved in four years of general college education followed by two years of professional study.

Child Welfare Services.—Salaries in child welfare services reflect much the same situation as that in public assistance, although the discrepancy between the professional preparation which is recognized as the desirable goal and the salary level for beginning workers is less marked than in public assistance. According to information available at the time this study was made, the salary of the local area worker is customarily $1,500 a year, with some differential up to $2,100 for workers with experience or for those assigned to special tasks. Field supervisors and case consultants are paid on a somewhat higher salary basis.

From this brief analysis, the variations in salary levels for workers performing the essential services to individuals is readily noted. Likewise, there is no evidence as yet that this variation has any relationship to personnel requirements or to responsibilities performed.

STAFF DEVELOPMENT

Viewed in relation to the services studied, staff development includes both formal in-service programs of training and provisions for leaves of absence to permit resident study in educational institutions.

Old Age Insurance.—Old age insurance did not place importance on graduate professional education for positions, on account of the belief that such educational facilities, especially designed to develop the particular competence required in this field, do not yet exist.

Among the services studied, old age insurance took the lead, however, in the development of elaborate in-service training programs. The administrators of this program have tried to develop, through introductory and continuing training of all personnel, a thorough and common understanding of the social objectives of the program and of preferable methods and techniques of administration. All administrative personnel, including field assistants, assistant managers, managers, and superior officers must complete the five weeks' training course conducted in Washington by the Training Division of the Bureau of Business Management of the Social Security Board. Topics presented in this course include: Survey of the Social Security Act, Insecurity in American Life, Growth of the American Social Services, Types of Insecurity, Comparison of Private and Social Insurance, Foreign Social Insurance, the Wage Earner and the Social Security Program, Social Security and Its Relation to Governmental Relief. The various titles of the Social Security Act are then considered in sequence, and the administrative policies of the Board are carefully discussed. Assigned readings and written exercises are required in addition to attendance at lectures. Materials in this course are presented fully and well, especially that subject-matter of the social sciences which is related to the social security program.

In addition to this original orientation, optional correspondence courses have been offered for clerical and for administrative staffs in old age insurance field offices. "Claims schools" have been conducted in the field by representatives from the adjudications section, and recently the responsible clerical personnel has been admitted to these schools.

The trainees who are being promoted to field assistant-ships undertake seven weeks' field observation, in addition to the five weeks' orientation program. They spend one week observing central record operations in the Baltimore office; another in the claims section in Washington, and a month in supervised work on "wage discrepancies" and "over-the-counter" work in the New York Administration.

Advantages and weaknesses in this program were observed during the study. The officials in Old Age Insurance administration throughout the country, especially those who had completed the Washington course, were aware of the broad social significance of their program, and in this respect they often stood out in sharp and happy contrast to persons in the other services visited. A five-weeks' training course, on the other hand, cannot compensate for basic deficiencies in knowledge of the social sciences. Nor can the program supply specific training for the complex task of serving people in a variety of situations. The importance of skills in human relations was emphasized, yet no attempt was made to equip the personnel with a basic understanding of behavior. Even those trainees who had completed the field work assignment lacked the interviewing skill which is emphasized in public assistance and in the employment service. Personnel equipped to train workers on the job is not available in the service. Likewise, the relatively small number of personnel involved in old age insurance administration in each state complicates a training program related to this service alone.

Such a training program cannot be finally evaluated until it has met the test of benefit payments beginning in January, 1940. If, however, any plan of in-service training can supply the deficiencies in pre-service training, it is the opinion of the study staff that the old age insurance program will achieve that result.

Although no leaves of absence on whole or part salary for university study have been provided, there was no attitude of antagonism to the practice. Appropriate extension courses might be welcomed, but the small and scattered personnel make such a course hardly feasible.

Unemployment Compensation and Employment Service.—The responsibility for staff development in the unemployment compensation and employment service naturally rests with the states, yet both the United States Employment Service and the Bureau of Unemployment Compensation have taken some leadership in the field.

In 1937 under the direction of a specialist, the United States Employment Service appointed seven training supervisors, each in charge of a geographical district. Each state service was authorized to appoint a state training supervisor to the administrative staff. Regional training conferences for state administrators and state training supervisors were organized, and materials were prepared and distributed to the training supervisors. These undertakings were interrupted by the developments in unemployment compensation administration.

Uniformly the state employment services recognize the importance of in-service training and devote considerable time and energy to it. Evidence of this is the agreement of the delegates at the International Association of Employment Officers in 1938 that staff training is a legitimate function of state administration because: (1) the employment service has developed as a professional service and now has a body of knowledge, techniques and skills and social attitudes toward applicants, employers

148   Education for the Public Social Services

and the community; (2) personnel in public employment offices is recruited from all walks of life, with related experience perhaps, but not specific experience in
public employment service work; (3) no specialized training is available in the schools; most university courses
are applicable generally rather than specifically; (4)
training increases efficiency, a fact recognized by industry; (5) training tends to establish definite lines of promotion, thus increasing both efficiency and morale.[22]

It is generally recognized that in-service training can
best be carried on by the line executive or under his
immediate supervision. The content includes group
meetings for the discussion of objectives, history, principles of organization, field observation, and training
supervision. It is interesting that this last aspect of the
program was stressed at the 1939 conference of public
employment officers.[23] State-wide conferences for interviewers and for office managers are frequently arranged,
and in a few instances regional conferences for state administrators and training supervisors have been arranged
by the United States Employment Service.

Manuals of procedure have been developed by training supervisors in most of the states studied. These range
from short descriptions of application forms to many-
volumed series designed for supervisory personnel, interviewers, and clerical personnel. The more elaborate manuals sometimes include such auxiliary material as the
history of the public employment services in Europe and
the United States and the general principles of organization and management. A considerable amount of prac-

22. Proceedings of the 26th Annual Convention of the International
Association of Public Employment Services, 1938, p. 60.
23. Proceedings of the 27th Annual Convention of the International
Association of Public Employment Services, 1939, p. 24.

tical psychology has been incorporated in the Pennsylvania and Indiana manuals for interviewers, and in Texas, basic instruction in Spanish has been prepared for interviewers serving Mexican applicants.

In-service training in the employment service has included the study of community industries or occupations through field visits and discussion groups. For example, in Connecticut, a group of interviewers specializing in construction work placement devoted a morning to inspection of a building addition in Hartford; in the afternoon, various "highlights of the job visit" were discussed, and specific problems considered. What type of workers should set gypsum planking? Should brick masons or stone setters be referred in answer to requests for layers of glass brick? In Milwaukee a group of younger interviewers constructed a model automobile so that each job in a local automobile factory could be analyzed. The field visit is an accepted technique of instruction.

In spite of these efforts, interviews with employment service administrators disclosed a widespread dissatisfaction with the results of in-service training. The training methods, however, were not criticized. Many administrators were convinced that the lack of success could be traced to deficiencies of pre-entry or post-entry education. In most instances, no program for correcting the situation had been developed, nor were many constructive suggestions cited. The following summaries of interviews are typical.

In one of the better state services visited, two administrators, not college graduates themselves, remarked that the employment service would never achieve high performance until it recruited college graduates. One qualified his statement by saying that he desired more "democratic college men, such as those found in the great plains states." The administrator of another state service, which is usually regarded as one of the best in the country, believed that a pre-entry college course in the social sciences was essential but stressed the importance of a course closely related to local office experience. He knew of no college capable of providing such training, and his state is considering an interneship plan for college men. Another state director expressed similar doubt of academic programs. To what extent these criticisms related to teaching methods is not known, but the interviews suggest that some inquiry in this direction would be helpful.

Post-entry education for the employment service is almost as undeveloped as is pre-entry education. In California, Connecticut, Michigan, Nebraska, New York, Pennsylvania, Texas, and Wisconsin, it was generally agreed that efforts should be made to supply to the staff basic knowledge in certain fields where gaps are especially noticed. Economics, psychology, social legislation, and public administration were cited. Some interest was expressed in the establishment of extension courses for employment service workers. No effective program was under way, however, partly because of uncertainty within the employment service as to its specific aims, but partly because of the inflexibility of academic programs. Workers in metropolitan centers were unwilling to undertake extension courses which did not carry degree credit, and universities were chary of granting credit to students not in full-time residence. In more remote local offices, the difficulty of securing sufficient enrollment for extension courses was obvious.

State programs to which the Bureau of Unemployment Compensation has given assistance are very similar. In practically all the states, claims examiners are given intensive induction courses in the law and administration of unemployment compensation. These courses vary from one to three weeks. Subsequent training seems in large part to consist of conferences on the procedures and on the trends of referee or appeal board decisions.

In a few states, unemployment compensation employees have shared in the more elaborate training programs of the employment service. In California, Michigan, Pennsylvania, and Utah, the same training supervisor carried responsibility for both services. It is reasonable to suppose that an increase in joint training programs will result from the integration of the Washington administrations.

The need for in-service training has been stressed in the employment service and more recently in unemployment compensation administration. In the employment services undergoing rapid expansion, new personnel should be taught the responsibilities of their positions and the ideals of their organization, and the experienced personnel needs a new and broader viewpoint. The efforts of the federal agencies to influence the states in this respect have not been significant, probably because of the uncertainties concerning reorganization within the United States Employment Service and the lack of experienced personnel in the Bureau of Unemployment Compensation. It is possible that administrative integration of the two services and the increasing interest of the Social Security Board in broad administrative training may have some positive effect in the future.

It is apparent from the study that the in-service training concept in this service obscures the place of pre-

entry education. It was suggested that the experience
requirements and the emphasis on in-service training are
due to the fact that educational institutions have not
anticipated needs, and the agencies therefore do not recognize the extent to which special preparation might be
substituted for the experience requirements. Some re-
thinking of the experience requirements is important if
men and women of good educational background are to
be recruited for the service.

Public Assistance.—In contrast to the two preceding
services, where the emphasis on pre-entry preparation is
slight, the in-service program in public assistance is in
accord with the conviction on the part of the Technical
Training Division of the Bureau of Public Assistance
that the long-range development in the service demands
a personnel professionally prepared in schools of social
work.

Staff development is conceived by the Technical
Training Division as "an integral part of administration
and as a means of strengthening administration through
improving competence of staff." All members of the staff
are to be included in the program, which is planned specifically to "meet the needs of staff in relation to work
expected of each employee towards achievement of the
agency's purposes." [24]

Possible activities for the development of staff include
an orientation period for new workers to "enable each
employee to make a satisfactory beginning on his part
of the agency's work," "supervision of the day-by-day
work of the individual employee so that there is result-

24. "Staff Development Programs in State Public Assistance Agencies,"
Division of Technical Training, Bureau of Public Assistance, Social Security Board, December 2, 1940 (mimeo.).

ing growth on the job," and other resources such as lectures, institutes, and planning for educational opportunities.

The orientation period is designed to (a) give insight into the broad purpose of the agency's work, (b) give a start toward familiarity with legal base, administrative structure, job function, rules, regulations, and office procedures of the agency, (c) give an understanding of the historical background of the agency and its relationships to the other services in the field, past and present.[25]

Supervision of the individual employee is designed to promote growth on the job. Among methods used are (a) staff meetings, held regularly, with content planned from the day-by-day work, with creative leadership, (b) individual conferences between worker and supervisor, held regularly, with preparation made by both workers and with positive educational value, and (c) group conferences for a specific purpose and for workers concerned with the same subject or problem.

Within the service itself differences of opinion are noted. Several administrators dissented strongly from the view held by the Bureau of Public Assistance and stated that in-service training should attempt to supply some of the basic deficiencies of staff members. It is not the policy of the Bureau to ignore the needs of the staff. Rather, the Bureau hopes, as indicated above, to recruit for operating level personnel college graduates with preparation in the social sciences, and for supervisory or specialized personnel individuals with professional education in social work. It further hopes that educational leave for study at schools of social work can

25. *Ibid.*

be provided for promising staff personnel.[26] Such a system of educational leaves has been established on a small scale in a few states. This training policy would be wholly consistent if it were accompanied by a more generous provision for educational leaves and for extension work by the schools of social work.

The present salary level is hardly conducive to investment in two years of professional education at the graduate level, which follows the recognition of professional training as pre-requisite for appointment to the service. Without far more extensive provision for "salaried leave" or for fellowships by schools of social work than is now available, the plan for educational leaves of absence is likely to make little headway, since the prevailing low salaries handicap workers from financing educational leaves. At first sight, extension courses might seem to be the solution. A time allowance for extension work was not infrequently found within the agencies visited. The nature of the course material available, however, was often criticized. Unquestionably the criticism is often justified, often not. For example, the criticism made by agency workers of course material offered by schools of social work through extension is justified when this course content does not follow the regular curriculum course content as given in the school. Criticism directed against the failure of a school to give a course which deals with the policies and procedures of a specific agency for the purpose of instructing workers in that agency procedure is not valid. Another source of friction is the limitation on academic credit for extension work.

26. See "Use of Federal Administration Funds for Paying Salaries to Staff Members on Educational Leave in Schools of Social Work," December 23, 1937.

In several states the universities were criticized for their general lack of interest in problems of social work. It should be noted here that more flexible and coöperative arrangements by schools of social work would be helpful in furthering the interest in education for social work, provided sound educational requirements and standards of professional education are safeguarded.

Child Welfare Services.—Since staffs are still relatively small and considerable pre-entry education is required, the in-service training programs in the child welfare services are not elaborate. Emphasis is placed first on training through supervision, which is indeed the most important of the three types of in-service training suggested by the United States Children's Bureau.[27] As the federal agency indicates, this method is effective only when well-qualified supervisors are available. In some cases qualified supervisors have been secured from other states on a temporary basis usually to travel throughout the state conducting an intermittent but intensive supervision of all child welfare workers. Frequently the influence of such appointments is far-reaching.

In the second place, emphasis is placed upon the specially-staffed training unit. These units are primarily intended to provide services for children in the community and only secondarily to supply a convenient training center for staff workers. They are sometimes established in areas adjacent to schools of social work and used as field practice centers. The extent of this type of development has not been very great.

27. Incidentally, it should be remembered that traditionally supervision constitutes a more vital aspect of in-service training in the profession of social work than in the new services included in this study.

Third, in the in-service training program are conferences, institutes, or discussion groups. These are considered as substitutes neither for professional education nor
for intensive supervision. While few institutes or conferences have been organized by state child welfare services, the workers in these services have actively participated in many which were fostered by public assistance
or other welfare departments or by private family and
child welfare agencies.

The U. S. Children's Bureau has consistently urged
leaves of absence for post-entry education. Two quarters
or one semester in an approved school of social work is
the customary provision. The number of persons in each
state to which the leaves may be granted is proportioned
to the total amount of child welfare appropriations and
the total number of workers for that state. Staff members
who have had some preparation in recognized schools of
social work are given first consideration. Those who have
the basic educational qualifications for admission to such
schools are given second consideration. It is believed desirable that federal funds be used only as supplementary
assistance, and the maximum grant for educational leave
per student cannot exceed $110 a month.[28] The Bureau
strongly urges that students select schools where field
work practice in children's agencies of high standard is
available. State supervisors are urged to confer with the
schools in which the students are enrolled, and in some
instances federal representatives have shared this responsibility.

28. U. S. Children's Bureau, "Policies on Training," August 1, 1939
(mimeographed) .

POSSIBILITIES FOR PROMOTION

Any discussion of possibilities of advancement in the services reflects two points of view toward promotion. First is the concept that the initial selection of persons for the positions at the lowest rank should be followed by a system of promotion based on seniority and service records. The second is that promotion embodies something more than seniority and satisfactory performance on a particular job. In many instances it involves the assumption of a new set of duties for which new skills may be required. This philosophy of promotion supports the suggestion that promotional examinations governing the transfer from one group of positions to another be open and competitive, so that qualified persons outside the service may compete. A review of the services studied gives evidence of both points of view in operation.

Old Age Insurance.—In a service as new as old age insurance there is little to be said on the subject of promotion. It must be remembered that the initial selection of managers was based on the Administrative Officer Register and later on the use of inter-departmental transfer. Field assistants were recruited from the Junior Administrative Technician Register or from the Clerical Register. According to study findings, promotions to field assistantships and assistant managerships have been based on general intelligence, general education, and service record. While it is too soon to tell, the conclusion from the data obtained in the study is that policy in old age insurance administration favors the closed system of promotions. The changing nature of the service with the introduction of survivors' benefits may, however, modify this tendency.

*Unemployment Compensation and Employment Serv-
ice.*—Opportunities for trained personnel to progress up
the administrative ladder are improving in both Unemployment Compensation and the Employment Service,
but it is as yet impossible to say just how great are those
opportunities. In most of the states studied, the highest
administrative positions were regarded, at least in part,
as rewards for political services. In unemployment compensation especially, partisan politics affected even the
less important positions, since the federal agency at the
time had no statutory power to require merit systems.
The recent amendment to the Social Security Act, which
requires merit systems in all states, may improve the situation greatly.[29]

Another important factor restricting promotional opportunities, especially in the employment service, is the
broad base of the administrative pyramid. In Ohio, for
example, 255 junior interviewers and 134 senior interviewers aspire to seven local administrative and eleven
state administrative positions. The situation in other
states is similar.[30] To what extent this situation is due
to the early development of the employment service is
not known, but the possibility is worth consideration.
It is interesting to note that unemployment compensation is without this pyramid picture, since the number
of jobs at the lowest level of service is proportionately
smaller than that in employment service. The study staff
concluded that this has the effect at present of providing
greater promotion possibilities.

The federal personnel in the United States Employment Service was recruited to a large extent from the

29. 53 *Stat* 1360. August 10, 1939.
30. Appendix B, Table No. III.

state services, and it is conceivable that promotion to the federal level in the Bureau of Unemployment Security will follow the same course and will also draw from subordinate positions in the federal bureau.

Public Assistance.—In public assistance, promotion from local to state offices is fairly frequent. In some states, there has been a tendency to stress other than professional qualifications in appointments to positions of administrative responsibility in public assistance. With the aid of the Board's new powers, the promotion of social workers with professional qualifications may be encouraged and extended.

In addition to the limitations imposed by residence requirements, a definite sex differential in public assistance was occasionally observed. In several of the states included in the study there was apparent discrimination against women in administrative positions. This practice may have been due to a desire to remove these positions from the possibility of attainment by well-qualified social workers, so many of whom are women. Proposals in the 1939 sessions of several state legislatures barring married women from state employment if the husbands' salaries are "adequate" would constitute a further restriction on some of the most promising personnel in public assistance.

Child Welfare.—The organization of the relatively small number of positions in child welfare is such that a competent well-trained person can reasonably hope for promotion from the ranks. It should, however, be noted that while political considerations do not as greatly affect the appointment to higher positions as has been true in public assistance, there are fewer administrative positions to be filled, and the pressure for appointment of

local residents is still great. One of the disadvantages
arising from the otherwise useful tool of federal grants-
in-aid is the tendency to consider those whose salaries
are so provided as "outsiders." Although their function
may be an integral part of a large state welfare department, few workers in child welfare services can hope,
under present circumstances, to secure general administrative positions in these departments.

FEDERAL LEADERSHIP IN PERSONNEL PRACTICES IN THE SERVICES

Within those services established by the Social Security Act, there is variation in the degree of federal leadership. Old age insurance is federally administered and
operated, while unemployment compensation, public
assistance, and child welfare are administered by a partnership of the federal government and the states, which
at first excluded the federal authorities from any responsibility for the qualifications, tenure, or compensation
of personnel employed by the states in the program.
Recent amendment to the Act provides for merit selection of employees in public assistance, unemployment
compensation, and child welfare services.[31] It is interesting, however, to note that the Social Security Board has
exercised leadership in the definition and standards of
personnel in the services administered under grants-in-
aid as well as in the service directly operated.

The initial selection of personnel for the administration of old age insurance was accomplished by the use of
federal civil service registers and inter-departmental
transfer, at a time when it is only fair to say that the job
of old age insurance was as yet undefined. The content

31. 53 *Stat* 1360, August 10, 1939.

of the administrative examination indicates that reliance was placed upon the traditions of private insurance at the time.[32] The four annual reports of the Social Security Board give no further attention to the qualifications or selection of personnel for old age insurance. And it is significant that the Second Annual Report comments on the organization as established to carry out a program which has been called "the world's largest insurance system," and the accounting processes necessary, "the largest bookkeeping operation in history." In the meantime, since the passage of the Act, substantial change in the scope and nature of old age insurance has been effected.[33]

In unemployment compensation, federal leadership has concentrated upon the use of civil service or merit systems for selection and upon the need for classification of personnel by the states. In this leadership the Board utilized its power of allocating grants to the states for administrative purposes, to withhold moneys should the administration of the state law be found to be unsound. To exercise this discretion, the Board quite early decided that the development of standards "against which state administrative costs might be measured" should include among other items the maximum salary scales for personnel.[34] Specifications for positions in state unemployment compensation administration were prepared and used in the development and promotion of standards in the states.[35] The firm conviction of the Board with reference to personnel is indicated in the following quotation from the First Annual Report. "Regardless of state law,

32. Administrative Register, *supra*, p. 126.

33. Amendments of August 10, 1939 establishing the system as Old Age and Survivors' Insurance, 53 *Stat* 1360, Title II.

34. First Annual Report of the Social Security Board, 1936, p. 43.

35. *Ibid.*

the state administration will succeed or fail in accordance with the quality of personnel selected to operate the service." [36]

The emphasis seems to have been placed upon merit selection and the in-service training program rather than upon the known qualifications for the job. The lack of sources for trained or experienced personnel in the area of unemployment compensation was cited as a difficulty and may have been the determining factor.[37] It is evident that the federal leadership had clearly in mind the broader aspects of the program, for in referring to the training program which it regarded as essential, the Board indicated that the entire program should be oriented definitely towards the situation which would obtain "when benefits are payable." Without it, the administration would develop into an organization "which merely collects and pays out money, with little appreciation of its larger responsibility." [38] The content of suggested training programs substantiates this goal.[39]

Considerable progress was made in the use of classification plans and in merit systems, and by the end of the fiscal year 1939, forty-two states had established such classification plans, sixteen were selecting personnel under civil service laws, and twenty-eight (including three with civil service laws just enacted) were selecting per-

36. *Ibid.*, p. 44.
37. Second Annual Report of the Social Security Board, 1937, p. 64.
38. First Annual Report of the Social Security Board, 1936, p. 45.
39. "Such a training program should include an examination of the problem of unemployment, the past methods of dealing with it, the development of unemployment compensation in this country and abroad, the events which led up to the enactment of the Social Security Act, provisions of the act, and an analysis of existing state laws. . . . In addition, advance knowledge is needed of the type of problems which available experience suggests as probable in the actual administration of the law." *Ibid.*

sonnel under merit systems established according to the rules and regulations issued under the state unemployment compensation laws.[40] Technical assistance in the development of personnel classification, policies, and training programs was made available on a continuing basis.[41] But the establishment of a personnel classification plan and the outlining of work duties and responsibilities of the proposed personnel constituted an essential which the Board required in the granting of administrative funds.[42]

In the administration of public assistance grants to the states, the Board lacked the responsibility for tenure and for compensation of state and local personnel, but the close relation of qualified personnel to its responsibility for the efficient administration of state plans was quickly seen. At first, the Board, while recommending no individuals nor saying anything about qualifications or compensation, urged upon the states the need for "competent administrators and for minimum objective standards of training and experience" and was prepared to help any state develop a program of training for its administrative personnel.[43] Later the Board decided to approve no plan "unless it contains provisions developed by the state which establish minimum objective standards for the selection of both state and local staffs." [44]

Qualifications of personnel are implied throughout. In the Second Report, for example, qualified personnel was defined as "equipped for its responsibilities by edu-

40. Fourth Annual Report of the Social Security Board, 1939, p. 73.
41. Third Annual Report of the Social Security Board, 1938, p. 60, and *ibid.*, 1939, p. 45.
42. Third Annual Report of the Social Security Board, 1938, p. 64.
43. First Annual Report of the Social Security Board, 1936, p. 34.
44. Second Annual Report of the Social Security Board, 1937, p. 34.

cation, training, and experience in public welfare." [45]
In further comment, the Report states:

> The effective administration of public assistance involves
> much more than the receiving and investigating of applica-
> tions for aid and the making of payments. Nevertheless, the
> successful performance of even these primary functions re-
> quires personnel capable of dealing with difficult problems
> of human relations, and with experience and judgment
> which can be relied upon in the making of decisions which
> will affect the lives of needy individuals.[46]

Requisite skills included the ability to secure and evaluate facts in the light of the total family situation, continuing service to recipients such as the aged who may
need medical care or who have personal difficulties which
cannot be met by money; service to mothers with dependent children in need of education, vocational training and social adjustment and to the blind who often
have an infinite variety of personal problems.

> The state and local staffs must be equipped not only to
> help recipients to meet such problems but also to contribute
> to the development of community resources for medical care,
> prevention and treatment of juvenile delinquency, voca-
> tional guidance and placement, and the like.[47]

The problem of obtaining such a personnel was early
recognized. The experience of the emergency relief program had made the recruiting easier in some of the states
but in others there was little recognition of the "professional character of such work." [48] In-service training was
recognized as important and the Board gave assistance

45. *Ibid.*, p. 34.
46. *Ibid.*, p. 35.
47. *Ibid.*, p. 36.
48. First Annual Report of the Social Security Board, 1936, p. 34.

to the states in this respect, yet it definitely stated that "in-service training is not regarded in any sense as a substitute for professional education in social welfare." [49] By the fourth year, the program of staff development to which the Board gave leadership, recognized in addition to in-service training for workers on the job, efforts to "broaden the base of knowledge and skill of employees through plans for general and professional education." [50]

With reference to the qualifications of personnel in child welfare services, the attitude of the federal agency was unequivocal. In the Third Report was the following statement which was reiterated in the Fourth Report.[51]

The importance of employing well qualified workers to carry on the local demonstration services has necessitated the development of state supervisory services and training programs, including educational leave for attendance at schools of social work, the establishment of training units, and the holding of institutes for the instruction of staff members.[52]

The amendment providing for merit selection has been passed since the material for the present study was gathered.[53] This substantiated the conviction of the Board that the "wording in the titles of the act which relate to federal grants to states should be amended to re-

49. Second Annual Report of the Social Security Board, 1937, p. 37.
50. Fourth Annual Report of the Social Security Board, 1939, p. 83.
51. *Ibid.*, p. 161.
52. Third Annual Report of the Social Security Board, 1938, p. 130.
53. Effective January 1, 1940, the amended act provides for the establishment of objective standards for merit systems for both state and local personnel as one of the conditions to be met by the states seeking federal grants. This extends to public assistance, unemployment compensation, maternal and child health services, and service to crippled children. Methods relating to the establishment and maintenance of personnel standards on a merit basis must now be included along with other conditions to be met. 53 *Stat* 1360, August 10, 1939.

quire state agencies to establish and maintain personnel standards based on a merit system and should include a provision prohibiting political activity on the part of state personnel." [54] The traditions upon which these systems can be built are clear in the area of public assistance and child welfare. A philosophy of broad basis of service is evident in unemployment compensation. That of old age insurance seems not yet defined. Yet an over-all view of the four services convinces the student that progress in the direction of defining and standardizing service has been continuous and effective.

SUMMARY

Within the services studied, definite progress is being made towards securing more adequate personnel. Old age insurance is giving most attention to outlining personnel policies, but has not given the same concern to the educational content of the job. In unemployment compensation and the employment services, the experience minimum required of all applicants for appointment bars graduates of colleges or professional schools without work experience from the entering level in the services. In public assistance and child welfare services a personnel prepared in schools of social work is the recognized goal. Progress towards this end is hampered by salary levels which hardly seem to justify investment in professional education at the graduate level. The child welfare services included in the study have made greater progress towards establishing salary levels commensurate with preparation.

Were the salary levels adequate, the numerical need of workers is out of proportion to the present supply. For

54. Third Annual Report of the Social Security Board, 1938, pp. 13-14.

example, in public assistance the number of operating level positions has been estimated as 25,000. It is interesting to compare this figure with the number of members of the American Association of Social Workers now estimated as 11,000 and with the number of students graduating each year from schools of social work estimated as 1,400. From these comparisons, the goal of a professionally trained staff seems far in the future. In some states, a sound basis has been laid by the appointment of college graduates with background of education in the social sciences. In other states the operation of political forces has handicapped this practice. Here the operation of the merit amendment to the Social Security Act should have a profound effect.

Civil service selection of personnel has been universally applied in old age insurance. In unemployment compensation and the employment service, merit systems have been established in general accordance with plans recommended by the United States Employment Service and the Bureau of Unemployment Compensation. Merit selection has been applied in public assistance in the majority of states, and except where state civil service systems have dictated otherwise the selection of workers in the child welfare services has been carried out according to qualifications specified in state plans developed jointly by the states and the U. S. Children's Bureau.

Experience with merit examinations revealed in the study indicates that the relative weighting of education and experience has varied widely. In addition to this problem, the residence barrier and certain administrative problems associated with the timing of examinations have presented serious difficulties to the schools of social work desiring to qualify their students. Many of the problems, it is recognized, are inherent in the present stage of development in the services. Experiments with examination methods are being encouraged and should lead to considerable improvement in the future.

Either by specific provision or tacit acceptance, residence requirements affect personnel appointments in all the services studied. In old age insurance, the federally operated service, residence needs no consideration, yet some evidence of a tacit requirement was revealed in the study. In unemployment compensation and the employment service, state residence is almost universally required, and a tendency to recognize local residence in appointments within the state was observed. Although generalization is difficult, state residence is usually required by law in the administration of public assistance, and except where the system is state operated, local residence requirements are a matter of accepted policy. The fact that personnel qualifications are specified by the federal authority makes it possible to avoid the state residence requirements in child welfare, yet sentiment for the appointment of persons having local or state residence is very strong and was observed in operation.

The entrance salary at the operative level was found to be highest in old age insurance among the services studied. In unemployment compensation and employment service, salaries are adjusted to some extent to the general state levels and thus vary widely. Those in public assistance do not compare favorably. Here where there is definite recognition of the need for professional education at the graduate level, it is obvious that salary levels are not commensurate with the financial investment involved in the two years of professional study. The variation in salary levels in all the services seems to have no relationship to personnel requirements or to responsibilities performed.

Old age insurance, which had not recognized pre-entry education, had taken the lead in the establishment of in-service training programs. The development of such programs in unemployment compensation and the employment service has been hampered in part by the transition period pending the integration of the two services. In public assistance and the child welfare services, where professional education for social work has been accepted as the pre-entry goal, the emphasis in the staff development training program has taken the form of educational leave for professional study.

Promotional possibilities vary from service to service and are dependent upon the philosophy of the services. Where there is less acceptance of pre-entry education, there is greater emphasis upon promotion based upon experience and service ratings.

The recognition of common elements in the services is to be encouraged in every possible way. Upon such recognition could be based unified plans for selection of personnel which would remove some of the marked discrepancies, make possible the use of inter-departmental transfer, and in general further more effective recruitment of personnel.

Chapter Eight

THE SCHOOLS OF SOCIAL WORK:
THEIR PROGRAMS

AT THIS POINT it is appropriate to examine what the schools of social work have to offer to the public social services and how they have adapted their programs to meet new demands more effectively. The contribution of the schools is expressed through the unique nature of the professional curriculum, through the work of graduates and former students in the development of the services, and through a very close relationship between the schools and the actual administration of the services. This relationship is expressed through the leadership of specific schools in the growth of the public services, through experiments in high standards of practice in these services, through research in the field, and through a variety of incidental services by members of these faculties. The following paragraphs relate to curriculum content and will be more significant if at the same time the reader bears in mind the training needs expressed by the personnel in the services and discussed in Chapters V and VI.

The professional curriculum in social work has two important characteristics which should be emphasized here. First, the scope of theory, field practice, and re-

search encompassed in the curriculum embodies the
essence of understanding human beings, the mastery of
methods in individualizing service to meet their needs,
the concept of administrative practice through which
these methods are applied, and the problems inherent
in establishing adequate provision for these services
within the community. Secondly, the concept of preparation for administration embodies the belief that the
mastery of professional content inherent in the service
and demonstrated capacity are the foundations upon
which specific preparation for supervision and administration can be developed.

The objective of the school of social work is to prepare
the student to assume the responsibilities of practice.
The development of intellectual maturity, emotional
balance, professional skill, and broad perspective are so
closely interrelated that one cannot be distinguished
from the others in the process. With the emergence of a
common content of practice in the agencies, the curriculum has lost much of its earlier agency focus and is
acquiring a professional focus. A general preparation
for a developing profession permitting interchange in
the field and enabling students to participate in agencies
newly created becomes the setting for student growth to
which the schools aspire.

The schools of social work further assume the general
preparation offered is the best foundation for leadership
in administration. Obviously certain individuals will
reveal capacities for leadership and others will not.
Usually these capacities are demonstrated in the employment situation. It is the opinion of the schools that general foundation in professional practice is a sound basis
for development of these skills. In contrast to a belief in

administrative theory which is universally applicable, the schools of social work consider preparation for the beginning job as equipment for the first rung on the ladder leading to a supervisory or administrative position in the field; the content of practice at the operating level as essential to the administration of the service itself; and a mastery of practice in the field as the logical basis for training in administration.

The professional curriculum offered in preparation for the field of social work is placed at the post-baccalaureate level and is planned for students with a general background in the social sciences. It is based on the theory that classroom instruction and field or clinical instruction are related organically, and is offered in a setting which makes such relationship effective. The scope of the curriculum, including courses and field work practice, gives concrete form to the basic skills and knowledge indigenous to social work, a program of social services through which these skills are applied, and the framework of government and of community to which they are related.

While the schools are committed to a curriculum which provides general preparation for the field of social work, and while the present study gives evidence of continuous progress towards this goal, yet a wide gap between objective and accomplishment is also revealed in the data assembled. Among the reasons to which this may be attributed are the following: (a) there is little real agreement as yet concerning the basic methods in the field; (b) there is a lack of agreement concerning the functional areas in practice, and consequently confusion regarding areas in the curriculum; (c) there is little common meaning in the term "general preparation" as it is

used by the schools. Until general preparation is more
fully defined, the Basic Curriculum [1] is the only meas-
urement which can be applied to determine whether the
school is interested in general or in special preparation
for the field. When adopted in 1932, this Basic Curriculum represented agreement by the schools concerning
the common content which should be offered. Subsequently, however, changes have taken place in the scope
of the social services and definite progress made in the
development of methods which can be applied. [2] The
schools, moreover, differ in their philosophy of curriculum planning. Some will emphasize the courses in basic
methods more than the framework and administration
of the services; some will emphasize field practice more
than instruction in the classroom. Some will rely more
upon the learning process of experience in the field than
upon the mastery of available literature. Some will emphasize the research process more than skill in administration. Yet regardless of these differences, there is an
essential agreement on objectives, when the total span
of the curriculum is considered.

The subject-matter offered in the curriculum can be
classified according to the following groupings: (1) the
structure and function of agencies, (2) public welfare
administration, (3) administration, (4) basic practices in
service to individuals and groups, (5) research, (6) field
work which provides a realistic experience in practice
as carried out by social agencies in the community and

1. Constitution and By-Laws, American Association of Schools of
Social Work, Appendix B.
2. Undoubtedly revisions in the Basic Curriculum which reflect this
change and progress will follow the present study by the Curriculum
Committee of the American Association of Schools of Social Work.

as given educational content by supervision closely related to the school program, and (7) the framework of
the community in which these services function. As indicated previously, this curriculum must be viewed as a
whole in order to determine its contribution. Much of
the discussion in the following paragraphs is related to
specific subject matter, but the reader should remember
that the scope of the entire course of study is at stake
when any evaluation of the role of the schools is attempted.

THE STRUCTURE AND FUNCTION OF AGENCIES

The objectives of social work are furthered through
organized social services, local, state, or national. One of
the distinguishing features of professional practice in the
field is the functioning of the individual social worker
through the social agency. The field, however, cannot be
limited by the scope of organized social agencies, since
social service functions are attached to agencies whose
primary objectives may be in other fields. Health and
Education are examples of services which have clearly
defined objectives, but whose operation necessitates the
recognition of the social service function for definite
purposes.

The structure and organization of the social services
is constantly changing, as new methods of social control
are developed and old ones discarded, as social and economic change dictates new needs, and as scientific knowledge is extended into new areas. The relating of structure and function of the social services to these changing
factors is one of the challenges to leadership in the profession. Fundamental to practice in the field is the un-

derstanding of the historical development of the social services and of their structure and functioning and inter-relationship at any one time from the local, state, and national point of view.

While emphases differ, the tendency in the schools is to treat the historical development of social services in England and the United States in very close relationship. In the study of the early efforts at prison reform, factory legislation, public health and public education, of the early social agencies for the care of the unemployed, for neglected and dependent children, and for the mentally ill and the delinquent, the student is given some perspective in relation to the problems of social planning and also some concept of the philosophic basis of his professional practice. Historical backgrounds may be treated as subject-matter common to the whole field of contemporary social work or as material related to the various functional fields. In some schools both methods are employed. The purpose is not so much to acquaint the student with the chronological sequence of developments as to give him perspective for understanding the present scope and nature of the social work program. Where the school recognizes the functional fields of family welfare, child welfare, probation and parole, medical social work and psychiatric social work, historical backgrounds may be developed in terms of the particular field.

These functional fields are so closely related that much overlapping may result from an effort to isolate specific backgrounds. Also in such a method of presentation, the student may lose sight of the picture of the whole. For the student who wishes to relate the history of social work programs to the social and economic trends, there is no adequate substitute for the general inclusive treatment of the subject.

The functional fields are subject to change and can only be generally identified at any one period.[3] The method of classifying the functional and structural aspects of the social services is subject to debate. Differences of opinion are not important to the present discussion. It is essential, however, to recognize the place in the professional curriculum for materials dealing with the mosaic of social and health services and their interrelationship. Scope, function, method, and financial support, are among the aspects to be considered. General courses offered in all these fields will include historical perspective, present structure, agency function, and the relationship to other functional areas in the total field of the social services. In some instances these functional areas can only be explained historically, but the knowledge of their place in the program is important to the student who expects to practice realistically in a community.

PUBLIC WELFARE

The structure and function of agencies established and supported by public funds is of especial interest to

3. A workable classification is that employed by the National Conference of Social Work in establishing major divisions through which its membership can function. At the present time, Social Case Work, Social Group Work, Community Organization, Social Action, and Public Welfare Administration are utilized for this purpose. The same general groupings are employed in many of the schools of social work, with the marked exception of Social Case Work, which includes the additional classifications of Child Welfare, Family Welfare, Medical Social Case Work, Delinquency, Probation and Parole. The field most frequently developed in this way is Child Welfare. Courses in Juvenile Delinquency and Probation and Parole are sometimes organically related as a functional field. In other situations, Juvenile Delinquency is related to Child Welfare.

this study. The courses in this area bear a variety of titles such as "public welfare," "public assistance," "social welfare," "social insurance," "child welfare," and "public housing." While a distinction is usually drawn between public welfare and social insurance services, in the last analysis the term "public welfare" may be used to encompass both, and for the purpose of this summary is permitted to do so.

Some public welfare content within this meaning is offered in all but two of the schools included in the study. Yet in plan and scope of material given and in competence of teaching faculty, there are vast differences in the resources of the schools. By way of explanation, three factors are indicated here.

First, the tradition of interest on the part of the school in the public welfare services determines the degree of attention which public welfare content has received in the curriculum. Second, the lack of agreement concerning the definition of the field is a source of conflict in curriculum planning. For example, the place of the institutional program in the public welfare plan is variously considered. In some situations the social services of the courts are included as a part of the social case work sequence and in others as a part of the structure of public welfare. Social insurance is considered by some schools to be outside the purview of public welfare, and by others to be a natural development of public welfare services.

In the third place, the degree of reliance which the school places upon the curriculum offerings of other schools or departments in the university is a determining factor in the scope of material offered by the school of social work itself. The use of related departments is by no means limited to the public welfare sequence, but it is very significant in this area. The development of courses in the political science and economics departments designed to prepare students for actual administration of some of the public social services has a significant relationship to the program of the school of social work in the same institution. At two universities, where Institutes of Public Administration have been established, the expansion of the curriculum in social work takes a direction different from that, for example, of a school of social work loosely affiliated with a university whose present interest in administration has fostered the development of a series of courses and a sequence of specialization in administration offered as an organic part of the professional curriculum.

Irrespective of these variables in the situation, certain trends in the development of public welfare content are indicated when the programs of the schools are studied. First is the introductory course in public welfare which deals with the structure and organization of public welfare services. Frequently this course is focused to a particular state, sometimes that in which the school is located with an opportunity given students to follow the same sequence of study in a state of their own choice. In some schools, this course emphasizes the actual services under public auspices. In others, more attention is directed to the general administrative relationships of the federal, state, and local units in the field. Second, frequently observed is the course in public welfare administration which is concerned with problems of administration in the public welfare setting. In some schools, historical material is emphasized in order to give understanding and perspective to the problems which are presented. In others, selected administrative problems which have peculiar connotation in the public field are the principal foci.

Third is the course in public assistance, which is concerned with administrative problems centering in programs of old age assistance, blind assistance, and aid to dependent children as expanded under the Social Security Act. And fourth, frequently offered in the sequence, is the course in social insurance, presumably emphasizing the relationship of public welfare services and the social insurances. As in all generalization concerning curriculum trends, the degree of error is very high and cannot be reduced pending an exhaustive analysis of course content and extended conference with instructors. Course titles and descriptions in the field are far from conclusive, and syllabi frequently do not give other than general clues to the situation.

The initial point of orientation to the public welfare field determines in large measure the emphasis made by the school. The variety and richness of curriculum offerings at one university, which has contributed both administrators and teachers to the field, have been focused upon the development of the entire field of the public social services. Structure and interrelationship of the services have been emphasized, both historically and with attention to public assistance and the newer aspects of the public welfare program. At least eight other schools have followed this general tradition.

On the other hand, the curriculum of a school loosely affiliated with a university has been directed to the process of administration from the operating level to the supervisory level. Emphasis upon the understanding of human behavior, with a shifting of accent from "the individual need to the individual in need," has permeated the approach of the school to administration of the public social services. A significant contribution has been made, especially in the development of practice in agencies administering assistance as a right.[4]

The development of public welfare content at the leading independent school had its origin in the interest of the school in problems of general administration in the field of social work. As social services under public auspices became more important, the courses in administration have been enlarged to introduce new content from the public field. Emphasis upon the generic content in all administration and especial reference to the particular setting in which it is applied seems to be a guiding principle in the development of the curriculum.

Among the public welfare fields of special interest to this study is housing. The analysis of curriculum offerings in the schools indicates that the schools believe that a general course in housing is a useful elective. Obviously, where offered, such courses would contribute to the preparation of individuals especially interested in some phase of housing management. That the subject-matter does not have a wide appeal to students was frequently suggested. In part, this may be due to the lack of competent teaching faculty in the field, and it may be due to the present insecurity of tenure in housing management positions and the lack of merit selection of personnel.

Generally speaking, all schools agree that the subject matter of public welfare should be a part of the preparation of every student whether he is going into public or private social service. In some instances this was empha-

4. See "Method and Skill in Public Assistance," *Journal of Social Work Process*, Vol. II, No. 1, Pennsylvania School of Social Work, 1938.

sized because students entering the private field must be equipped for sound working relationships with public agencies. In other instances it was stressed because various follow-up studies have shown that, irrespective of the first job placement, many students now graduating eventually enter the public welfare field. In still others, the organic relationship of public and private social services is recognized as basic in curriculum planning.

Whether through the curriculum of the school or through that of related departments of political science or public administration, an increasing number of schools are making available to students the series of courses in public administration. The impression gained is that these courses follow rather than precede the courses in public welfare administration, and that they are elective rather than required. The integration of this material with the content of public welfare administration needs a sympathetic and understanding approach by both the schools of social work and the schools of public administration. In furthering a solution of this problem, the study of training for public administration undertaken by George Graham, of Princeton University, for the Public Administration Committee of the Social Science Research Council will yield pertinent data.[5]

ADMINISTRATION

Social workers operate within the framework of social services and are inherently a part of the administration of a social agency program. Thus students preparing for the field should be equipped with a knowledge and understanding of the concepts of administration and the

5. George Graham, *Education for Public Administration*, Public Administration Service, Chicago, 1941.

procedures and problems involved in management in order that they may carry their own responsibilities effectively. According to the philosophy of social work, preparation for administration of social programs is based on the mastery of the content of practice and demonstrated ability in the field. The schools of social work believe that general preparation offered in the professional curriculum is the best foundation upon which to develop capacity for supervisory and executive functions. Only mature individuals who have demonstrated these capacities are encouraged to undertake additional and special preparation. Obviously, such a philosophy of preparation for administration envisages contributions to be made from a wide range of course materials and educational experience.

Administration as a tool subject emphasizes the problems of organization and management of social agencies from the standpoint both of the staff worker and of the executive. The subject matter includes principles underlying organization; the function and relationship of the board, executive, and staff; personnel policies and practices; problems of finance and budgeting; and office equipment and management. The social worker is not only a member of an agency staff and thus a part of an administrative structure which he should understand and accept, but the management of his own job demands of him the capacity to organize and plan a work load. Thus the administrative techniques used by the individual worker will receive attention in such a course. These materials are usually assembled under the title "Administration of Social Agencies" and offered as such or under similar titles by all except a small number of schools.

In addition to the general courses, some special content applicable to particular fields is offered, as for example, the Community Chests and Councils, Institutional Administration, or administrative problems in particular agencies. Courses in Social Work Interpretation are classified here as a special skill in administration. In order to delineate the field of Public Welfare Administration as it is developed in the schools, the courses that relate exclusively to public social agencies have been considered in the section on Public Welfare.

A word should be said here with reference to the courses in supervision which are closely related to administration. A distinction is made between the clinical supervision of case loads carried by workers in the agencies and administrative supervision which would combine with it some oversight of a general administrative nature. Both are inherent in the work of an agency. The courses developed in the schools and offered as "Supervision" deal primarily with the clinical supervision of case loads. Some few have been organized about the more general problems of supervision in an agency. The seminar offered by one school of social work in the summer of 1939, entitled "Field Service in Public Welfare" is an example here. As the catalogue description indicates, "this seminar will be devoted to the consideration of problems of administrative supervision, focused particularly upon the activities of the field staffs of state and federal public welfare agencies. . . . Following are some of the topics to be included: the differentiation between a supervisory and an operating agency; functions of a supervisory field staff; field staff organization; technical consultation in relation to administrative supervision; the place of the financial audit in a field service program; personnel development as a part of field supervision." [6]

Preparation for supervision and administration as indicated earlier is offered in the schools of social work for students who have had a satisfactory experience in the practice of social work. The general curriculum of courses and field work has presumably laid the foundation for successful performance and promotion to positions of further responsibility. Efforts are being made by the schools to lay this general foundation in the early instruction of the student. Those with satisfactory experience in the field who desire further preparation for the responsibilities of administration are usually encouraged to broaden their equipment by electing courses in Community Organization, Social Planning, Public Finance, Governmental Fiscal Control, Social Legislation, Public Welfare Organization, and Research. Programs are usually individualized in terms of the student's background, and it is difficult to generalize except in emphasizing the conviction that the mastery of practice in the field and a broad background of knowledge of the setting in which social work functions constitute the objectives in any specialized equipment for administration.

Here and there field work practice in the problems of administration is arranged, but, as the discussion of field work will indicate, the nature of the administrative process does not lend itself readily to the educational experience which is inherent in any satisfactory program of field work.

6. *Bulletin of the New York School of Social Work,* Summer Quarter and Seminars. January 1939, p. 13.

PRACTICE COURSES

Case work, group work, and community organization are considered as basic methods or tool courses which acquaint the student with the processes of practice in the field. Within this group, case work is the most highly developed; yet encouraging progress is being made in a clarification of the group work process and its place in the field. Although it has long been accepted as a subject taught in the schools, community organization is hardly recognized as a "process." There is an increasing tendency to consider it so, however, and it is therefore included here.

As the individual in society is the focus of interest in social work, the understanding of his behavior mechanisms and manifestations is fundamental to case work, group work, and community organization, accepted as basic to the field. For this understanding, social work has looked to the related fields of medicine, psychiatry, psychology, and social anthropology. Courses in the professional curriculum which deal with individual development, physical, mental, and emotional, are offered under descriptive titles such as Psychiatric Information, Psychiatric Aspects of Social Work, Mental Hygiene, Medical Information, Medical Aspects of Social Work, Psychological Growth Problems, and similar designations. Physical growth from the prenatal period to old age and mental and emotional development from infancy to maturity have formed the central theme or subject matter offered in the first courses. Deviations from the normal are included either at the same time or in subsequent courses. The teaching responsibility for these subjects is usually carried by members of the respective professions chosen for special competence both in their own professional discipline and in the understanding of the social implications with which the social worker is concerned. Competent instruction is a very great problem in this particular field, especially for schools located at some distance from centers of modern psychiatric practice.

The effective adaptation of materials from medicine, psychiatry, and psychology is possible only when the students are prepared in the undergraduate years with an adequate basis for understanding. Thus it is encouraging to cite progress made by the schools in defining the social and biological sciences as general prerequisites and to note that fewer students are attempting professional study in the field without basic preparation in psychology and physiology.

The basic course in medical information emphasizes the various periods in physical development, including pre-natal, infancy, childhood, adolescence, maturity, and old age. Throughout the material as usually offered, the social implications of the growth and the organic deviations are emphasized. Attention is also given to the major physical disorders which may affect such growth. The subject matter is correlated with the basic case work course and field work experience.

It is important to indicate here the scope of the material from medicine and public health which has been considered essential to the preparation of students for the practice of social work. In outlining desirable content, the American Association of Medical Social Workers has taken leadership, and the recent report of the Sub-Committee of the Education Committee of the

Association [7] is a valuable guide to the schools of social work. The objectives of the Committee imply "an appreciation of the continuous relationship between health and disease, between prevention and cure, between individual care and public health, between illness and social factors." [8] Suggested content in the general curriculum would include (a) Medical Information, presenting discussion of medical care, the meaning of health, disease, disability, diagnosis, treatment, prognosis and prevention, followed by descriptions of a selected number of diseases with emphasis on individual care; (b) Public Health Information, including concepts of prevention and control and treatment of all illness, the various programs for medical care; (c) Social Aspects, including the social and the emotional factors causing, precipitating or complicating illness, and (d) the use of medical resources, including a knowledge of standards and facilities for medical care and effective use of available programs.[9]

The presentation of this subject matter varies according to the curriculum of the school. Invariably one and usually two courses dealing specifically with content of medicine and public health are offered. In addition, such material is frequently included or cited in such courses as public welfare, social insurance, child welfare, and community organization.

The basic course in psychiatric information follows the same sequence of development in the mental and emotional life of the individual. The tendency is to emphasize the phenomena of normal development and at-

7. American Association of Medical Social Workers, *Education Committee*, "Medical and Public Health Information in the Curriculum of the School of Social Work." January, 1941 (mimeographed).
8. *Ibid.*
9. *Ibid.*

tending conflicts. Such a course is found in all schools of social work. In addition, subject matter dealing with mental and emotional deviations is found in such courses as psychopathology, neuropsychiatry, social psychiatry, behavior disorders of children, and child psychiatry.

To a lesser extent the schools have been influenced by the belief that specific adaptations from the field of psychology have a place in the professional curriculum. Two schools have offered such materials. Four others have introduced courses in the specific area of tests and measurements. Courses in related departments may be utilized by other schools, but the extent of this use is impossible to determine. To the importance of this material in the curriculum, the findings of the present study of professional education have given ample testimony. Graduates of the schools of social work were frequently criticized as unable to understand the use of mental measurements and their place in the study of personality.

The expansion of the public social services has influenced some modification in these courses. In the adaptation of material from psychiatry, a greater emphasis upon normal behavior was suggested as desirable in the light of the changes in social work programs. Such a trend is an encouraging offset to the vigorous criticism made by certain agencies visited that the schools are over-emphasizing psychiatric content in the curriculum. In the adaptation of content from medicine, it is clear that the newer concepts of prevention have been emphasized by an integration of the public health and clinical contributions. In a small number of instances the basic course has been extended to two semesters. In this connection the increasing importance of programs of medical care or public organization for medical care was emphasized, and the close relationship of this material to that of public welfare was suggested.

The inter-dependence of these materials in any effort to understand the manifestations of human behavior is easily seen. The study of curriculums indicates that such content overlaps the practice courses in many instances, not infrequently forming the substance of courses in case work; [10] yet it also indicates the wisdom of separating these areas of content.

An interesting effort to integrate the materials which present this understanding of the individual is that of a newly-established school which is experimenting with the course, Social Aspects of Individual Growth, conducted according to the following plan:

A synthesis of selected knowledge from the related fields of medicine-psychiatry-psychology is presented in order to give students an understanding of the interplay of physical-emotional-intellectual forces which describes the normal individual from the pre-natal period through old age. In addition to the lectures, student committees and the group of instructors hold periodic panel discussions of questions arising out of student social work practice. Observation of the infant is arranged with hospitals; of the pre-school child,

10. Analyzing the psychiatric information courses offered in the curriculum was especially difficult because of the merging of the psychiatric and social material in many instances. Course titles therefore did not describe content. The course in psychiatric social work might be either a course in psychiatric information or a course in case work with psychiatric emphasis. A practical limiting factor was the field of the instructor, and therefore data are based on the analysis of such courses known to be taught by psychiatrists.

Because of this limitation, a large number of courses very closely related have been excluded, and a true picture of any one school can only be given by including them in the study. Courses which for want of more accurate information have been classified as psychology, and numbers of courses classified as case work need to be examined if the resources of any one school are to be compared with any other.

with nursery schools; and of the older children, through public schools and settlements. Demonstration of mental testing.[11]

Inasmuch as the material is basic to work with individuals and with groups of individuals, an argument can be made for its organization and presentation to all students concurrently with practice courses in the specific area. Thus the student is helped to master some understanding of the individual motivation quite apart from the practice of case work or group work which attempt to provide service to him.

Case Work.—Case work is the method by which the service of a social agency is made available to the individual. The assistance rendered by the agency will vary according to the objectives of the agency, and the case work methods will vary correspondingly. Divergent concepts of case work have naturally developed and when not related to the function and programs of the agencies, frequently cause conflict and differences in professional practice.[12]

Case work practice applicable to all social case work agencies and case work practice adapted to agencies having special functions constitute a subject matter which is fundamental in curriculum planning in all the schools of social work. The materials offered in these courses include the principles of case work practice and their application; the process of social study; the analysis of

11. University of Pittsburgh, School of Applied Social Sciences, Catalogue 1940-1941, p. 28.
12. The present study has led the writer to the conviction that the divergent concepts of case work practice held both by practitioners and educators in the field constitute one great source of present confusion concerning the differences between public and private agencies and thus the place of case work in the public agency program as it is administered in many communities.

factors present and the activity of the case worker in dealing with problems. Case material which is the recorded experience of the agency with the individual or family group constitutes the principal teaching resources in such a course. In some situations use is made of the case records prepared and edited for teaching purposes, and in others the emphasis is placed upon the day-by-day experience of the student engaged in field work practice in an agency at the same time. The tendency to teach from the student's field work experience is noticeable.

With few exceptions, the student elects the course in case work practice and undertakes field work in a social case work agency at the same time. The organic relationship of theory and practice in the field is everywhere recognized, and increasing efforts to integrate the two are attempted. In one sense of the word, theory and practice are two segments of a single educational experience.

Courses in social work which recognize a specific agency function will include: in child welfare, such titles as Foster Care of Children, Children with Special Handicaps, Problems of Childhood, the Delinquent Child, and the Child Presenting Behavior Disorders; in medical care, such titles as Medical Social Work, Health Problems in Social Case Work; in psychiatric care, such titles as Psychiatry and Social Case Work, or Psychiatric Aspects of Case Work; in work with adult offenders, such titles as Parole Case Work or Probation and Parole, or Case Work in Penology; and in social work in the schools, such titles as Visiting Teacher in the Schools, or Case Work with the Schools.

The range of content in case work practice has been

evident for some time.[13] Possibilities include on the one
hand, case work as individualized service to an applicant
for public assistance and, on the other hand, case work
as the individual therapeutic relationship of worker to
client with the emphasis upon understanding and modification of attitudes such as might be characteristic of a
voluntary relationship in a guidance clinic. At first, case
work practice in unemployment relief was focused to the
need of persons "out of work through no fault of their
own." Later, with the prolonging of the depression and
the extension of public assistance under the Social Security Act, other factors emerged in relation to the individual need. The appearance of mass need and the development of emergency agencies whose patterns of practice
have carried over have suggested to some practitioners
and to some administrators that a specific content of case
work is characteristic of the public field. Certain adaptations are definitely indicated. Private social agencies, on
the other hand, relieved of the pressure of mass need,
undertook to re-define their function and practice. In
many instances, the result was a highly specialized form
of case work practice, perhaps suitable only to a voluntary relationship between client and agency.

The extent to which specialized content is needed for
one or the other is a question of very great interest and
importance. The schools whose faculties accept an inclusive definition of generic case work will tend to favor
modification and broadening of the content of the general case work courses, leaving to the field work experience the specific application in terms of agency function.
Others tend to develop a more specialized content which

13. Fern Lowry, Editor, *Selected Readings in Social Case Work*, New
York, Columbia University Press, 1939.

is labeled as applicable to a particular field. The first point of view is illustrated by the following comment of a member of a school faculty: Case work has two aspects, "an individualization of an administrative service, a way of doing administrative service, and a counselling relationship voluntary on both sides. The counselling either in public or private is a generic thing, only colored by the situation in which it occurs. The administrative service is different in the situation in which it occurs. Thus the public field would require the same generic case work training plus more training in administration which would differ in different lines, public or private." [14]

In this study, there has been an attempt to learn the nature and extent of the modification within the basic case work courses occasioned by the impact of the public social services. The schools are unanimous in the statement that generic case work is the sound basis of preparation for the public welfare services. To some, it forms the basis upon which specialized case work content can be learned. To others, it forms the entire content of the case work practice and is applicable to specialized as well as generalized agencies.

School programs, however, do not always substantiate this general statement. In one, the case work faculty accepted no essential difference between case work practice in public and private agencies so far as the teaching of case work and field work is concerned. At the same time, the teacher of case work has had long experience in the private family agencies only, and the students have been assigned to field work in private case work agencies only. That a generic content is sound was stated by another

14. Bertha Reynolds, Comment in Joint Faculty Discussion, Washington University, St. Louis, February, 1939.

faculty, yet there did not seem to be agreement concerning the extent to which field placement in the public agency would make any contribution, for the reason that "the experience afforded by the public agency would necessarily have less security." Another faculty which recognizes no inherent differences as between public and private agencies saw no need to develop field practice centers except to meet the numerical problem, and no field work placements were arranged in the public agencies at the time of the study. In this school as in many others, however, the number of students with previous employment experience in the public field is noticeable.

In reply to the question concerning modifications which have been accomplished to meet the demands of expanding public programs, there were several suggestions. Most frequently, it was stated that case material had been changed in important respects, so that a selection of cases from a wider variety of agency situations could be presented in the basic case work course. It was also suggested that clarification of agency function had been found to be helpful, so that the setting of the public agency might be understood. In another instance, it was believed that the school's emphasis upon the understanding of individual behavior as distinct from the teaching of case work has developed a universality in application which has met the needs of the situation. The integration of field practice in both public and private agencies with the teaching of generic case work, so that the student preparation at least in the first year may equip him with basic skills for practice in either area, is another device frequently used.

The increasing emphasis placed by the schools in selecting case work faculty with a background of general practice is the most encouraging sign. Of thirty-seven schools, in which the experience background of teachers of courses in basic case work was examined, it was shown that nineteen have had both public and private experience, seventeen have had private agency experience only, and one has had public agency experience only. In one where the teaching is shared by four members of the faculty, three have had private agency experience and one has had both private and public experience.

Group Work.—Group work is a method of utilizing the processes of interaction within groups for the individual development of members of the group and for the development of the group as a whole. The subject-matter of group work method includes the understanding of group interaction; the method of group organization; the nature of group leadership and principles to be utilized in the direction of group work processes, and the analysis of group procedures. The objectives of group work agencies, the place of supervision, and the planning of group programs will also be considered. Materials presenting the records of group process, the operation of leadership, and the process of program-planning are utilized in the teaching. Such records, however, are as yet inadequate and poorly developed.

The basic course in group work method may either be the first of a series of courses in a specialized sequence designed to prepare students for practice in the group work field, or it may be an orientation to group work practice for students who plan to prepare themselves for the case work field. Where a sequence of specialization in group work is offered, the first course in Principles of Group Work is one of a series which may include, among others, courses in Group Analysis, Adult Education and Group Discussion, Supervision in Group Work, and Special Skills in Group Work.

Where the course serves as orientation, it is an enrichment of the student's general preparation for the field of social work. The objectives for such a course have been suggested as the following: (1) to examine the factors in group relationships and activity by utilizing the recorded experience of a specific group; (2) to analyze the techniques utilized by the social worker in relation to the purposes and programs of groups with which social work is concerned; (3) to survey the field of group work, the philosophy, organization and programs of agencies providing group work service, both as to their distinctive and common objectives and methods; (4) to examine the relationships of the emphases and methods of other social work procedures to those of group work; and (5) to indicate problems and progress in coördinating services of group work agencies to other types of social institutions in the community.[15]

There is an increasing tendency to offer this orientation course only in connection with a period of field work practice in a group work agency. Where field work is required there is the problem of when and for how long the students should be placed in the field work center. Because of the nature of activities programs, the planning of the field work experience does not lend itself as easily to the semester or quarter unit as does the case work experience. Here and there this problem has been met in an interesting way, as for example at a school

15. Clara Kaiser, "Group Work Courses for Students Preparing for Other Fields," American Association of Schools of Social Work News Letter, July 1, 1937, mimeographed.

where students seeking group work orientation along with case work carry a very limited field practice assignment in group work concurrently with the customary field work assignment in case work. Frequently this limited assignment involves responsibility to a single group or activities unit.

Trends in the offerings of group work courses which are especially significant for the present study are: first, the increasing use of these orientation courses by those students preparing for general case work or supervisory positions. For example, in the rural child welfare programs under the general auspices of the Children's Bureau, workers equipped with the knowledge of group work or community organization are especially needed.[16] A second discernible trend is a reciprocal recognition of orientation to case work theory and practice within the specialized group work curriculum. As the personnel needs of the housing management program are reviewed in another section of this general report, this particular tendency assumes special significance.

Community Organization.—Community organization is included here as the third of the basic practice courses in the field. Yet it is understood that certain leaders consider the content as a part of administration and not a distinct process in itself. As a matter of fact, if titles are at all descriptive, course offerings in the field may be classified according to the following emphases: (a) the community, (b) community organization, (c) community or social welfare planning, and (d) community prob-

16. Hazel Hendricks, "The Rural Plus in Social Work," Address given at National Conference of Social Work, June 23, 1939 (mimeographed by the U. S. Children's Bureau), p. 6.

lems.[17] These classifications indicate clearly that community organization is not yet accepted as a basic process in inter-group relationships. However, a tendency towards this recognition is pronounced in the recent discussions of the subject.[18]

Community organization as a process attempts to effect mutually satisfactory relationships between groups through formal or informal contacts and to use these contacts to further selected goals such as a program of child care in the community, adequate relief, proper sanitation, hospitalization, housing, recreation, or education and similar goals.[19] Its goal is effective social planning in fields of social assistance, health, and recreation. The basic course as defined by the Sub-Committee on Community Organization of the Curriculum Committee attempts:

To give some understanding of what community organization is, and what the methods, the techniques and processes are, but not to prepare the students to assume the responsibility for that specific area. It might be called community organization in relation to social work. Perhaps the basic course can go no further with techniques than helping the students see the relatedness at different levels in their work whether in case work or some other area.[20]

17. The classification indicated was made by the Sub-Committee on Community Organization of the Curriculum Committee, American Association of Schools of Social Work, June, 1939.

18. *Ibid.*

19. W. I. Newstetter, Content of the Curriculum in Group Work, American Association of Schools of Social Work, News Letter, November 1, 1937 (mimeographed).

20. Minutes of Round Table Discussion, June 20. 1939, American Association of Schools of Social Work. Pittsburgh, 1939 (mimeographed).

As with group work, this basic course may be one of a sequence of specialization for the field of community organization work offered to mature and experienced students only, or it may be the single course offered for the enrichment of the preparation of the student interested in case work or group work or in general administration. At one school where a sequence of courses in community organization is offered in preparation for community chest and council administration, auxiliary courses in the field include: The Community Chest Movement, Interpretation of Social Work, The Social Worker and Community Groups, National Social Work Agencies and Local Programs, Budgeting Community Social Work, and related courses.

Where a single course is offered for the enrichment of the student's general preparation, it will frequently include: recognizing the social and health needs in the community and developing programs to meet them, the analysis of the functions of coördinating agencies in the community, the process of social planning, the principles and methods of organizing communities for social welfare purposes, understanding the social forces which affect the community life and the social program, and interpretation of the agency social program to the community. Such content is effectively expressed in the description of such a course as offered by a second school of social work: "A detailed study of the methods by which a social worker may assist in developing a progressive social program for the community. The methods for analyzing community needs; the problem of inter-relating the work of public and private agencies to meet these needs. The securing of community interest, leadership and support for social work. Organization and problems of city-wide or local councils of social agencies." [21]

The extent to which course offerings in this area have been affected by expansion of public welfare programs can only be suggested. Reference has previously been made to criticisms from the employing agencies that the graduates of the schools of social work do not understand or appreciate the significance of the community or of community forces which affect the social work program. In the majority of schools visited there was an expressed conviction that the materials and objectives of the courses in community organization need review in the light of the increasing importance of tax-supported efforts and the changing functions of voluntary activities in the field. There was several times the suggestion that the material of these courses had not received as much attention as might be warranted and the implication that objectives and methods focused principally to private social work practice might still be in use. The difficulty of obtaining adequate teaching material from the public agency field was many times indicated. It is encouraging that the Sub-Committee on Community Organization is turning its attention to the development of case material that will be suitable for teaching purposes.

RESEARCH

The basic course in research may serve to acquaint the student with methods in the field, to develop on his part the attitude of scientific study of programs or procedures, and to give him some basis for understanding and eval-

21. New York School of Social Work, General Announcement, New York, 1939, p. 26.

uating social data. Such a source may also serve as the
introduction to a sequence of specialization which will
equip the student to undertake independent investigation and to carry on the work of research agencies. As
stated by one school, "the work in social research is
planned to serve two purposes: (1) to provide adequate
preparation for professional positions in the field of
social research; and (2) to develop in future social workers an interest in the research aspects of their own work
and to enable them better to formulate the social welfare program which they may administer and more com-
pletely to evaluate the results of their own work." [22]

The materials of this basic course will include: the
collection, summarizing and presentation of social data;
the application of statistical methods to social problems
and the analysis of social data; some practice in schedule-
making, tabulation, charting, and analysis. In most instances such a course is designed to prepare the student
to undertake the thesis or project required of degree
candidates. Observations and discussions in the course of
the study indicate that the subject matter of this course
emphasizes the quantitative rather than qualitative
method. Its application, therefore, to research in the field
of social treatment has been less successful than its application to research in analysis of social conditions.

For the teaching of social statistics and social research,
there has been some tendency to utilize similar courses
offered in the departments of sociology, economics, and
psychology. Experience has revealed that students are
able to relate very little from such courses to the analysis
of social data as used in the professional schools of social

22. University of Chicago, School of Social Service Administration,
Announcements, 1939-1940, Chicago, May 10, 1939, p. 16.

work. Furthermore, the ability to understand and utilize social data has become increasingly important, especially as the administration of social services under public auspices has been extended. The result has been an increasing conviction in the necessity of course content at the graduate level which emphasizes facility in the use of social data as a tool essential to professional competence.

From the analysis, it is not possible to say how many of the schools provided for the teaching of statistics by a member of the faculty who is professionally qualified and how many depend upon courses in related social science departments. A few of the schools have long maintained that such courses should be taught by members of the faculty disciplined in the field of social work. Others have customarily relied upon the teaching of courses in related social science departments as substitutes for courses which might be offered by the school of social work. With few exceptions the successful teaching observed in the course of the study was found where the courses are integrated with the professional curriculum and where course materials and teaching are related to the field. This does not preclude the possibility of utilizing additional courses offered by related departments as adjuncts to these offerings provided by the schools of social work.

For specialization in research, knowledge of the field of social work practice as well as the mastery of research methods is required. Students are therefore encouraged to elect a substantial number of courses and field work practice from the general curriculum. In research, as in administration, it is necessary to know the field which is to be studied.

For students specializing in research, field work in research methods is planned in addition to the field work practice offered in connection with other courses in the curriculum.

FIELD WORK PRACTICE

The nature of the social work services implies a high degree of individual responsibility on the part of the practitioner. The social worker should be able to individualize people and situations and to base important judgments upon the analysis of factors which may exist in a unique relationship. Understanding and discretion are therefore very important and are best developed, according to the philosophy of educators in the field of social work, by actual experience in practice as carried out by social agencies in the community and as given educational content by supervision which is closely related to the school program.

In one sense, field work is a course of instruction in case work or group work offered as practice in the social agency setting and with tutorial guidance by selected supervisors. As such it closely parallels courses in the same area of practice offered in the curriculum. In no sense is field work a laboratory demonstration. It differs also from clinical work in the medical school in that the student is not supervised "as he works" but is asked to carry responsibility alone and away from the agency, almost from the day he undertakes his field work assignment. As in the preparation for other professions, student work in the field is the point at which theory becomes real and at which the various courses in the curriculum assume an organic relationship to each other and to practice.

The philosophy of field work practice varies from school to school, as the following statement will illustrate. "The student," according to the plan at one university, "is ordinarily assigned to two different field work centers, spending normally a full academic year in each. At the agency he assumes controlled responsibility for a limited number of cases or functions. This practice is carried on under the guidance of an agency supervisor, who, as the student's field work teacher, organizes his program in coöperation with the field work director of the school. The student has regular consultations with his supervisor, participates in agency meetings, and confers frequently with staff members of other organizations. These opportunities enable the student to make use of the thinking and experience of a wide circle of professional associates. The Field Work Department of the School, composed of full-time staff members, is available at all times for conference with both students and supervisors. Its function is to give unity, variety, and continuity to each student's field work program." [23]

"By means of coöperative relationships with local social and health agencies," according to another school, "the conditions prescribed for field work are agreed upon and maintained between school and agency. Thus field work is carried on under actual conditions of professional work to meet the educational needs of students. In field work the student has an opportunity to apply subject matter of the classroom and to acquire skill in the processes that are utilized in social work. The content of field work includes knowledge of the organization and methods of social agencies and of the health and

23. Fordham University School of Social Service, Announcement, 1939-40, New York, March 1, 1939, p. 15.

welfare program of the community. In the course of the field work, each student becomes familiar through visiting and personal conferences with various social and welfare organizations, and has occasion in conferences with the supervisor and in group meetings in the agency for discussing their several functions. The time spent in field work varies in the different fields of specialization, the minimum schedule being ordinarily three days a week for two academic years." [24]

At a third school, "there are four special training centers in public agencies ... where first year students are placed. Each one is under the supervision of a university instructor who gives full time to this phase of social work education. Beginning students are expected to spend at least two quarters in one of these training centers. For advanced placement, agencies operating in special fields are chosen, and the student is placed under the direct supervision of an agency staff member. Advanced students are expected to spend at least two quarters in one agency. Rural field work is available to a limited number of advanced students under a plan worked out in cooperation with the State Board of Control whereby the student is placed full time in a rural county for a three-month period." [25]

While there is a general agreement as to the nature of the experience, variation in length of time and in emphasis of activities and in the nature of the supervision is indicated. These variations are not the central point of interest in this particular study, however.

Field work is recognized as an integral part of the

24. Western Reserve University, School of Applied Social Sciences, *Bulletin*, 1940, p. 24.

25. University of Minnesota, Department of Sociology and Social Work; The Graduate Course in Social Work, Minneapolis, May 1939, p. 7.

preparation for practice in a particular area. Thus the basic methods courses in case work, group work, and community organization are linked to field work practice in these fields. As indicated earlier, administration and research are ordinarily regarded as cutting across these fields of methods and are elected by the student interested in a general course of study. Here and there, however, greater emphasis is placed upon the preparation of the student for administration or research, and where this is done, field work practice forms, as in the other areas, an integral part of the student's program.

Field work practice in case work, which forms the backbone of the field work programs in the schools, provides for actual experience in carrying through the processes of social case work under supervisors selected or provided by the school. Usually field work practice is carried concurrently with courses while the student is in residence. Other variations of this plan are in use here and there. Under this arrangement the student is assigned to a case work agency in the locality, spends from two to three full days a week in the agency where he carries a small case load of families or individuals under the careful supervision of a field guide selected by the agency and the school or a field instructor provided by the school and placed in the agency.

The policy determining the selection of field practice placements for students is an important indication of the extent to which a broad preparation is secured in the first year and the extent to which field placement in the public agency can serve this purpose. From the data of the study, it may be said that the objective in the first placement of the student is a generic experience and that family and child welfare agencies are most frequently utilized for this purpose. As to whether the auspices shall be public or private, a considerable difference of opinion exists and a general conclusion is impossible. In a few instances, medical social agencies are used for the beginning experience, but such a plan is limited to a very few schools.

For advanced students, there is a decided tendency to recognize the need of the student for experience in a specialized area and in the area which approximates his own interest as far as this is practicable. The student's own needs, however, are recognized as important and are definitely balanced against his expressed desire for experience in a particular field. The material examined gives the impression that the placement of advanced students is highly individualized.

Field work practice in group work is designed to give the student experience in group leadership, in the supervision of volunteer group leaders, and in committee participation and administrative procedures in group work agencies. Because of the nature of agency activities, the field work schedule, while concurrent with courses, coincides usually with the academic year.

Field work practice in community organization work is much less standardized than in case work and in group work. The principal reason is that the process of community organization has not yet been defined in a way to which the profession and the schools subscribe. This has been discussed earlier in the chapter. Those who emphasize the process of community organization are interested in student placements which provide experience in the "inter-group" process. Those who emphasize community organization as a part of administration are interested in placements for students which emphasize the social planning aspect of the social work program. Everywhere, however, there is agreement that field practice in community organization is suitable only for mature and advanced students.

Field work in administration is still highly experimental, and there is no widespread agreement that a sound educational experience can be provided for students in the area of administrative practice. Experiments, however, have been undertaken which deserve scrutiny. As an example, the report of a recent experiment is briefly cited.

General principles to which agency and school agreed were: that the student must have as definite a segment of staff responsibility as that afforded a student in case work; that the student in administration must in some way develop as close an identification with the staff as possible; and that the student on his own should make a contribution to the agency, assume some definite phase of executive function and carry it through alone without supervision or direction. The actual outline for the student experience, which extended over two days a week, was centered around board development, administrative responsibilities, the community and the agency in the community, and agency interpretation. The areas in which the student assumed the greatest responsibility were: planning meetings of committees and the board, studying the problems presented by other agencies, and in planning newspaper and copy work.

In a summary of the experience it was pointed out: "First, great care must be given to the selection of the student for field work in administration. He must possess genuine professional integrity. He must share many professional confidences with the executive; for example, salary schedules, evaluation of workers and board members, and delicate inter-agency problems involving standards of personnel in other agencies. Second, the student must see the whole executive job, the relationship of each part to the other, each part to the whole, and the ever-changing nature of the job. Third, the agency gets from the experience what it puts into it in planning and supervision. Fourth, the student in administration must have a real experience in assuming executive responsibility. The value of the field work in this area is dependent on the degree of reality experienced by the student. He is a staff member, he does assume actual responsibility, and he is making a real, although perhaps not the most important, contribution to the program." [26]

The emphasis upon supervision as a vital aspect of the public agency job has prompted some schools to experiment with field practice in this area.

Field work in research is less experimental, yet there are few such placements attempted by the schools. Where it is provided, placement provides for practice in an agency which specializes in studies and research, including participation under "supervision in a statistical study in the field of social work which gives practice in interviewing and obtaining data from original sources." [27] "Field research should not be 'practice work' but should be planned to yield results of scientific value and to provide at the same time educational work for the student investigators." [28]

26. Howard M. Slutes, "An Agency's Experience with a Field Work Student in Administration" in "The Range of Experience in the Field Work Program," American Association of Schools of Social Work, 1936 (mimeographed).

27. Simmons College, the School of Social Work, *Bulletin*, 1939-40, Boston, May 1939, p. 20.

28. University of Chicago, *op. cit.*, p. 16.

The selection and approval of social agencies as field practice centers where students can be placed under school or under agency supervision is an undertaking which calls for special skill, and with almost no exception the school faculties include one or more persons competent to develop a field work program.

Criteria for the selection of agencies suitable for field work placements include the professional standing of the agency, the interest of the agency in the future development of its own staff and acceptance of a share in the training of future social workers, established personnel practices, satisfactory physical facilities to permit the placement of students, quality and extent of suitable clinical material and available supervisory personnel.

Criteria used in the selection and approval of field supervisors include the certificate or degree from an accredited two-year school of social work as professional equipment; eligibility for senior membership in the American Association of Social Workers, or membership in a cognate professional organization which would seem to be more nearly applicable; professional experience of two or more years in a satisfactory agency; experience in supervision or demonstrated ability as a supervisor, and ability or capacity for teaching in the supervisor-student relationship. Apparently exceptions are made or equivalents accepted in several respects, especially in the case of supervisors of long and satisfactory experience but without professional equipment.

The expansion of the public social services has affected the field work programs in the schools in a number of ways. In the first place, genuine conviction has developed on the part of the majority of schools that the public agencies should be more generally used as field work centers than ever before. Executives in the field have indicated the changing character of the social worker's job occasioned by the setting of the public agency, and are unfavorably inclined towards any suggestion that supervised field experience and employment experience in private agencies are conducive to the best adjustment and performance in public agencies. Thus the school preparing students for general social work practice at a time when job placements in the public field are expanding, turns its attention to the use of field centers in the area which will give acceptable generic practice.

With very few exceptions, the schools visited are making decided efforts to develop field practice centers in the public agencies. Here it should be said that in those areas of public social work where the content of social work practice has been demonstrated for some time, field experience for students is not a new phenomenon in many of the schools. For example, the use of medical and psychiatric agencies under public auspices and to some extent the use of the probation or parole agencies has become an established part of the program of field work. Here reference is made primarily to the extension of assistance to families and to individuals under public auspices on a wide scale, sometimes in areas where it was not known before 1930, and to the establishment of forms of social insurance not heretofore a part of the national picture.

In the second place, the extension of the public social services has suggested new types of field experience which might be suitable preparation for students anticipating practice in the public field. Some of these have been indicated in the previous paragraphs. In the third place, the modification in content of field practice in par-

ticular areas is clear and definite. The field of public
assistance practice may be cited as an example. Here in
many instances the content of the student experience is
more closely related than before to agency function.
Also the content of the field work program includes a
wider scope of experience in order that the student may
be acquainted as never before with the setting and the
problems in which the agency function is performed.

Problems in the use of public agencies relate to the
thus far undefined nature of the job in the public agency
and the lack of available and competent supervision for
the direction of students. An important trend within
the various schools is the assumption of more responsibility for the cost of student supervision as a part of the
school's budget. Resources within the school budget for
the employment of supervisors to carry responsibility for
student supervision in the agency are thus available.
That adequate field teaching can only be secured in this
way has long been the conviction of one school, where
the major part of the field work program had been organized on this basis from the beginning. Four others
have applied the principle to first-year students. All subscribe to the method as the one way in which a satisfactory experience can be obtained for beginning students.
In another group of schools, traditionally adhering to
the principle of agency supervision of students as edu-
cationally sound, there are experiments with the use of
direct supervision in the public field.

THE FRAMEWORK OF THE COMMUNITY

So far, the curriculum analysis has been concerned
with the method and skill utilized by the social worker
in understanding the individual and in modifying the

relationship between him and society. Obviously such skills can only be applied by a worker who has some understanding of the nature of the environment in which he practices. Thus it is logical to turn to that phase of the curriculum which is concerned with the social and economic framework of society in which social work programs are developed. A number of difficulties, however, are presented by this segment of the curriculum.

Here and there courses in social planning or regional resources, in rural or urban social problems, in propaganda and public opinion, provide a broad orientation to the student interested in community organization or administration. On the whole, however, except where they may be available through related departments and thus not listed in the catalogue, there seem to be few attempts to offer such material. The impression gained from the present study is that more such courses are desirable. They should be planned, however, to meet the needs of advanced students interested in professional practice and thus interested in orientation to culture patterns in which their practice must be undertaken.

In a number of schools the use of the material from social economics in the professional curriculum is confined to the elementary courses in labor economics. At the same time there is increasing awareness of the importance of the subject matter. Problems of industrial organization and standards of living take on new meaning for students confronted with the reality of human adjustment in present-day society. Sub-standard wages for full-time employment and the relationship of industrial disputes to family well-being appear in a new light when seen in a given family situation which the student meets in his field work experience. Whether or not this orientation can be accomplished by the use of electives in related departments of a university is still an open question. A study of the offerings in the related departments at some universities might give an affirmative answer. A study of a university whose economics courses have a business administration focus might give a negative answer.

A few schools of social work have attempted a more complete integration of economics with the professional curriculum. At one school, one of three full-time members of the faculty carries responsibility for a seminar in the field of labor economics and for integrating the field work experience in the employment services. Observation and discussion during the field visits lead to the conclusion that the students in this school have an unusual grasp of the economic implications of various phases of the social work program. Careful selection of students and much individual instruction have contributed to achievement, but the answer seems to lie principally in the use which is made of the material of social economics.

At a second school, through the use of courses supplemented by offerings of related departments, a high degree of integration is possible. At a third, one faculty member holds a joint appointment with the department of economics. His training and experience and the subject matter offered make for effective orientation of the students. For a number of years a labor economist on the faculty of a fourth school has had the same opportunity to relate economics to professional content in the curriculum. A fifth school has begun an experiment with two courses in Labor Organization and Social Work under a part-time member of the faculty selected because of special experience in the trade union and in social reform movements. A sixth school has for some time offered a substantial number of courses from the field, such as the Economic Basis of Social Life, Industrial Relations, Industry and Human Welfare, Economic Aspects of Personnel Administration, and Social and Economic Backgrounds.

So far as the subject matter of government or political science is concerned, increasing reliance is placed upon courses in Local Government, Public Finance, and Public Administration. Some further reference to this subject has been made in the discussion of public welfare content.

THE EFFECT OF EXPANSION IN THE PUBLIC SOCIAL SERVICES

The expansion in the public social services has stimulated the schools to re-examine content of the basic courses and field work practice, to expand content of courses in public welfare, public medical care, and social insurance, to develop field practice areas, and to enrich the entire curriculum either by the use of additional subject matter from economics and political science or by the use of certain courses offered by these related departments. The schools believe a general preparation to be desirable equipment for Public Assistance and Child Welfare. It must be remembered, however, that the general curriculum is more heavily weighted than formerly with materials from the public welfare field and that field practice in public agencies is more generally used. Students admittedly interested in the administration of public assistance are encouraged to take additional courses in the public welfare sequence; to undertake field practice in the public agencies, and for electives to look to the subjects related to administration. Students who are interested in the public child care programs are encouraged to select additional courses in content of child welfare, case work, public welfare, and to undertake field work practice in a child welfare agency.

The study of the training needs in the public services indicates certain special problems of the rural areas. For example, in the employment service, there is the recruiting of farm labor, especially to meet harvest demands, the counselling of young workers, and the transferring in and out of labor to meet local demands.[29] The problem of medical care is acute in rural areas. The inclusive nature of social work in a rural community has also been suggested. Intake, home visits, case recording, budgeting, correspondence in treatment and wide community contacts are all a part of the rural social worker's job, for "he must be administrator, community interpreter, and organizer as well as case worker."[30]

The needs of the child welfare services have been especially emphasized, but it must be remembered that these services are reserved for rural and distressed areas.[31] Rural child welfare workers should know the proper relation of the work of the child welfare division to other divisions in the department of public welfare. In addition to professional knowledge, they should have an inexhaustible variety of working skills; good undergraduate

29. Atkinson, Odencrantz, and Deming, *op. cit..* pp. 127-28.

30. See articles by Josephine Strode: "Rural Social Workers Do Everything," *The Survey,* Vol. LXXIV (October, 1938), pp. 308-09, "Publicity By Way of the Barn Door," *ibid.,* (November, 1938), pp. 345-47, and "Learning From the Job," *ibid.,* (December, 1938), pp. 380-81.

31. 53 *Stat* 1360, Title V.

preparation in the social sciences; necessary basic social work courses; understanding of cultural differences; local vocabulary and customs; and an understanding of social laws and the economic and political framework of the community. Great emphasis is placed upon adequate personality for the task. In summarizing observations made by child welfare workers in forty-seven states, Hazel Hendricks, U. S. Children's Bureau, comments that "although human experience may be fundamentally the same in city and country, case work procedures and the way skills are utilized may be entirely different, though aims and techniques are the same." [32]

As the social services have been extended to the sparsely settled areas, especially in the South, the Middle West, and the Far West, the attention of the schools has been called to the necessity or importance of preparing personnel for rural areas. The tendency to carry over practices learned and applied in urban areas to localities different in many important respects such as resources, community attitudes, and social pressures, has been cited by many critics. The responsibility of the schools for a failure to prepare students for both urban and rural practice is stated clearly by some leaders in the field. It is said by others that the demands of rural areas are sufficiently unique to warrant the establishment of special schools in distinctly "rural" settings.

Some who emphasize the differences in the social setting and in the culture patterns of the rural community are sceptical of the ability of any school located in an urban environment to provide the kind of preparation suitable for practice in the rural area. They advocate the establishment of graduate schools of rural social work

32. Hazel Hendricks, *op. cit.*

218   Education for the Public Social Services

within the land grant colleges as a solution, maintaining
that these colleges understand rural life, that they are
already operating in every county and community
through the extension division and the experiment sta-
tions, and that rural people look to these colleges for
leadership.[33] Others, including the staff who prepared
this study, believe that the differences between rural and
urban practice are largely those of culture patterns, and
maintain that skills and knowledge basic to the one are
basic to the other. A broader and better preparation is
believed to be the answer. It is the suggestion of the
Sub-Committee on Rural Materials, Curriculum Committee, that this broader preparation should include
provision for the study of rural culture patterns and
social welfare organizations in their relation to the practice of social work in rural communities.[34]

The entire question of preparation for rural social
work is now the subject of inquiry by a special committee
of the American Association of Schools of Social Work.
Here it is only necessary to say that the use of field work
centers in strictly rural areas is not yet regarded as essential by the majority of schools, and where attempted it
has presented a variety of almost insuperable problems
from the standpoint of educational planning. Universities and colleges located in rural areas are confronted
with these problems as well as many others in their efforts to develop field work programs, and the solution
for the slight amount of rural field work practice available to students is hardly to be sought in the establish-

33. "Report of Joint Committee on Accrediting Representing the Land
Grant Colleges and State Universities," Proceedings of the Association of
Land Grant Colleges and Universities, 1938, pp. 330-33.

34. Memorandum from Gertrude Vaile, Chairman, *Sub-Committee on
Rural Materials*, January 20, 1941.

ment of schools of social work in institutions so located.

The findings of the present study clearly indicate that the schools should make greater efforts to prepare students to understand the social and economic forces which have such profound effect upon the service programs and to understand public officials and others who represent these forces in the community. "The importance of public relations" and "knowing how to work with politicians" were phrases frequently quoted by those whom the study staff interviewed. The end result of the two-year professional course should be students grounded not only in skill and method of "getting things done," but also in the factual basis for understanding psychological, political, and economic factors which may make or break the program. The practitioner needs not only professional competence; he needs perspective and understanding that enable him to function as a member of a profession in a changing world.

When a student enters the professional school, he should know something of the world in which he lives. He should have a sense of social responsibility and some awareness of his role as an individual member of the community. All of this suggests that he should come to professional study well-equipped by a general education. For the development of these qualities, the undergraduate years of study carry a heavy responsibility. However, the problem is by no means limited to the area of general education. More and more the professional schools have come to realize that skill and content in the methods of the field can only be successful when related to the social and economic setting in which they are applied. This recognition carries the subject matter of the social sciences into the area of the professional curriculum.

The nature of the material which belongs in the undergraduate and in the graduate years must be clarified. Students entering the graduate schools must have basic knowledge of the social sciences before much progress can be made with this problem, for the nature of the material in the professional curriculum will depend in large part upon the education and development of the student who undertakes it. Further study of this problem has been undertaken by the Committee of the American Association of Schools of Social Work on the Pre-Social Work Curriculum. Additional progress might be made if schools which are fortunate in their relationship to strong social science departments should undertake further research and experimentation.

So far as the social insurances are concerned, the schools believe the basic skills as taught in the professional curriculum to be adaptable. The employment of graduates in these services is frequently cited. Quite as frequently is cited the discomfiture of the graduates over the conflicts between their preparation and the content of practice they find to be applicable in the agency setting. The conviction of the schools is that general preparation as offered has some relationship to the future demands of good administration in these services. While the connection is not as yet specific, much can be said for broadening the curriculum in order that the students may add to their basic preparation from the known content of social insurance administration.

Chapter Nine

RELATIONSHIP OF THE SERVICES
AND THE SCHOOLS

PROFESSIONAL FUNCTION IN
THE SERVICES

THE ESSENTIAL FOCUS of this study has been the exploration of training needs in the public social services and of the role of the schools of social work in preparing personnel for the services. Because of importance and suitability for study, the social services expanded or developed under the Social Security Act were selected for analysis. Old Age Insurance, Unemployment Compensation and the Employment Service, Public Assistance, and Child Welfare comprise the programs reviewed. The analysis of training needs as revealed from interviews with the personnel in the administering agencies has indicated both skills and knowledge which are common to the services and certain skills and knowledge which are related specifically to the services in accordance with defined functions. At the operating level these needs were found to be (1) the knowledge of the organization of the social services and their place in the structure of government, (2) the knowledge of agency function, (3) the mastery of necessary administrative procedures, (4) a professional attitude, (5) the understanding of human behavior, and (6) the understanding of political and economic forces in the community. At the supervisory and administrative level these common needs were found to be the knowledge of the operating job in the service, ability to work with administrative groups, understanding of budget planning and operation and of administrative research methods, knowledge of methods of staff development, capacity for executive direction, and the capacity to develop public opinion in support of the program.

As specific needs in unemployment compensation and the employment service, the knowledge of employment trends, of trades and occupations, of vocational guidance, and of labor relations were indicated; in the administration of public assistance, the need for individualized service identified as social case work, knowledge of medical and social resources, of laws relating to persons and property, of vocational guidance and occupational opportunity; in child welfare services, additional knowledge of laws relating to child welfare and special case work procedures relating to child placing, home finding, and adoption were cited.

No valid attempt can be made to identify within the framework of the present administration those factors which determine whether or not the service has a professional content. For, in the opinion of the study staff, the picture of present needs in the services is not final and conclusive. It is safe to say, however, that professional practice may be observed in some services; in others, the elements of a professional attitude exist and the future development of professional service can be assured; while in others, the future is quite uncertain on account of the structural changes which may be affected by legislative action at any time and by the dominating leadership.

To observe and record meticulously the various component parts of the individual worker's present performance gives little guidance in determining whether or not the service is or may become a profession. Seen in isolation from each other, these component parts assume a simplicity which would justify their early discard as routine or non-professional. To some extent, this is even true of the older professions. In law, for example, the establishment of fact or the various processes that enter into a title search, present little more than routine tasks, no one of which would identify the occupation as a profession. The diagnosis of a sunburn or the reading of a thermometer does not require three years of graduate study in a medical school. Taken together in their constellation, however, these tasks present a different picture. They appear as skills or knowledge in a particular setting and against a background of intellectual discipline. The necessity for intellectual training of a special sort becomes very clear.

In the present study it has been possible to discover this constellation in certain of the services. In others, it is seen only in component parts, or it is seen in the making. One of the criteria is the extent to which the services provide a place for independent action as well as for the responsible use of traditional skills. All of the public social services do not yet offer a field for the use of skill and knowledge for which professional education is necessary. They may do so under conditions which future developments will determine.

In selecting personnel for the line services in these agencies, old age insurance has recruited college graduates who qualified on a general information examination; unemployment compensation and employment service has used several combinations of education and experience, all of which specified the minimum of one year's paid employment in specified fields; public assistance and child welfare recognized professional study in schools of social work. Child welfare services had more nearly achieved this goal than had public assistance.

As the initial stage of development in the services is completed and as civil service or merit systems are extended under the amendment to the Social Security Act, less attention will probably be given to recruitment of numbers of applicants, and more attention will be given to establishing standards and uniformity in all aspects of the selection process. In public assistance and child welfare it is clear that this stabilization will be in terms of professional education in the schools of social work. In old age insurance, more attention to the educational content of the job is necessary before any conclusion can be drawn. And in the unemployment compensation and employment services a re-examination of the need for actual employment experience and the extent to which field practice work can be successfully substituted must be accomplished before the content of pre-entry education can be outlined.

The study has shown conclusively that progress is being made in raising personnel standards in all these services; and has given promise of further attention to the residence requirements, promotional plans, post-entry education, and salary levels. The development in the programs however has been uneven, with greater perception in some than in others as to the basis of satisfactory administration. Some of the services are fortunate in having the traditions of related fields upon which to rely; others have years of experience to evaluate. Some have been developed as if there were no experience in any related field upon which to build. Some have been more amenable than others to the influence of partisan politics. Some have been fortunate in effective federal leadership; others have been dependent upon the best and worst leadership of which state autonomy is capable.

Yet with all this variation, the evidence of progressive development in standards of service is unmistakable. So far as the services provided and extended under the Social Security Act are concerned, the annual reports of the Social Security Board to which reference has been made are alone sufficient evidence of this tendency. The recent amendment providing for merit selection predicts further progress in the future.[1] So far then as the quali-

1. See Fifth Annual Report of the Social Security Board, 1940, pp. 131-33, from which the following excerpt is quoted: "As of June 30, 1940, there were 18 jurisdictions in which general civil service systems were applicable to the state social security agencies. Rules for joint merit systems had been adopted in 19 jurisdictions, in 10 of which the systems served the health department as well as the employment security and public assistance agencies. In 13 states separate merit systems had been established for the employment security and public assistance agencies, and in 4 of these states the health department and the public assistance agency were served by the same system. In one state plans were being formulated for a joint system to operate until the state civil service system becomes effective on July 1, 1942. The Board recognized that it was impossible to have fully functioning merit systems by January 1, 1940, but considered it necessary to obtain from each state either the rules and regulations under which the state would administer its personnel program or an acceptance of the Board's standards together with a statement of the steps which would be taken to put those standards in operation. . . .

"Requests from the states for technical assistance in the development and administration of effective systems of personnel administration increased sharply. During the year technical services were extended to all 48 states at the request of the State officials. These services included consultation on personnel rules and regulations, assistance in the development and installation of classification and compensation plans, assistance on problems of construction and administration of examina-

fication and preparation of personnel are concerned, it is important that present practices be scrutinized in relation to the light they throw upon possible future trends. This the study staff endeavored to do, and in assembling data concerning the present situation recognized in the dynamic nature of the services the direction in which the services seem to be moving. This method gave substantial evidence that the administration of old age insurance, unemployment compensation and the employment service, public assistance, and child welfare justifies the application of knowledge and skill which is appropriate to professional education.

TRENDS TOWARD RECOGNITION OF THIS FUNCTION

The inter-relationship of developments in the schools and developments in the public social services is vital at every stage. It is important, therefore, to reiterate questions relating to the nature of the services, the basic concepts of administration, and policies governing recruitment and promotion of personnel which will determine the ultimate future of these services.

The qualifications and preparation of personnel have a direct relationship to the nature of the service. Sharp distinctions between social insurance and public assist-

---

tions, and advice on internal personnel administration. Attention was necessarily concentrated upon the more urgent requests for assistance in connection with the immediate problem of conformity with Federal standards. A course for merit system supervisors was held in Washington in May, and another was scheduled for July, 1940. Bibliographies on various phases of merit system administration were prepared, and suggested examination materials for public assistance and employment security positions were developed for consideration and possible adaptation by the States to their particular circumstances. Periodic review of merit systems was instituted."

ance and between the nature of personnel needed in each instance have been made by certain students in the field. To them, the establishment of claim to benefit on the basis of demonstrated employment and the establishment of eligibility to assistance on the basis of individual need are clearly differentiated. The latter function they would assign to professional personnel presumably with preparation in schools of social work. The former they regard as an insurance function calling for administration by non-social work personnel.

An examination of the text of the Social Security Act as originally passed gives some support to this argument, since from a fiscal and administrative point of view the insurance provisions were carefully separated from the assistance provisions. Yet it must be admitted that the sponsors of the act had in mind the concept of a total framework of security for the protection of the worker. In transmitting the Report of the Committee on Economic Security to Congress, for example, President Roosevelt spoke of unemployment, illness, and old age as the normal risks of contemporary life from which each citizen should be protected.[2] The right to assistance and the need for assistance were not differentiated.

Experience with the Act and its subsequent amendments clarify the philosophy of the statute. In the first place, the distinction between the covered and non-covered employments must be remembered. The provisions concerning old age insurance and unemployment compensation excluded workers in agricultural labor, domestic service in private homes, governmental employ-

2. President's message transmitting the Report of the Committee on Economic Security, January 17, 1935, Congressional Record, Vol. 79, pp. 545-46.

ment, and in certain non-profit organizations. The old age insurance sections made no provisions for the self-employed worker in industry, business, agriculture, or elsewhere. The unemployment compensation provisions imposed the payroll tax on industries employing eight or more persons. These exclusions have been justified wholly from an administrative point of view.[3] No theoretical distinction between the non-covered and covered workers is implied, and no deep-seated conviction bound up with the reality that the covered worker is protected by the insurance principle and the non-covered worker only by the assistance principle. The movement from covered industries to the non-covered industries and back, which has been greater than anticipated, is an interesting aspect of the problem.[4] Perhaps it is further evidence of artificiality in the distinction.

In the second place, the experience with lump sum benefits under old age insurance is significant. Claims for lump sum payments to eligible workers' or survivors' estates became payable on January 1, 1937. Application could be made by the worker himself, by the guardian of such worker legally incompetent, by wife, husband, parent, child or grandchild of the deceased worker, or by the executor of his estate.[5]

3. The Advisory Council, the Social Security Board, and President Roosevelt have all recommended extension of coverage as rapidly as administrative provisions could be devised.—Fourth Annual Report of the Social Security Board, 1939, p. 35.

4. *Ibid.*, p. 35.

5. The lump sum payments represent $3\frac{1}{2}$ per cent of the taxable wages received by the worker for employment after 1936 and prior to his sixty-fifth birthday or his death prior to that age. Lump sum benefits at the age of sixty-five, were discontinued on August 10, 1939. Lump sum payments on behalf of workers who die after 1939 will be made when the worker meets certain qualifications and leaves no survivor entitled to a survivor's benefit for the month in which death occurred. *Ibid.*, p. 29.

Two other facts quickly became apparent. The need of the worker actually to maintain himself in his old age without recourse to public assistance and the need to protect his wife and children in case of his death were inherent in any system to prevent old age dependency. The inadequacy of this system of lump sum payment was early recognized. "Further, the size of the death payment was likely to be inverse in proportion to the need for protection." [6] Subsequent amendment to the act in 1939 provided benefits related to average rather than accumulated wages according to a formula which gives a relatively higher benefit to those with lower earnings and supplementary benefits for the wife aged sixty-five or more and for dependent children aged less than sixteen, or eighteen if they are regularly attending schools. "This change recognizes the greater presumptive need of families in which the wage earner has such dependents." [7] In this a deviation from the insurance principle of claim to the assistance principle of need is certainly implied.

In the third place, the limitation upon the number of weeks during which unemployment compensation is payable suggested either by provisions for payroll tax under the Social Security Act or by state acts through which it has been offset does not coincide always with the period of involuntary unemployment. The waiting period, the length of benefit payment, and the minimum benefits allowable under some statutes may be criticized as failing to provide the worker and his dependents with protection from the normal risks of unemployment. Some integration of the principle of claim to compensation with the principle of eligibility to assistance is again implied,

6. *Ibid.*, p. 36.
7. *Ibid.*, p. 168.

and it is substantiated in the following quotation from the *Second Report* of the Social Security Board:

> The problem of providing a means of subsistence for unemployed workers who have exhausted their rights to benefits or who have been unable to accumulate benefit right, and the related problem of the integration of unemployment compensation with supplementary relief and work relief, will continue to demand the attention of the states and the federal government.[8]

These instances are cited not to stimulate the argument of need versus right, but merely to indicate that in the spirit of the Act, as administered and modified, no such rigid distinction is implied. In the amendments cited above, the years since the act was passed have seemed to minimize rather than sharpen any such implications, as the right to protection in terms of individual need is more clearly understood.

The dominating philosophy of administration in the services is not yet clear. Future developments may recognize within the group to be served only those who present special problems. An example from the history of workmen's compensation in New York will illustrate a differentiation of service to individuals presenting special needs from the service provided for all those eligible to compensation under the Act.[9] Here in an otherwise uniform service to individuals, the After-Care Division has been established with certain special objectives, and the quality of service has been protected by standards of personnel especially equipped. Will the employment service and unemployment compensation differentiate

8. Second Annual Report of the Social Security Board, 1937, p. 59.
9. Appendix A.

service to young persons seeking their first jobs and to adults who are "hard to place" and maintain a routine service for others? Will old age insurance provide especially for the administration of survivors' benefits? Here will be a smaller group of individuals for whom the community accepts a peculiar responsibility. The administration of estates involves problems of guardianship and the care of dependent children in stable and in unstable homes. Similar problems are inherent in this program.

The present study has indicated that skilled service can be utilized in the day-by-day administration of benefits of various kinds. If the needs of a special group are recognized, as in workmen's compensation, small service divisions may be established with professional personnel while the general administration of the agency remains at a simple clerical level. If supervisory and administrative positions were filled from open and competitive examinations, professional education would be justified in preparation for these upper levels. If, however, these positions are a part of the "career hierarchy," they would be governed by the "stockroom to the front office" philosophy of training.

The preparation of personnel has also a direct relationship to personnel standards in the services. If the merit amendment to the Social Security Act extends the present basis of selection throughout the country and adds thereby certain procedures of civil service, it is very possible that a "permanent" personnel will be fastened upon these services, with relatively little opportunity for recruitment of workers from employments outside the program. If promotional examinations can be placed on an open competitive basis, on the assumption that additional qualifications other than "efficiency" are needed in the new responsibilities, opportunities will be available to trained persons to enter at various levels. Otherwise the main inducement to a well-equipped person to enter at the "lowest rung of the ladder" in a "career" framework is that in certain of the services, such as old age insurance, the entrance salary is actually higher than that in public assistance. Whether this would content the competent person through the long period when he is establishing seniority is another matter.

This problem was summarized in comment by a member of the study staff who said, "In other words, there is no profession at the present time (in the social insurances). There is no agreement regarding the most suitable educational experience background for these positions. In selecting personnel for the line services, old age insurance has gone farther than any of the other bureaus in moving toward requiring a broad general collegiate background. In the other insurances, however, in the absence of any accepted technical requirements for any positions, a career service may prevail which is almost totally lacking in pre-entry requirements. The possible effect of this is shown in what has evolved as the career systems in workmen's compensation in New York State. The entering point of a person who wishes to engage in workmen's compensation in New York State is a clerical position paying $900 a year. During the depression it has been possible to recruit persons with academic and sometimes legal training who are willing to remain at even the low entry level of $900 for an indefinite length of time with the hopes of gradually rising in the service, but this appears to be exceptional. Particularly because of federal participation the entrance salary in other insurances is higher, but in many of them it appears that per-

sons without academic or specialized training will be
able to rise from minor positions to the upper brackets."

IMPACT OF THE SERVICES UPON THE SCHOOLS

The schools of social work, as indicated in the previous
chapter, have effected certain adaptations in their efforts
to provide a competent personnel for the social services
developing under public auspices. Those to be emphasized briefly here relate to structure, curriculum, faculty,
and students.

One-Year Schools.—The structural adaptations have
been few in number because there is widespread conviction on the part of the schools that the present organiza-
tional base is essentially sound. Yet attention should be
called to the establishment of two types of schools which
may now be approved for membership in the American
Association of Schools of Social Work. The recognition
of one-year and two-year programs was in part the result
of the work of two committees considering the facilities of the state universities and land grant colleges desiring to establish professional curriculums in order to meet
local demands for additional personnel.[10] As indicated in
an earlier chapter, the new classification makes no basic
change in the place of the two-year professional curriculum at the graduate level as sound preparation for the
field. It recognizes, however, two factors: first, the dependence of the schools upon field practice resources and
upon adequate teaching faculties, and second, the exist-

10. Advisory Committee on Training and Personnel in connection
with the Social Security Act. Minutes 1937-1938 (mimeo.), American Association of Schools of Social Work.
Committee on State Universities and Membership Requirements,
Report, American Association of Schools of Social Work (mimeo.), 1939.

ing salary levels which encourage students to seek employment after one year of graduate study. The plan makes possible the limited functioning of a university in a region where resources do not justify the establishment of a two-year course of study and where for financial reasons few students could remain to complete such a curriculum if it were offered.

Curriculum.—Curriculum adaptations which have been effected have been discussed in relation to curriculum areas in the previous chapter. To summarize briefly, these adaptations have included greater emphasis upon the normal physical and emotional development of the individual in the courses adapting material from psychiatry and medicine; greater efforts to develop generic content in the teaching of case work; re-examination of course content in administration and community organization in order to present subject matter which is common both to public and private agencies; an expansion of course content in administration in part by the use of curriculum offerings in related departments; an enrichment and expansion of the subject matter of public welfare and the addition of courses in social insurance and in organization and development of resources for medical care, and finally, a further effort to orient the curriculum to the social and economic setting of the larger community.

Further work in curriculum study by the schools is clearly indicated. The material analyzed in this study, while indicative of substantial progress both in curriculum content and in quality of teaching, has also revealed much confusion with reference to content and teaching methods and with reference to the objectives for which the schools are preparing students. Here and there, schools are making substantial effort to study their curriculums.

Faculty.—The nature of the field for which the schools are preparing personnel and the content of the professional curriculum which is thereby necessary, point emphatically to the need of faculties broadly trained, highly competent in their own fields, and conversant with the problems of professional education in the whole field of social work. The study has provided evidence for genuine encouragement in this direction.

While the number of full-time faculty is increasing slowly, due to budget limitations which confront the schools, it is apparent in the selection of new faculty personnel that broad preparation is being emphasized. This is especially true of the faculty carrying responsibility for the practice courses. The schools of social work even more than the schools of law and medicine recognize that leadership in the professional school must be oriented to the institutional forms in which the particular practice is carried out.[11]

There is still the tendency here and there to isolate or protect the teaching of practice and to recognize skill in the area as the sole determinant in faculty appointment. Evidence suggests that social case work has been singled out for a special kind of protection in the program of educational leadership and that some of the problems of curriculum planning and modification have their origin in this situation.

The increasing importance of the field of public wel-

11. For example, the attitude of the faculty of a medical school towards public medical care provisions may have been a factor of slight importance in medical education twenty-five years ago. The interests of members of a law school faculty in the field of administrative law may have been of slight significance to the student at the time.

fare administration is shown by a recent expansion in full-time faculty in schools which have previously not emphasized the public welfare content. New appointments at five schools may be cited in support of this observation. Additional appointments of full-time instructors at two others are also significant.

Some of the criteria considered important by the schools in the selection of faculty suggest some of the reasons why adequate faculties are difficult to recruit. The importance of advanced degrees indicating the mastery of professional content as distinguished from academic content alone; especially in the social treatment fields, the weighting of professional experience both authoritative and recent in content; the emphasis upon general experience in both public and private social work; and finally demonstrated teaching capacity are all desired. Devices of additional study and leaves of absence for practice develop the further skill of present faculty and vitalize teaching through recent contact with the field. Some schools have utilized these devices more than others. In a field in which the inter-relationship of education and practice is so intimate, such recognition is especially important.

Students.—Policies covering the admission of students have been modified to some extent to meet the new situations which the expansion of public social services has created. The probability of employment in the field and the demands of agencies for a higher standard of personnel are stimuli which help the schools to be more selective. The prospect of placement in the public field has been an encouragement to able students to apply for admission, and where the public agencies have begun to develop personnel standards a positive effect upon the

recruiting of competent students for the schools is noticeable. On the other hand, the low standards which have
recently been set by certain civil service commissions,
and the insecurity of tenure and low salaries characteristic of some of the social services where civil service does
not operate continue to be deterrents toward effective
recruiting.

Special concessions are frequently made to students
granted educational leave for study and who plan to
return to their former jobs after a period of residence
work in a school. In at least twenty-two of the schools,
definite consideration is given to students on leave from
state or local welfare agencies. Frequently students selected for educational leave do not satisfy the stated requirements for admission to the schools. In almost every
instance they are enrolled in the schools for limited
periods and thus schedule-planning must be greatly individualized to meet their needs. In special instances
requirements relating to age, to the content of the pre-
professional work and to the academic average or to
credentials from non-accredited institutions may be
waived. In most instances the candidate who presents a
record of successful employment in the field of social
work when applying to a school is in the more favorable
situation so far as the waiver of requirements is concerned. In general, the schools require some reassurance
that the student applicant is physically able to carry the
program of study and the responsibilities of practice following work at the school. More and more attention is
being given by the schools to an evaluation of personality
attributes which may predict success or failure.

Here and there, agencies and schools have worked co-
operatively in the development of policies affecting such

students.[12] Yet it must be said that the schools and the agencies do not always agree as to the evaluation of candidates for special concessions in admission requirements.[13] The leadership of the Bureau of Public Assistance and the United States Children's Bureau in clarifying policies governing the selection of workers for educational leave has been especially helpful.[14]

The increasing number of part-time students in the schools indicates that registration in regular and in special courses has been extended to many workers employed in the public agencies.[15] In general the policies covering admission of part-time students to courses in the regular curriculum coincide with policies relating to full-time students. Yet the privilege of electing all courses in the curriculum or of becoming candidates for the degree or certificate is rarely extended. The difficulty of arranging field work on a part-time basis and the isolation of field work from other courses are very real problems in this type of educational planning. The schools regard field work placements for part-time students as limited in number and undesirable except as special provision for a few students who could otherwise not complete the minimum requirements for membership in the

12. Note especially the states of New York and Washington.

13. Round Table Discussion, American Public Welfare Association, December 7, 1940 (mimeo.), American Association of Schools of Social Work.

14. *U. S. Children's Bureau:* Recommendations to States Granting Educational Leave (mimeo., n.d.); *Bureau of Public Assistance,* Social Security Board: policy governing Administrative Costs in states granting educational leave; Minutes Advisory Committee on Training and Personnel to U. S. Children's Bureau and Social Security Board in Connection with the Social Security Act, 1936-1940 (mimeo.).

15. These should not be confused with "Staff Workers Courses" which are non-credit and which are fundamentally not to be distinguished from in-service training programs except that the school carries the responsibility.

professional organization [16] or who for certain emergent reasons are unable to continue the work of the school in residence.

Extra-mural courses sponsored by the school or accepted by a school for credit and offered as non-resident courses outside the city in which the school is located are devices by which the resources of the school can be extended to social workers employed in agencies of adjacent communities. In the majority of instances the schools either question the wisdom of such course offerings or have had no experience upon which to base conclusions. Few have actually experimented with the plan.[17] As a general rule the schools do not consider extra-mural field work sound, due to the lack of adequate supervision from the school and the depletion of faculty resources involved.[18]

One school of social work is conducting an interesting experiment in extending facilities to a near-by community. Here, with the coöperation of certain local agencies in the community, a member of the regular faculty of the university maintains residence and carries responsibility for teaching and planning additional lecture courses. The students electing courses are registered at the university and obtain credit from the school of social work in the customary way. An evaluation of this experiment may reveal the wisdom of similar experiments by other institutions.

In placing limitations upon extra-mural work, for reasons that they believe to be sound, the schools are at variance with the desires of the agencies as revealed

16. American Association of Social Workers (New York), *Membership Requirements*, 1933.

17. Seven schools reported such courses in 1937-1938.

18. Yet the entire program of one school of social work is extra-mural.

through the interviews carried on by the study staff. Further study of the problem is no doubt necessary.

The Graduates of the Schools in the Services.—Graduates of the schools interested in public social service have found their way into the field through direct placement by the schools, or through a shift to public agency employment after a period of employment in private agencies.

In an effort to learn the extent to which graduates of the schools are being placed in public and private agencies, the schools were asked to indicate for 1937-1938 the number of graduates placed and the types of agencies in which placement was made. The twenty-one [19] from which data were secured, reported a total of 259 graduates placed in public agencies and 349 placed in private agencies that year. The inquiry was limited to the placement of graduates alone, and it is not known how many students who had completed some part of the degree program were placed in either type of agency. Of the schools in the group reporting twenty-five or more students directed to employment, the placements by Boston College, New York, the Pennsylvania School, Simmons College, and the College of William and Mary were predominantly in private agencies. Placements by the University of Chicago and the University of Minnesota were about evenly divided between public and private agencies. These figures are verified by the Joint Vocational Service study in 1938-1939 which attempted to learn the number of school graduates during the previous two years who were placed in private and public

19. Of the thirty-three schools included in the inquiry, eight indicated that no statistics were available or that no placement was undertaken by the school. Three did not reply to the question and one stated that no students had been graduated from the degree program that year.

agencies. Ten of the schools reported 988 students placed, of whom 538 or 54.5 per cent had their first jobs in private agencies and 450 or 45.5 per cent in public agencies.[20]

These data do not warrant a conclusive statement but are indicative of trends in the schools.

Inter-Play Between School and Community.—The school of social work is a functioning unit in the development of higher standards of administration in the field of the social services. Present leadership in the schools reflects a close relationship to public welfare administration. Twelve deans or directors have served in administrative and supervisory capacity in the state or federal public welfare services. Faculty members have been selected with "recent and authoritative experience" in the field in addition to their professional equipment. They have been encouraged to maintain close contact with current trends in the field of practice, and the study indicates that the schools have given generously of faculty time and skill in a variety of services to the community agencies. Of particular significance here are the services in connection with examining boards, institute leadership, and consultation in connection with in-service training programs and research in the field.

A few instances may be cited as concrete illustrations. One school has made a great contribution to the clarification of practice in public agencies in its local community; the origin and development of a state department of public welfare is closely linked with the school of public welfare at a state university; a third school has given outstanding leadership to the public social services

20. Arthur Dunham and Dorothy Bourne, *The Future of Vocational Service for Social Work,* New York, Joint Vocational Service Bureau, 1939.

in the far south. A fourth school has an enviable history in its vital connections with the development of standards in the public agencies in a large metropolitan center, among which is the county bureau of public welfare and the minors' service division of the county bureau. Under a coöperative program with the department of welfare, one state university supplies a service of research and community organization throughout the state. A school in a municipal university contributed to the establishment of the public recreation program in the city and at one time shared the services of a member of its faculty with the city administration. A school located in an eastern women's college has had a significant interest in the employment services. A seventh school, independently organized, supplied leadership for the first organization of the temporary emergency relief administration in the state and has made professional service by faculty widely available through a generous policy of leaves of absence.

A school of social work serves also as an interpreter of the field to the community. This service is not the sole prerogative of the school, but it becomes an important demand upon the time of the faculty of any school. There is an increasing desire on the part of other professional groups for more information about the functioning of the social services. The home economists, the public health nurses, the public health officers and the teachers work closely with the members of social agency staffs. The expansion of the public services has intensified this relationship, especially in the rural areas. The need to exchange information about function and method is very great at the present time and constitutes a challenge to the schools which must be faced.

Problems Yet To Be Faced.—The future contribution of the schools of social work will depend upon the internal and external factors in their relationship to the social services as a whole. The previous paragraphs have considered the internal factors of curriculum, faculty, and student body. Recent progress has been cited and strategic points for study and development indicated. Two additional aspects should be emphasized.

In predicting the potential contributions of the schools of social work to the public social services the present limited financial resources of the schools must be considered. In 1934-1935 the total budget of 22 out of the 29 schools was slightly over $1,100,000. Forty-seven per cent of that amount was expended by the three largest schools.[21] When the data for the present study were assembled in 1937-1938, the total expenditures by the 33 schools was between $1,500,000 and $2,000,000, of which more than one-third was included in the budget of three schools. The costly nature of experiment and expansion present particular problems to the private institutions whose incomes from endowments are decreasing. The state universities have yet to recognize the significance of professional education for social work. With one exception, no tax-supported institution has taken a significant step to increase substantially the resources available for this purpose. Without a more secure financial basis, the schools may be forced to limit their efforts or to resort to practices which may have income-bearing potentialities.

A second major problem of adaptation yet to be faced grows out of the specific place of post-entry education in

21. Mildred Mudgett's Report to the Executive Committee, American Association of Schools of Social Work, August, 1935 (mimeo.), p. 4.

244 Education for the Public Social Services

the services. Obviously it belongs to both the school and the agency. Merit systems are being established during the formative period of the services. The importance of post-entry preparation thus becomes very great. To date, educational leave is used extensively in child welfare services. However, it is making slow progress in public assistance, in spite of the encouragement from the Bureau of Public Assistance of the Social Security Board. There seems to be no reason why it cannot be used in other services, but to date the instances are very few. Is reliance to be placed solely on educational leave? Are the schools only to prepare students for replacements in the services? Is development to wait solely upon the standards which can be achieved in the civil service over a period of years? Or can the schools and the services jointly face the situation, recognizing that the problem cannot be solved by either alone?

The conviction remains that school resources are wisely invested in those areas in which the professional function has been clarified and where there is an established demand for trained personnel. The study has clearly revealed the contribution which can be made by schools of social work in preparing personnel for the administration of public social services. It does not show how far the schools are justified in directing students to these services other than to Public Assistance and Child Welfare, where professional standards have been well established. With limited budgets and the demand from certain fields for qualified social workers the investment of resources in uncharted fields cannot be warranted. Confusion concerning the professional function and political control of placements are sobering factors to schools accepting the responsibility of preparing young persons for professional practice in the field. No school believes it should use a major part of its resources in preparing for a field where qualified personnel is frequently rejected.

The needed skills and knowledge revealed in the study suggest that a professional content can be developed and the direction in which the services are moving would justify the preparation of personnel for employment in the services. The study also indicates that the subject matter offered in the professional curriculum is applicable to practice and administration in a variety of social services, and with certain modifications can be widely useful in preparing this personnel. The problem to be met is the extent to which these two parallel developments will converge in a coöperative effort to raise the standards of administration in all the public social services.

Appendix A

ADDITIONAL SERVICES

IN ADDITION to social services immediately within the scope of this study, others may be cited which have important implications for educational institutions interested in preparing personnel for the field.

First to be listed are the state and local public welfare agencies, other than those whose functions are administered in connection with the provisions of the Social Security Act and therefore the subject of the detailed analysis which has just been presented. Programs are many and varied but include, for the most part: general assistance, services to dependent and delinquent children; licensing and supervision of child caring organizations and other social agencies; services to the physically handicapped; and services to the mentally handicapped, including the mentally ill, defective, and epileptic. These programs both local and state are now so inter-related with federal programs, and subject to so much variation, depending upon the flexibility of the federal program and the degree of coöperation in the states, that a state-by-state analysis is necessary if an accurate picture is to be obtained.

Secondly, provision for the treatment of juvenile delinquents should be cited, including the work of juvenile courts, which in 1938 served between 200,000 and 250,000 delinquent children,[1] and institutional care in state or local schools for delinquents. Likewise provision for the treatment of adult offenders, including probation, institutional treatment, and parole, made by both county and state authorities constitute a large segment of such services. It is estimated that of the 3,072 counties in the United States 1,596 have probation service in the juvenile courts and 1,244 have adult probation service. According to an estimate of the National Probation Association, there were 4,800 probation officers serving in the United States in 1937.[2] No centralized source of information concerning function and standards of personnel is available, and here again a state-by-state analysis is necessary to provide an accurate picture of needs.

Third should be included workmen's compensation which, as the oldest form of social insurance in the United States, has a special interest for the student concerned with the development of standards of practice in the newer services.

Workmen's compensation laws are state enacted and state administered, with the exception of laws covering certain employees of the federal government, private employees of the District of Columbia, and longshoremen and harbor workers, which are federal in character. Exclusive of these federal statutes there are some fifty acts in effect in the United States and territories,[3] each with its own provisions about awards, procedures and the like, although all center around the function of making a decision which will result in compensation to the worker who has been injured in the course of his employment.

Variation in coverage and in standards is so great that it is impossible to determine the total number of workers protected in any way by the fifty acts in operation. Nor is it possible to estimate the number of personnel employed. Ac-

1. Marjorie Bell "Probation," Social Work Year Book, 1939, New York, Russell Sage Foundation, p. 203.
2. *Ibid.*, p. 302.
3. Forty-seven states (Mississippi excluded), and three territories.

cording to the estimate of the United States Bureau of Labor Statistics, not more than 40 per cent of the total gainfully employed workers are actually protected by workmen's compensation coverage. On December 1, 1938, when approximately 42,500,000 workers were employed, about 17,000,000 would be so covered.[4] No figures are available to indicate the number of employees engaged in the administration of workmen's compensation in the several jurisdictions. The material which follows is limited to an analysis of New York State experience.[5]

The "compensation clerks" carry the principal responsibility for routine administration of the compensation procedure in New York. To them is assigned the procedure of answering inquiries from applicants, handling insurance company inquiries, effecting adjustments, and arranging for medical treatment; examining folders in preparation for use by the referee and arranging calendars for the referee; checking when payments stop; checking on "future date" cases to see that the items which caused the postponement are now available; preparing monthly and quarterly reports; arranging for special hearings, such as those in hospitals and homes, when claimants are not physically able to travel; arranging through the Assistant Director for impartial specialists to examine the claimant and to testify; dealing with claimant's complaints about the amount of compensation; deciding whether claimants are entitled to or need hearings; dealing with bills from physicians when questions arise over the amount and time of payment, obtaining out-of-state data when necessary; and coöperating with the After-Care Department.

The enforcement of the Workmen's Compensation Law to make sure that employees are covered according to law is

4. Marshall Dawson, "Coverage Limitations of Workmen's Compensation Laws," *Monthly Labor Review*, Vol. 48, June, 1939, p. 1269.

5. In New York State the coverage under the Act was approximately 3,500,000 in 1935, and the number of persons employed is approximately 800.

in the hands of the "compensation claims investigator," who spends most of the time in the field visiting places about which there is some question. Special attention is given to hazardous types of work. Information or "leads" from other state departments, such as the Factory and Mercantile Divisions, insurance company cancellations, the City Building Department, and the general public are referred to the investigator. He also serves summonses on violators, testifies in magistrate's court, assists claimants under some circumstances to obtain the full benefits of the law, and follows up claimants who do not appear for hearings.

Cases which involve complications or relationships with outside agencies are sent to the After-Care Department by various workers in the Compensation Division, including referees and the assistant director. It is the only department which employs social workers. Here the claimant is interviewed, his record read, and steps taken in accordance with the need suggested. An early hearing may be in order because of an emergency in the claimant's financial condition. Medical treatment may not have been adequate and may be urgently required. Complications over medical bills are usually handled in the After-Care Department. Considerable discussion and counsel with the claimant may be called for in reference to procedure, such as reopening cases, lump sum situations, and the use of impartial specialists. Referrals are made to the Rehabilitation Department, employment agencies, legal aid society, or to a list of approved attorneys, Home Relief Bureau, and to various other social agencies. Referral for financial relief may be necessary when all possibilities of payments of compensation have been exhausted.

Other duties include assisting in the location of claimants, witnesses, and others; supervising the spending of money awarded to minors or incompetents; arranging for special hearings in homes and hospitals; securing immediate small payments before hearings when emergencies exist; helping claimants to travel to other parts of the United States and to other countries when it seems wise to do so; attempting to adjust domestic difficulties and referral to the Domestic Relations Court or elsewhere if that is indicated. Unusual situations arise which require a great deal of time and thought. Obtaining the coöperation of claimants who refuse medical care is frequently difficult. Complex cultural and emotional factors may be present. When minors receive either regular stipends or lump sum payments, a supervisory responsibility is indicated to see that the money is used constructively. Lump sum payments generally need careful investigation and supervision.

In the After-Care Department the same worker carries a case throughout its history, and the average case load is about 150 a month per worker. Most of the work is done in the office, but field work is also involved.

The senior compensation clerk, the principal compensation clerk, and the head compensation clerk are sequential steps in the hierarchy of supervision in workmen's compensation administration in New York State. The principal compensation clerk is in charge of a small unit such as index and calendar, involving the supervision of about seven employees. Aside from the fact that the work is somewhat more complex, the content of the position is like that of the senior compensation clerk. It is, however, difficult to draw a clear line between the classifications.

The head compensation clerks are in charge of "up-state offices" and of specific units in New York City. There may be greater variation in the content of duties performed here than is true at the lower levels. Special cases arise which do not fit into the regular units and are referred to the head compensation clerk who usually decides on the disposition. He also answers inquiries on law and procedure which are of unusual complexity. Under some circumstances, he performs the duties of referee. Since the latter are central in importance, it can be seen that the head compensation clerk occupies a significant position requiring a full background. The director or assistant director carries responsibility for general administration and supervision of the Division of Workmen's Compensation. Upon occasion, they also act as referees.

In Workmen's Compensation administration, almost no specific content was suggested for the various compensation clerk positions. Skills in interviewing, including understanding human nature and evaluating statements, were believed to be important. Office procedure was emphasized. The knowledge of local conditions or of the basic social and economic structure of society was not considered to be important. Whatever is desirable in the way of special training was believed to be obtainable through experience on the job.

In New York State, the first general level of jobs, including typists, stenographers, and junior clerks, from which many promotions are made, has a salary range of $900 to $1,460. The assistant compensation clerk has a salary range of $1,100 to $1,700 and the senior compensation clerk has a range from $1,300 to $2,000. The principal compensation clerk has a range from $1,800 to $2,500 and the head compensation clerk from $2,420 to $3,100. The compensation claims investigator has a range from $1,420 to $2,200; social workers, from $1,800 to $2,300 and senior supervisors from $2,400 to $3,000. The referee, who holds a key position, has a salary range from $4,000 to $6,000. The assistant director's salary range is from $5,200 to $6,450.

In New York State, to which the study is limited, recruitment of personnel is regulated by state civil service rules. For the clerkships which are most likely to supply the higher levels of compensation clerks, the minimum age of appointment is eighteen and the minimum educational requirement is high school graduation, with special credit usually given for further education.

The position of social worker in the After-Care Department is one of the few positions for which previous experience in the labor department is not required. For these positions which number four, and for the positions of physician, attorney, and engineer, professional school education is usually required. In New York State the requirements for appointment in workmen's compensation include residence of one year and citizenship.

New York, the state chosen for study, is committed by law to the promotion principle in large sections of its civil service, including Workmen's Compensation. With few exceptions, it is necessary to move through the lower levels to reach the higher ones. The starting point is apt to be the junior clerk position for which the requirements call for a high school education and sometimes a year in business or some other type of experience. During the depression, college and even professional school graduates have entered the service at this level. Progress is very slow, and in spite of the policy of assigning duties consistent with ability, dissatisfaction is likely to be present. There is some doubt about the advisability of urging professionally trained individuals to embark upon a career which will make it necessary for them to spend years of waiting until they are able to maintain a reasonable standard of living. There are few promotions or positions for which previous experience in the Division or in the Labor Department is not required.

* * *

It is possible, also, to present briefly the scope and function of certain of the federal programs, some of which are functioning through long-established state agencies and some of which have required the establishment of separate agencies. Those included here are: The Bureau of Prisons and Administrative Office, U. S. Courts; the United States Veterans' Administration; the Vocational Rehabilitation Service of the Office of Education; the Office of Indian Affairs; the Work Projects Administration; the National

Youth Administration; the Farm Security Administration; and low cost housing programs aided by the United States Housing Authority. A brief reference to function, content of the service job, training needs, and personnel policies will be made in each instance.

Bureau of Prisons, U. S. Department of Justice and Administrative Office, United States Courts.—To the Bureau of Prisons has been assigned the general supervision of the federal penal institutions, federal prisons, and prison contracts, and questions arising under the parole laws. Likewise, the Bureau supervises the federal prison industries and has jurisdiction over all employment and vocational activities in the penal institutions.[6]

Under the direction of the Federal Supervisor of Probation, Administrative Office, U. S. Courts, there are 220 probation officers appointed by the U. S. district judges and attached to the 90 district courts. In 1937, there were 34,650 federal offenders on probation under supervisors.[7] These probation officers carry responsibility for the pre-sentence, pre-institutional, and post-sentence investigations and later for supervision of offenders on probation or parole. Pre-sentence study includes a tentative plan of probation treatment for use in the event that probation is granted, indication of the type of institution to which the offender should be committed in the event a sentence of imprisonment is imposed, and if possible a tentative parole or conditional release plan. The pre-institutional study assembles all available information pertinent to the case for use by the institutional authorities. The post-sentence investigation is made in event that pre-sentence study has not been completed or supplementary material revealed during the trial. Depending on the type of sentence, it will include a plan of probation treatment, the type of institution to which the offender should be committed, and if possible, a plan of

6. U. S. Government Manual, February, 1940, p. 107.
7. Bell, *op. cit.,* p. 302.

254 Education for the Public Social Services

parole or conditional release. The work of the probation officer is essentially a case work service.[8]

To qualify for an appointment as probation officer, the candidate must be a citizen of the United States. Graduation from a college or university of recognized standing or equivalent practical training in probation work or in an allied field is required, with the provision that one year of study in a recognized school of social work may be substituted for two years of college training. In addition, he should have had at least two years full-time experience in probation work or two years full time experience as a case worker in an accredited professional family service agency or other social case work agency or equivalent experience in an allied field. At the present time, most of the probation officers have backgrounds of education or law, although a few have had preparation for or experience in the field of social work.

Appointments are made by the federal judge in the district, in consultation with the Supervisor of Parole in Washington. Civil service selection is not used. Where more than one probation officer is appointed to a district, one is designated as chief probation officer. The salary range for the probation officers is from $2000 to $2900, with a range to $3200 for chief probation officer.

The in-service training program consists of annual three-day conferences organized on a regional basis. There is some interest in the establishment of short institutes under the auspices of the schools of social work. To meet the needs of the service, the schools of social work are encouraged to offer more courses in the field of delinquency. Educational leave on the workers' own time and expense can be arranged, but there is no premium on additional preparation so far as promotion in rank or salary is concerned.[9]

8. See "Probation," Vol. II, Attorney General's Survey of Release Procedures, U. S. Dept. of Justice, 1939.
9. Interview with Richard A. Chappell, Federal Supervisor, March 26, 1940.

United States Veterans' Administration.—The Veterans' Administration administers all laws providing benefits for former members of the military and naval forces. Benefits extend to veterans and to dependents of deceased veterans of all wars and to veterans and dependents of deceased veterans who served in the government, military and naval establishments during times of peace. In addition to compensation and pensions, the following services are provided: government insurance, military and naval insurance, adjusted compensation, emergency officers' retirement pay for veterans of the World War, and hospital and domiciliary care for veterans of all wars.[10]

Under the general supervision of a Chief of the Social Work Section of the Medical Service 97 social workers are assigned to the regional offices and its hospitals for neuropsychiatric, general and tuberculosis patients. The responsibility of the social workers is to secure social data of significance to the diagnostic and treatment process in the case of Veterans' Administration patients and to help promote the medical objectives for them by giving attention to the social and psychological factors that directly affect their health. To do this the workers study the history and environmental conditions of patients; analyze and submit data to the physician to aid him in arriving at a definite diagnosis and in outlining a course of treatment; further, they consider, report upon, and treat the social environment to which a convalescent patient may go or be expected to go.

Requirements for appointment as a social worker include the completion of two years of post-graduate study in an approved school of social work or one year of post-graduate study in social work, including courses in psychiatric social work or psychiatric field work; or one year of post-graduate study in social work with six months of experience in psychiatric social service work under supervision; or nine months of experience in medical social service work which

10, U. S. Government Manual, *op. cit.*, p. 454.

involves the handling, in collaboration with a psychiatrist, of at least ten psychiatric cases.[11] Of candidates with two years of post-graduate work, no experience is required, although higher ratings are given those who do have such experience.

These workers, all of whom are classified as psychiatric social workers, are selected from the United States Civil Service Register for the position in psychiatric social work. The salary range for these positions is from $2000 to $2600, with of course a higher range for the position of Chief of the Section.[12]

Vocational Rehabilitation.—The Vocational Rehabilitation Service of the Office of Education assists the states in establishing, promoting, and improving programs for locating physically disabled persons and preparing them for and placing them in employment. Grants-in-aid to the states established under the original act of 1920 [13] have been extended and expanded in scope under the provisions of the Social Security Act. Through this service, aid is also given to the states in initiating and maintaining programs for establishing blind persons as operators of vending stands in office buildings, in discovering opportunities for employment of the blind, and in placing blind persons in employment.[14]

The state acts which implement the federal statutes provide in general for the "promotion of vocational rehabilitation of persons disabled in industry or otherwise and their return to remunerative employment." Administration of the act within the states is within the State Departments of Education. By July 1, 1939, 46 states, the District of Columbia, Hawaii, and Puerto Rico had accepted the provisions of the national act.[15]

The program has a vocational guidance emphasis, with the

11. U. S. Civil Service Announcement, 1938.
12. Letter from Charles M. Griffith, Medical Director, April 16, 1940.
13. 41 *Stat* 735, June 2, 1920.
14. 49 *Stat* 1559, June 20, 1936.
15. Fourth Annual Report of the Social Security Board, 1939, p. 4.

ultimate objective of placing the individual in suitable employment. Individualized service to applicants, therefore, is essential. In the plan for rehabilitation is included a study of the applicant's disability, his education, occupational experience, intellectual capacity, personality, financial resources, attitude toward rehabilitation and his attitude toward employment. The development of the plan and continued assistance to the individual until satisfactory placement has been effected complete the cycle of this service.

Within this service there are employed 47 supervisors or directors and 328 case workers or rehabilitation agents. The salary range for the case workers is $1800 to $2700; for supervisors, $3000 to $4000, and for directors, $4000 to $6000. State positions are not covered by civil service except as provided for under state civil service acts.[16]

For the position of case workers, requirements include two years of work in a college or university of recognized standing and successful experience of two years in one or more of the following: vocational rehabilitation, education, personnel management, public employment service, social welfare, and business. Desirable qualities are good judgment, initiative, social-mindedness, comprehension of requirements of good public service, and knowledge of occupations and of training facilities and methods. In the opinion of the Washington administration, the engineering, legal, and vocational fields have yielded the best personnel. A few qualified social workers have been appointed to the state staffs.

For the position of state supervisor, requirements include graduation from a college or university of recognized standing, and demonstrated leadership ability in full-time paid employment in an administrative or supervisory capacity totalling at least five years in one or more of the following fields: vocational rehabilitation, education, personnel management, public employment service, social welfare, and

16. Interview with Terry C. Foster, Vocational Rehabilitation Division, March 26, 1940.

workmen's compensation. Qualifications for assistant state supervisor are the same except that the length of experience is shortened to three years.

For the position of Federal Supervisor, applicants must have been graduated from a college or university of recognized standing, with a major in economics, sociology, vocational education, or general education. In addition, requirements include five years of progressive experience in vocational education, educational administration, workmen's compensation administration or personnel management or in full-time paid employment with organized social work. At least three years of the required experience must have involved administrative responsibility in organized rehabilitation activities, preferably in an organized public civilian rehabilitation program.[17]

In-service training consists of five- to ten-day summer institutes held every other year. Each institute considers one particular phase of the program. Schools of social work have occasionally coöperated in staffing these institutes. Leaves of absence for training are encouraged only after some experience in the service. Such additional preparation should emphasize courses in physical health, vocational training, and testing. Schools of social work interested in offering successful programs for this service are encouraged to emphasize these areas of the curriculum.

Office of Indian Affairs.—Under the direction of the Secretary of the Interior, the management of all Indian affairs and of questions arising out of Indian relations is carried by the Office of Indian Affairs. "These include the economic development of the Indians, both tribally and as individuals, through the effective use of their resources and the acquisition of new resources necessary to provide subsistence; a land-use program, involving land consolidation, acquisition and management, to the end that all Indians able and willing to work on land will have the opportunity to do so;

17. Circular, U. S. Office of Education, n. d.

forestry and grazing, including sustained-yield forest management, fire protection, prevention of erosion, and proper utilization of the range; irrigation, including construction, operation and maintenance; construction and maintenance of roads and bridges on Indian lands; emergency conservation work and other emergency activities, including the Indian Division of the Civilian Conservation Corps; construction and up-keep of buildings on about 200 Indian reservations." [18]

The Office is also responsible for the operation of boarding schools, day schools, and community centers for adult as well as juvenile education, and guides or supervises the education of 50,000 Indian children in public schools. The operation of hospitals and other activities for the improvement of health and sanitation on the reservations is also under the direction of the office.

Under the direction of superintendents who are the administrative officers of jurisdictions, twenty-five social workers have been appointed, of whom six are Indians. The social worker in the Indian Service is required to do a general child care, family care and visiting teacher's job and act as liaison officer between the Indian families and public assistance agencies. The responsibilities as defined by the United States Civil Service Commission are to make social case work investigations of home conditions of children considered for enrollment in Indian boarding schools; to arrange with the proper authorities for the adequate schooling and social adjustment of Indian children in transition from boarding school to local school facilities; on Indian reservations and in regions where Indian children attend government day schools or local public schools, to apply case work techniques in helping the school and family make necessary social adjustments, to make studies of schools and communities as a basis for determining educational policies appropriate for the various groups of the Indian population.

18. U. S. Government Manual, 1940, *op. cit.*, p. 143.

Requirements to be met by applicants for these positions include graduation from an accredited college or university, supplemented by a post-graduate course of not less than eight months' duration, including field work in an approved school of social work and at least one year's successful paid experience in the field of education. Applicants who have had 12 semester hour credits in sociology and technical social work courses may substitute for each of two years of required education one year's successful experience as paid, full time social case worker or family social worker in an established social agency, provided that one year has been under direct supervision. Additional credit is allowed for experience in rural communities as a visiting teacher, social case worker or class room teacher and extra credit allowed for "evidence of progressive professional advancement." Applicants must be between 25 and 50 years of age. In addition to meeting a standard of physical health, they must be able to drive automobiles.

These workers, with the exception of Indian appointees, are selected from the United States Civil Service Register of Social Work-Visiting Teachers. Indian applicants must meet the requirements, but are exempt from civil service examinations. The salary range is between $2300 and $2900.

As a part of the general in-service training program of the Indian Service, a series of partly self-supporting summer institutes are scheduled for teachers and other employees. These emphasize the practical problems and theoretical problems of Indian administration and life.

The Work Projects Administration.—Under the authority of the Emergency Relief Appropriation Act of 1935 the Work Projects Administration was established on May 6, 1935,[19] to operate in coöperation with local, state, and federal sponsors a program of useful public work projects and to aid needy unemployed persons by providing work on such projects. This program is clearly "emergency" at the

19. Formerly called Works Progress Administration.

present time. Work Projects Administrations have been established in each state under the direction of a State Work Projects Administrator and State Directors of the Divisions of Operations, Professional and Service Projects, Employment, and Finance. The registration of workers eligible for these projects is the responsibility of the United States Employment Service. It is required that at least 95 per cent of the persons employed on projects shall be persons referred as in need of relief by the public welfare agency and certified as eligible by the Division of Employment of the Work Projects Administration. Regulations with reference to the certification of workers have been developed by the federal administration and administered in the states through the State Supervisor of the Intake and Certification Section of the Employment Division.[20]

According to the regulations of the Administration, the State Director or Assistant State Director of the Division of Employment shall be a social worker, whose appointment is approved by the Regional Director and the Assistant Commissioner in charge of the Division of Employment. In the nine regions, eleven social workers are employed (four as chief regional supervisor and five as regional supervisors and two as assistants). The salary range is $3800 to $5200. A sufficient number of qualified social workers to perform the functions of the Intake and Certification Section are to be appointed and are to serve under the supervision of a social worker in the State Division of Employment.

In each of the State Work Projects Administration offices there is employed at least one social worker, who in small states has charge of the Intake and Certification Section and who in larger states has the help of an assistant social worker who carries this responsibility. There are approximately 75 to 150 employed. In a large percentage of instances the state social workers have had preparation in recognized schools of social work, and practically all have had social work experi-

20. U. S. Government Manual, 1940, p. 262.

ence with other agencies in addition to their experience with the Work Projects Administration.[21]

In the beginning, social workers were appointed to the staffs of state administrations "to see that people on relief get these jobs and to act in a liaison capacity between the Work Projects Administration, the relief agencies, and the employment agencies." With the establishment of new agencies and additional legislation, the responsibilities of the social workers have increased. Whatever form the work program takes, this field will remain, and there must be persons to act as clearing centers with other agencies serving the unemployed, knowing where the services of the work and other programs meet, supplement, and dove-tail; to be a medium of understanding between the unemployed and the community, and to bring to the unemployed who need and want them the available resources of the community which are unknown to him. The social worker in a work program must know the needs of the individual and how to meet them and how to determine the employability of those seeking work; must be a master in the technique of short contacts; must be familiar with the function and scope of all the community resources; must know how to work with politicians and all organs of government and labor; and most of all must be a good practitioner so that he or she may know when to give and when to withhold services.[22]

State Work Projects Administrations are divided into districts, the number and size depending on the volume of work. Each District office has a complete administrative unit with an Intake and Certification Section as a part of the Division of Employment. In districts where volume of work and traveling distances warrant it, there are area offices comprised of one county or more, serviced by the district offices. These area units, however, are staffed by social workers

21. Maude T. Barrett, Director, Intake and Certification, Work Projects Administration, Letter, April 10, 1940.

22. Alice Yonkman, Assistant Director, Intake and Certification. Letter December 23, 1940.

operating entirely within the field of the need and employability of the unemployed.

County Supervisors of Employment of whom there are "several hundred" are responsible for the certification of workers in the local communities. The actual number of persons employed in the social service function of the Work Projects Administration approximates 2,500.[23] At the present time, no definite standards or recruitment policies have been formulated, although progress is being made with the classification of personnel. No Civil Service selection is used.[24]

National Youth Administration.—Under the authority of the Emergency Relief Appropriation Act of 1935, and therefore "emergency," the National Youth Administration was established to aid young people in four aspects of their life in which their needs are greatest by "(1) providing funds for the part-time employment of needy secondary school, college, and graduate students from 16 through 24 years of age, so that they may continue their education; (2) providing funds for the part-time employment of out-of-school youth from 18 through 24 years of age, chiefly from relief families, on projects designed not only to afford valuable work experience but to benefit youth generally and the communities in which they live; (3) encouraging the establishment of job-training, counseling, and placement services for youth, and the preparation and distribution of occupational information; and (4) encouraging the development and extension of comfortable leisure time activities." [25]

Under the Federal Administrator, State Youth Administrations have been established in each state, New York City, and the District of Columbia, with a State Administrator and a voluntary state advisory committee for each. These are supplemented by district and local directors and advisory committees so that the program in each community is

23. *Ibid.*
24. Maude T. Barrett, Director, Intake and Certification, Work Projects Administration, Conference, April 20, 1940.
25. U. S. Government Manual, *op. cit.,* p. 229.

adapted to the needs of its local youth.[26] The State Administrators are appointed by the Federal Administrator at Washington. The state personnel is selected by the State Administrator with the exception of the Division Directors in the States who are subject to approval by the Federal Administrator. There is no civil service selection of personnel. The selection of state personnel depends upon the special needs of the area and depends also upon the special requirements which the state director believes to be desirable. No uniform requirements for state personnel have been established.

On January 1, 1940, the National Youth Administration employed 10,449 project supervisory employees and 1997 administrative employees. With few exceptions, the administrative employees are located either in the Washington office or in the State headquarters offices. The project supervisory employees are at work in practically every county in the country. The project supervisor's work is as varied as the types of projects carried on by the National Youth Administration, and it is "impossible to state general qualifications for this reason." [27]

Within the program, the Division of Counselling and Guidance and Placement of Out-of-School Youth has special interest for this study. It is the responsibility of the staff of this division to see that youth seeking employment are properly certified as needing employment and are placed on jobs. Knowledge of "guidance, industry, and trade journalism" is believed to be necessary equipment for work in this Division.

The salary scale for "professional workers" ranges from $1500 to $1800, for State Project Directors $4000, and for State Administrators $3600 to $6000.

Farm Security Administration.—Within the Department of Agriculture, the Farm Security Administration authorizes

26. *Ibid.*, p. 228.
27. Aubrey Williams, Administrator, National Youth Administration. Letter, March 21, 1940.

loans to competent farm tenants, sharecroppers, and farm laborers to enable them to become farm owners. Under the Farm loan program, county committees composed of three farmers appointed by the Secretary of Agriculture are authorized to examine applications for loans, appraise the farms to be purchased, and recommend applicants who have the character, ability, and experience to make successful farm owners. Applicants must be citizens of the United States, and preference must be given to persons who are married or who have dependent families, who are able to make initial down payments, or who own livestock and farm implements necessary to carry on farm operations.

Under the rural rehabilitation program the administration makes loans to destitute and low-income families for the purchase of farm supplies, equipment, and livestock, for the refinancing of indebtedness, and for family subsistence. Such loans are limited to families on relief or near relief that are unable to obtain adequate credit from any other source. Each standard loan is accompanied by a farm and home management plan providing for intelligent farm operation and soil conserving practices. These plans usually call for the production of vegetables, milk, eggs, and meat to feed the family and for enough feed and forage crops to take care of the livestock. Ordinarily they may also provide for two cash crops. Emergency loans and grants are made in cases of extreme distress in farm areas devastated by drought, flood, and similar catastrophes.[28]

The responsibility for completion and management of 194 homestead projects initiated under other federal agencies has been assigned to the Farm Security Administration, but there is no authority to initiate new projects. The homesteaders are, in the majority of cases, families which became stranded in worn-out farming areas, cut-over forests, and exhausted mining communities which could not maintain themselves in their former situation, but which could not

28. U. S. Government Manual, p. 167

266   Education for the Public Social Services

undertake a new venture without assistance. The Administration has also constructed 28 migratory labor camps, and three additional camps in other areas are nearing completion.[29] These camps are built to house 6,981 migratory families seeking employment in the farming and fruit-growing sections of the country. As many as 12,000 to 15,000 families may use the camps in a single year.

Regional and county family service aides are appointed to assist in selecting suitable families for resettlement, tenant purchase, and rehabilitation programs and to carry other responsibilities in connection with family adjustment and re-location. These aides are directly responsible to the community managers and technically responsible to the regional chief of family service. For appointment, preparation in a school of social work or experience in the field of social work is required. The salary range for these positions is from $1,800 to $2,300.

Home Economists, of whom there are 1,500, are employed on all agricultural projects. In addition to preparation in home economics, which is required, some knowledge of the social work field is considered to be desirable although not essential.

The County Supervisors carry the responsibility of advising on crop rotations, erosion control, livestock and equipment purchases, and other farm problems. The degree of Bachelor of Science in Agriculture and work in the social sciences is considered desirable equipment.

The project managers, of whom there are 194, and camp managers, of whom there will be 31, meet the educational standard of college graduation with a major in social sciences. Business experience and "an ability to understand people" are additional requirements. Regional directors, of whom

29. Stationary camps are found as follows: California—12; Arizona—3; Texas—4; Idaho—2; Florida—2; Oregon—1; and Washington—1. Mobile camps number three and are located in California.—W. W. Alexander, "Rural Housing—Today and Tomorrow," Housing Year Book, 1940, p. 147.

there are 12 in the program, should have executive ability in addition to knowledge of agricultural life.[30]

Although the jobs in Farm Security Administration have been classified by Civil Service, there is no civil service selection of personnel. The regional directors are appointed by the Washington administration, and regional personnel recommended by the regional directors and appointed from Washington.

United States Housing Authority.[31]—The purpose of the United States Housing Authority is to assist the states and their political subdivisions to remedy the unsafe and unsanitary housing conditions and the acute shortage of decent, safe, and sanitary dwellings for families of low income. The Authority may make loans to public housing agencies to assist in the development, acquisition, or administration of low-rent housing or slum-clearance projects. It may also make annual contributions over a period of years, or capital grants, to assist in achieving and maintaining the low-rent character of a housing project.[32]

By the end of 1939, there were 12 housing projects constructed with United States Housing Authority assistance. During 1940 it is expected that 29 will be opened, and in 1941 the completion of 240 is planned.

Management personnel includes the Housing Manager, the Management Aide, and the Community Relations Aide or Resident Counsellor. The following information concerning the content of their jobs and training needs was obtained by the representative of the U. S. Housing Authority in interviews with members of twelve management staffs.

The Housing Manager is responsible for the operation of the project, including maintenance, management, and rent

30. Wendell Lund, Farm Security Administration; March 27, 1940, Interview.

31. Material summarized from *Study of Project Management Staffs, Low Cost Public Housing*, United States Housing Authority, 1939, by Robert Graham.

32. U. S. Government Manual, p. 259.

collections, and for tenant selection and adjustment. He has general supervision over the management staff employed on the project.

Tenant interviews consume no small part of the manager's time and energy. Some managers estimated that they interviewed three to five tenants a day on an average, others as many as ten to fifteen. Tenant disputes, marital difficulties, financial troubles, loss of job, complaints about neighbors, and other personal problems are brought by the tenant to the manager. Rent delinquency, violations of the lease contract, changes in family composition, and increase in income are types of problems which may take manager to tenant, or cause the manager to send for the tenant. The handling of tenant disputes is seldom exclusively the duty of the manager. Where there is a Community Relations Counsellor, many disputes may be settled without the manager's assistance, but all serious problems in tenant relations usually become his concern at some time during their course of history.

Interviewing applicants is another type of duty which brings the manager in contact with people. Usually he interviews all applicants who appear to be eligible for project residence according to statute and local regulations. Staff members subordinate to the manager conduct the investigation and submit a recommendation, but final review of the application is left to the manager.

Public relations has been an extremely important part of the manager's job. Prior to initial occupancy it was necessary to educate many communities to the purposes of public housing, the rent levels to be put into effect, and the rules of eligibility. While this aspect of the job may become less important as the housing movement grows and becomes better understood, it will continue to be important in any community in which projects are being constructed for the first time.

The manager must make use of the resources of the com-

munity in which the project is located. He finds it important
to know, and to be in a position to ask advice and assistance
from city officials and representatives of welfare, educational,
and recreational agencies, and he reports on most of these
matters either to local authorities or to the United States
Housing Authority or both. There is also a considerable
volume of correspondence to be handled. Since the manager
is responsible for the accuracy of income and expense reports, a knowledge of accounting is important. In the interest of efficient and economical office operation, he must know
enough about the various types of office work to select personnel and organize routine intelligently.

Managers of projects are learning that the job of management is in large part one of effecting and maintaining good
community relations. Good relationships among the tenants,
and between tenants and management, mean lower maintenance costs and less delinquency in rent payments. Sound
programs of activities providing educational and recreational opportunities and health services for the tenants
create good community relationships.

The Community Relations Counsellor is one of the titles
used to designate the person responsible for supervising or
operating the program of project activities. He may also be
called the Resident Counsellor, Assistant or Junior Management Aide, or Community Relations Aide or Counsellor.
And in small projects, the manager himself carries the duties
inherent in this function. The job of the counsellor consists
in organizing and supervising programs of tenant maintenance; scheduling the use of laundries, and handling complaints; taking applications for dwellings; investigating and
rating applicants; giving instructions and enforcing rules of
occupancy, and assisting in the investigations of delinquent
rents. He usually has charge of all indoor community space,
schedules its uses, and determines what supplies and equipment are needed. He assists the tenants in organizing the
educational and recreational activities they may desire.

The programs of activities on the various projects differ considerably in content. While one small project had virtually no program at all, most projects possessed a variety of opportunities for the tenants. The type and quality of the program appeared to depend on the amount and quality of supervision, and the number and types of facilities available. In most cases the Community Relations Counsellors have succeeded in expanding the opportunities available to the tenants beyond the limits of project facilities and paid leaderships. Facilities in the neighborhood of the project have been secured for tenant activities, and volunteer supervisors and instructors have been enlisted from the tenant group, particularly in connection with the operation of nursery schools.

In the early months of project operation, the community relations counsellor ordinarily attempts to stimulate the founding of clubs and a tenant association. From these groups he determines the recreational and educational wants of the tenants, and assists in organizing the activities. The growth is slow, but gradually a great variety of activities spring up, such as tenant newspaper, credit union, nursery school, library, health services, athletics and sports, groups engaged in music, drama, arts and crafts, and dancing, and groups studying parent and homemaking education, health and safety education, and coöperatives.

Home Economics has proven a particularly valuable type of education, both to tenants who have become interested in it, and to the management. The tenant learns to make the family income go farther through wiser budgeting, purchasing, and menu planning, and the management costs are reduced because tenants improve in the care of their dwelling and its equipment.

It is the policy of most community relations counsellors to provide only such assistance as is essential to the project program. The tenants are encouraged to conduct their own activities and manage their programs, depending on the management only for technical assistance. In practice, tenant management of community programs has not proven wholly successful. Although the programs are too new and the number included in the scope of this study were too few to permit sound generalization, it appears that there is a continuous need for skilled stimulation of tenant interest and technical guidance of the activities.

There is a tendency for the person in charge of the community program to function as assistant to the manager, and to act as manager in times of his absence. Probably some of those now acting as assistant managers will be offered managerial jobs on projects now under construction. It can, therefore, be argued that the type of training provided the community relations counsellor should differ from that provided the manager only as an emphasis on training in recreational skills, equipment and activities.

On the other hand, there is also some indication that local authorities, when they become responsible for the management of several projects, will have a specialist on the authority staff acting as a technical advisor on community relations problems and programs. For this position, the persons would require a comprehensive knowledge of types of activities as well as a knowledge of group work methods and project management.

The manager will probably be selected from the residents of the community. Applicants from other parts of the state or country may be better qualified in terms of academic training and occupational experience, but a local resident will almost surely be the choice of the Authority. Selection of project management staffs of local housing authorities is not governed by civil service selection. In the study it was learned that experience in property management had apparently been the most important criterion in the selection of managers. Academic training may have been considered in determining the final choice, but experience seems to have been the basic criterion. It is probable that this policy will continue.

The salary range for the Housing Managers is $2000 to $4600, and for Management Aide, Community Relations Aide or Resident Counsellor from $1620 to $2100. Opportunity for promotion on project management staffs is not great. The only change which would mean a real promotion for an individual in any of these subordinate jobs would be to the position of manager. Generally speaking, the worker who has had experience on a project probably has a better chance of being selected for the manager's job on a new project than a person who has a more impressive academic record but no experience.

Social Services in the Public Schools.—The administration of the public school system once narrowly conceived now includes a variety of services for special groups justified by the necessity of meeting special needs if the entire system is to serve the community. The services commonly found are those of the attendance officer and visiting teacher, the administration of employment certificates, counselling and guidance, job placement, child guidance and to a lesser extent the provision of glasses, clothing, and luncheons for disadvantaged children. A recent study by the Educational Policies Commission indicates that there is considerable variation in the functional distribution of these services between the schools and other agencies. In the cities of over 100,000 there is a tendency to provide these welfare services under the school system itself, while in the counties the tendency is to rely on other agencies or to make no provision at all.[33] A functional distribution recommended by the Commission would assign the provision of material assistance to children to the welfare authorities, except where emergencies might dictate otherwise.[34] In guidance and placement there may be an overlapping with the employ-

33. National Education Association of the United States, Educational Policies Commission; *Social Services and the Schools,* Washington, 1940, p. 140.

34. *Ibid.,* p. 103.

ment service in the community. A close relationship is certainly implied; a functional relationship to both school and employment services may be justified.

Personnel needed to carry certain of these services has been the subject of recent study by Margaret Huntley, Chairman of the Committee on Membership Standards of the American Association of Visiting Teachers, from which the following material is summarized.[35] According to the study, limited to seventy-nine members of the American Association of Visiting Teachers who returned questionnaires, the visiting teacher [36] is a social worker assigned to an elementary or junior high school and in some instances to high schools for work with individual children who constitute behavior problems in the schoolroom or in other school activities. While usually the assignment of the visiting teacher is to an individual school or schools, in some systems the service is centralized within the office of the Board of Education and available for children throughout the system.

The social case work service so provided is distinct from any other offered in the school system. The visiting teacher "supplements school personnel and offers another point of view on the problems of the individual. In larger school systems where varied personnel services are obtainable, she often acts as a coördinator unifying the efforts of all in the interest of the individual child. She builds in the community a better understanding of the school and its functioning. She serves as a school representative in planning many community welfare activities." [37]

The recognized training for visiting teacher work includes

35. Margaret Huntley, "The Visiting Teacher at Work in the United States," American Association of Visiting Teachers, 1940 (typewritten).

36. The visiting teachers in the school systems are also designated as school counsellors, attendance officers, school visitors, counsellor for personality and character development, welfare officer, dean, social worker.

37. "Who, What and Where of the Visiting Teacher and Her Work," National Committee for Mental Hygiene, New York, 1940.

graduation from a recognized college or university and the completion of a two-year course in an approved school of social work. In some systems, both experience in social work and in teaching are required. Of the seventy-nine visiting teachers included in the Huntley study, seventy had had teaching experience and fifty-two had had experience in social work. For membership in the American Association of Visiting Teachers, credits in education which enable the visiting teacher to work effectively in schools and to meet the local and state requirements of certification are also specified.

Of the group included in the Huntley study, seventy-three had completed the work for the B.A. degree and thirty-seven had completed the work for the M.A. degree. Of the thirty-seven, sixteen degrees were in education, twelve in social work or social administration, and nine in liberal arts studies.

In general the salary of the visiting teacher corresponds to the salary of the high school teacher in the system.

, *Public Health and Medical Care.*[38]—Protection of the people's health and care of the sick and the handicapped are public services which are distributed among many agencies. State and local departments of health and departments of welfare, while carrying out their own immediate responsibilities, are at the same time taking part in nationwide health movements under federal leadership.

No health program for a community is complete without facilities for care and prevention of both physical and mental illness. Nevertheless for purposes of this report it is expedient to treat mental hospitals and clinics separately. They are not included, therefore, in the following discussion.

Any effective program of preventive medicine contributes to both health and welfare and calls upon all the special

38. Statement prepared by Antoinette Cannon, Chairman, Joint Committee, American Association of Medical Social Workers and American Public Welfare Association, directing the Study of "Medical Social Work in Tax-Supported Health and Welfare Agencies," published by the American Public Welfare Association, 1940.

agencies of the community for coöperation. As programs are now organized, however, they are themselves considerably specialized and designed to reach more or less well defined groups. For example, there are the programs for maternal and child health and those for crippled children, aided and promoted by the Children's Bureau; the state and county services for control of syphilis, tuberculosis, and cancer, some of these receiving aid through the United States Public Health Service; and there are many state and city public welfare programs which include the provision of medical care under specified conditions.

Generally speaking, the functions of the programs carried on by public health agencies include the following: providing diagnostic facilities, making the public aware of the existence of such facilities and of how and why they should be used, finding cases, following diagnosis by planning for treatment in individual cases, providing treatment and convalescent care facilities, organizing the use of existing facilities, and enlisting the coöperation of other agencies in the community in carrying out plans for care and rehabilitation of the sick and disabled, individually and in groups. The functions of the medical care programs carried on by public welfare agencies include the payment of costs of medical treatment for recipients of general assistance, provision of drugs and appliances for them, organization of some system by which medical diagnosis and treatment is available in the homes of recipients, payment for nursing care and for housekeeping aid, making of policies governing financial and administrative relations between state and local offices, and between the public welfare agency and other agencies and professional groups in the community, especially with doctors and nurses, and facilitating the use of all existing institutions for health care.

In order to perform these functions many agencies, both public health and public welfare, have included medical social workers among their personnel. This situation has recently been studied by the American Association of Medical Social Workers and the American Public Welfare Association.[39]

Fourteen agencies gave data on twenty-one divisions of public service which they severally administered. These twenty-one services were selected, (a) as illustrating the recognition within tax-supported programs of a medical-social function and use of medical social workers, and (b) as illustrating the distribution of certain responsibilities for health among both public health and public welfare agencies throughout the country.

Of the total number, six were services providing medical care to recipients of public assistance; they were under local and state administration, and served the general assistance recipients and also some categorical groups, such as Aid to Dependent Children, Old Age Assistance, and Aid to Blind. In this latter capacity they are among "those whose functions are administered in connection with the Social Security Act." [40]

The fifteen services which were not directed to the needs of relief recipients as such were for the most part under the auspices of departments of public health. The few exceptions were in programs set up under the Social Security Act, for crippled children and for the blind, under special circumstances. All have a primary purpose of conserving the public health. These services include, besides those for the blind and for crippled children, cancer control, tuberculosis control, maternal and child welfare, and health units in decentralized health department services.

Usually the programs of state, county, and city departments of health include the maintenance of hospitals, clinics,

39. "Medical Social Work in Tax-Supported Health and Welfare Services," a Report of the Joint Committee of the American Association of Medical Social Workers and the American Public Welfare Association, by Margaret Lovell Plumley. Published by the American Public Welfare Association, Chicago, 1940.
40. *Supra*, p. 57.

and other medical institutions. Such institutions are also administered under public auspices other than health departments. The responsibility of such institutions for a social service in connection with medical care is well established, and does not differ essentially from that of the voluntary hospital.

The social work function is ordinarily performed by medical social workers on the staff of the institution. The study shows that this is true in the hospitals which were included in the programs it covered. In them medical social workers were employed in their usual capacity as social case workers, as supervisors of medical social work, and as administrators of medical social work.

As the governmental hospitals and clinics serve not only relief recipients but also other persons in need of diagnosis and treatment, they have a problem of defining eligibility in terms of their public health purpose and of administering their policy when it is defined. In this policy-making and selection of eligible patients the social worker has a part to play which may influence the working relationships between hospital and community in important ways.

The hospital and clinic are necessary to the effective activity of any community health plan, and conversely the institution is incomplete as a health agency without the extramural activity of the department of health, the voluntary health organization, and the social agencies which uphold certain standards of living. The extra-mural program may be more or less thoroughly related to that of the institution, but it is evident that the two supplement and condition each other. In the services studied medical social work has been found to be required in that part of the health program which is centered in the community as well as in the part which centers in the hospital.

In these extra-mural positions, which carry responsibility for social work for the sick, yet which are not hospital or clinic positions, medical social workers serve usually in supervisory, advisory, and consultative capacity. In such capacity, though they may spend relatively little time in direct service to individual sick persons, they are required to be experienced in medical social case work and in coöperating on cases with doctors and with medical institutions, in order to be able to help other members of the staff when judgments have to be made regarding medical care for individuals or policies as to medical care.

Supervisory positions carry administrative responsibility and therefore require experience in administration. Supervisors and directors "are able to assist in the formation of general policies in their agencies since they have, through their workers, the most direct knowledge of the way in which the medical needs of the agencies' clients affect, and are affected by, their social needs." [41] It is desirable, therefore, that their previous experience include such formulation of policies. It should also include participation in community conferences, since the medical social worker plays a part in the establishment of working relationships between the public department and the other social and health agencies of the community.

"The data gathered in this study indicated that there are seven main categories into which the activities of medical social workers in public agencies can be grouped: administration (including supervision), consultation and guidance, case work, education, community leadership, program development, research." [42]

"In no agency do all of a medical social worker's activities fall exclusively into one category. Administrative duties in particular are closely related to the other activities. Consultation, for example, may be part of administration, as when it relates to policy-making and planning. Similarly, community relationships may be administrative, as in developing

41. Margaret L. Plumley, *op. cit.*, p. 17.
42. *Ibid.*, p. 16.

agreements with medical agencies and professional groups."[43]

At the time of this study (1939) appointments were made by use of civil service examination in 14 of the 21 divisions of service studied. Civil service requirements, however, varied. In the agencies in which civil service was not a requirement, definite qualifications had been set up as prerequisite to appointment. Persons interviewed expressed opinion that experience in a hospital social service department was essential, that experience as case supervisor in public relief was definitely valuable, and that a varied experience was needed, the type and amount dependent upon the specific position to be held.

"Among 18 directors of divisions of service, supervisors, and consultants, the lowest salary reported was $1800 and the highest $3200...." "The salaries for 102 staff workers (including 3 workers in hospital social service departments) ranged from $1500 to $2600." "Over half the workers, and probably a considerably larger proportion, received salaries of $1800 or above..."

"On the basis of this information and what is known about salaries of medical social workers generally, it would be difficult to make a comparison between rates of pay in public health and welfare agencies and rates of pay in hospitals, voluntary or public. In the two fields, positions which bear the same titles often do not have the same requirements in activities and especially in administrative responsibilities. Consequently, salary rates in public health and welfare services probably should be determined on the basis of the type of work required, the responsibilities to be carried by the medical social workers employed, and the established rates of pay for positions of similar rank in the field of public service." [44]

* * *

43. *Ibid.*, p. 17.
44. *Ibid.*, p. 15.

The previous paragraphs have included a partial list of social services which will supplement the present study. Some, it is indicated, are in the nature of provisions needed to insure the proper functioning of programs which have a broad function and which serve the entire population. They represent a type of service extended to a smaller group than the entire service comprises and to a group which presents needs not shared or suggested by the average or normal beneficiary. Others are in the nature of provisions which should be insured to every beneficiary.

Appendix B

TABLES

TABLE 1

Number and Distribution by States of Employees in Old Age Insurance Offices, February 9, 1939.

STATE	TOTAL	MANAGERS	ASSISTANT MANAGERS	OTHERS
Total	1643	309	152	1182
Alabama	38	8	2	28
Arizona	15	3	2	10
Arkansas	17	5	1	11
California	94	12	4	78
Colorado	21	3	2	16
Connecticut	27	5	3	19
Delaware	19	6	1	12
District of Columbia...	14	1	1	12
Florida	28	6	2	20
Georgia	36	8	2	26
Idaho	13	3	2	8
Illinois	94	14	7	73
Indiana	53	12	4	37
Iowa	22	4	1	17
Kansas	18	4	4	10
Kentucky	14	4	1	9
Louisiana	34	5	5	24
Maine	13	3	3	7
Maryland	22	4	1	17
Massachusetts	67	13	7	47
Michigan	45	6	6	33
Minnesota	31	5	2	24
Mississippi	21	6	1	14
Missouri	45	8	3	34
Montana	16	4	0	12
Nebraska	13	3	2	8
Nevada	7	2	0	5
New Hampshire	9	4	0	5
New Jersey	46	10	6	30
New Mexico	5	1	1	3
New York	163	21	20	122
North Carolina	39	9	7	23
North Dakota	10	4	1	5
Ohio	56	8	4	44
Oklahoma	25	5	1	19
Oregon	25	5	2	18
Pennsylvania	94	17	11	66

STATE	TOTAL	MANAGERS	ASSISTANT MANAGERS	OTHERS
Rhode Island	16	3	1	12
South Carolina	28	7	3	18
South Dakota	8	3	0	5
Tennessee	39	7	4	28
Texas	91	15	7	69
Utah	11	2	1	8
Vermont	7	3	1	3
Virginia	28	6	3	19
Washington	32	5	3	24
West Virginia	27	6	1	20
Wisconsin	36	8	5	23
Wyoming	11	3	1	7

TABLE 2

Number of Permanent and Temporary
ment Compensation and Employment

STATE	TOTAL PERSONNEL U.C. & E.S.	UNEMPLOYMENT COMPENSATION PERSONNEL		
		Total	Permanent	Temporary
United States	36,246	20,691	17,288	3,403
Alabama	471	239 (a)	202	37
Alaska	23	10 (b)	9	1
Arizona	127	71	71	0
Arkansas	231	110	108	2
California	2,460	1,868	1,843	25
Colorado	250	142	117	25
Connecticut	783	567	567	0
Delaware	137	86	82	4
District of Columbia	313	185	185	0
Florida	327	158	146	12
Georgia	470	198	198	0
Hawaii	82	64	58	6
Idaho	143	83	82	1
Illinois	881	398	397	1
Indiana	1,032	653	620	33
Iowa	434	191	190	1
Kansas	307	168	166	2
Kentucky	525	354	267	87(d)
Louisiana	475	244	244	0
Maine	328	229	229	0
Maryland	581	375	375	0
Massachusetts	2,209	1,500	1,106	394
Michigan	1,865	993	933	60
Minnesota	804	494	270	224
Mississippi	234	100	94	6 (e)
Missouri	913	454	412	42
Montana	87	55	40	15
Nebraska	258	118	101	17

(a) Includes 19 employees who were to be released before
June 1, 1939.

(b) Does not include three permanent commission members
because they received no compensation during May.

(c) Includes 23 part-time janitors.

TABLE 2

Employees Engaged in State Unemploy-
Service Activities as of May 31, 1939.

EMPLOYMENT SERVICE PERSONNEL			PERCENT U.C. PERSONNEL IS	PERCENT E.S. PERSONNEL
Total	Permanent	Temporary	OF TOTAL	IS OF TOTAL
15,555	14,384	1,171	57.1	42.9
232	232	0	50.7	49.3
13	12	1	43.5	56.5
56	55	1	55.9	44.1
121	108	13	47.6	52.4
592	582	10	75.9	24.1
108	100	8	56.8	43.2
216	216	0	72.4	27.6
51	51	0	62.8	37.2
128	105	23	59.1	40.9
169	154	15	48.3	51.7
272	272	0	42.1	57.9
18	16	2	78.0	22.0
60	57	3	58.0	42.0
483	483	0	45.2	54.8
379	379	0	63.3	36.7
243	209	34 (c)	44.0	56.0
139	138	1	54.7	45.3
171	169	2	67.4	32.6
231	217	14	51.4	48.6
99	99	0	69.8	30.2
206	202	4	64.5	35.5
709	705	4	67.9	32.1
872	872	0	53.2	46.8
310	309	1	61.4	38.6
134	116	18 (f)	42.7	57.3
459	459	0	49.7	50.3
32	26	6	63.2	36.8
140	126	14	45.7	54.3

(d) Includes 32 employees hired in local offices during bitu-
minous coal strike.

(e) Includes two employees on unemployment compensation
merit examination payrolls.

(f) Part-time janitors.

TABLE 2 (*continued*)

STATE	TOTAL PERSONNEL U.C. & E.S.	UNEMPLOYMENT COMPENSATION PERSONNEL		
		Total	Permanent	Temporary
Nevada	77	41	35 (g)	6
New Hampshire ..	185	126	126	0
New Jersey	1,467	922	755	167 (h)
New Mexico	118	52	52	0
New York	5,216	2,437	911	1,526 (i)
North Carolina ...	752	391	376	15 (k)
North Dakota	114	44	44	0
Ohio	1,673	1,151	980	171
Oklahoma	415	171	171	0
Oregon	360	253	253	0
Pennsylvania	3,910	2,051	1,615	436
Rhode Island......	355	301	292	9
South Carolina ...	407	252	224	28
South Dakota	94	47	47	0
Tennessee	525	258	246	12
Texas	1,162	392	392	0
Utah	167	114	99 (m)	15
Vermont	114	71	69	2
Virginia	580	393	382	11
Washington	448	250	250	0
West Virginia	613	445	445	0
Wisconsin	644	358	358	0
Wyoming	100	64	54 (n)	10

(g) Includes three probational employees.

(h) Includes 51 temporary employees on emergency payroll.

(i) Includes 518 temporary line-item and open-competitive provisional employees.

(j) Includes 659 temporary line-item and open-competitive provisional employees.

TABLE 2 (continued)

EMPLOYMENT SERVICE PERSONNEL			PERCENT U.C. PERSONNEL IS	PERCENT E.S. PERSONNEL
Total	Permanent	Temporary	OF TOTAL	IS OF TOTAL
36	34	2	53.2	46.8
59	59	0	68.1	31.9
545	534	11	62.8	37.2
66	66	0	44.1	55.9
2,779	1,947	832 (j)	46.7	53.3
361	361	0	52.0	48.6
70	68	2	38.6	61.4
522	432	90	68.8	31.2
244	219	25 (l)	41.2	58.8
107	107	0	70.3	29.7
1,859	1,827	32	52.5	47.5
54	54	0	84.8	15.2
155	155	0	61.9	38.1
47	47	0	50.0	50.0
267	267	0	49.1	50.9
770	770	0	33.7	66.3
53	53	0	68.3	31.7
43	43	0	62.3	37.7
187	187	0	67.8	32.2
198	198	0	55.8	44.2
168	168	0	72.6	27.4
286	286	0	55.6	44.4
36	33	3	64.0	36.0

(k) Includes 15 employees on unemployment compensation merit examination payrolls.

(l) Part-time janitors.

(m) Includes one employee engaged on interstate conference work and four probationary employees.

(n) Includes two commissioners, one merit examination supervisor, and two probational employees.

TABLE 3 (a)

Number and Distribution by States of Employment Service Personnel.

STATE	STATE ADMINIS- TRATIVE	LOCAL ADMINIS- TRATIVE (b)	SENIOR INTER- VIEWER	JUNIOR INTER- VIEWER
Total	276	934	2531	4534
Alabama	7	13	50	61
Arizona	3	5	15	13
Arkansas	6	11	20	33
California	2	34	91	207
Colorado	6	4	27	34
Connecticut	5	18	37	80
Delaware	3	5	8	15
District of Columbia	2	13	7	16
Florida	6	7	28	33
Georgia	11	17	52	72
Idaho	5	6	17	8
Illinois	13	47	121	150
Indiana	11	31	94	72
Iowa	5	13	51	58
Kansas	0	9	39	19
Kentucky	5	14	23	47
Louisiana	7	8	43	84
Maine	2	8	17	25
Maryland	5	10	20	65
Massachusetts	7	49	213	163
Michigan	11	101	109	264
Minnesota	6	15	86	74
Mississippi	4	10	32	25
Missouri	9	19	62	126
Montana	?	4	16	27
Nebraska	5	7	24	39

(a) This table is not a valid basis for administrative comparisons. Since it covers different periods of time and the classification of positions has been arbitrarily curtailed by the study staff, to use the table for judgment of administrative efficiency would be quite unjustifiable.

(b) Includes district managers, assistant managers, supervisory interviewers, and division chiefs.

Appendix B   289

TABLE 3 *(continued)*

STATE	STATE ADMINIS-TRATIVE	LOCAL ADMINIS-TRATIVE	SENIOR INTER-VIEWER	JUNIOR INTER-VIEWER
Nevada	3	3	9	7
New Hampshire ..	4	8	15	10
New Jersey	9	28	121	140
New Mexico	3	5	12	25
New York	3	96	244	835
North Carolina ..	9	51	30	63
North Dakota	3	8	10	19
Ohio	11	7	134	255
Oklahoma	7	15	44	68
Oregon	4	10	35	24
Pennsylvania	18	106	215	436
Rhode Island	6	5	6	17
South Carolina ...	4	8	25	38
South Dakota	3	3	14	11
Tennessee	9	8	65	79
Texas	6	16	88	408
Utah	3	5	13	10
Vermont	1	0	13	7
Virginia	6	11	44	60
Washington	4	10	35	67
West Virginia.....	5	20	34	37
Wisconsin	7	29	15	101
Wyoming	2	4	8	7

TABLE 4

Number and Distribution by States of
Professional and Administrative Child Welfare Workers
Supported by Federal Funds (as of January 3, 1939).

STATE	LOCAL WORKERS (a) Full-Time	Part-Time	STATE PROFESSIONAL STAFF Full-Time	Part-Time
Total	342	78	266	75
Alabama	13	—	4	9
Alaska	—	—	1	—
Arizona	3	—	2	—
Arkansas	9	—	5	1
California	8	2	10	—
Colorado	5	—	4	—
Connecticut	4	—	1	—
Delaware	—	5	—	1
Dist. of Columbia	—	—	4	—
Florida	10	—	2	—
Georgia	15	—	2	1
Hawaii	4	1	—	1
Idaho	—	5	1	1
Illinois	7	—	9	—
Indiana	5	—	8	—
Iowa	10	—	2	—
Kansas	7	—	4	—
Kentucky	3	5	12	—
Louisiana	19	—	3	1
Maine	2	1	4	4 (b)
Maryland	6	7	2	—
Massachusetts ..	2	—	1	—
Michigan	10	—	3	—
Minnesota	7	15	3	17
Mississippi	1	—	5	1
Missouri	12	—	4	—
Montana	7	1	2	—
Nebraska	3	12	4	1
Nevada	2	3	1	—
New Hampshire.	4	—	1	1
New Jersey	6	—	5	—

(a) County, town, parish, district.   (b) In training.

STATE	LOCAL WORKERS (a)		STATE PROFESSIONAL STAFF	
	Full-Time	Part-Time	Full-Time	Part-Time
New Mexico ...	7	—	—	1
New York	2	—	10	—
North Carolina .	17	—	4	1
North Dakota ..	—	11	1	9
Ohio	9	—	10	—
Oklahoma	21	1	7	—
Oregon	10	—	3	—
Pennsylvania ...	12	—	8	—
Rhode Island....	2	1	3	—
South Carolina .	6	—	5	1
South Dakota ..	10	—	2	1
Tennessee	11	—	4	7
Texas	15	1	9	—
Utah	10	1	—	2
Vermont	4	—	1	—
Virginia	7	—	3	13
Washington	8	—	3	—
West Virginia...	4	—	4	1
Wisconsin	3	6	5	—
Wyoming	—	—	—	—

TABLE 5

Number and Classification of Schools of Social Administration which were Members of the American Association of Schools of Social Work, indicating date of Admission to Association, 1939.

SCHOOL	STATE	MUNICIPAL	PRIVATE	DENOMINATIONAL
Atlanta University.....			1928	
Boston College				1938
Boston University......			1939	
Bryn Mawr College....			1919	
Buffalo, University of..			1934	
California, University of	1928			
Carnegie Institute			1919	
Catholic University ...				1937
Chicago, University of..			1919	
Cincinnati, University of		1935		
Denver, University of..			1933	
Fordham University ...				1929
Jewish Social Work....				1928
Indiana, University of..	1923			
Iowa, University of....	1938			
Louisville, University of		1937		
Loyola University				1921
Michigan, University of	1923			
Minnesota, University of	1919			
Montreal School.......			1939	
National Catholic School				1923
New York School of Social Work			1919	
Northwestern University			1936	
N. Carolina, U. of	1936			
Ohio State University..	1919			
Oklahoma, University of	1938			
Pennsylvania School....			1919	
Pittsburgh, University of			1934	
St. Louis University....				1933
Simmons College			1919	
Smith College			1919	

SCHOOL	STATE	PRIVATE
So. California, University of		1922
Toronto, University of.	1939 (a)	
Tulane University		1927
Washington, University of	1934	
Washington University.		1928
Western Reserve University		1919
William and Mary College		1919

(a) Provincial University.

TABLE 6

Number and Classification of Schools of Social Administration Not Yet Members of the American Association of Schools of Social Work, Indicating Year of Establishment, 1939.

SCHOOL	STATE UNIVERSITY & TERRITORIAL	STATE AGRI-CULTURAL COLLEGE	MUNIC-IPAL UNI-VERSITY	NATION-AL INSTI-TUTION	PRIVATE INSTI-TUTION
1. Florida State College for Women..	1939				
2. Howard University				1937	
3. University of Hawaii	1937				
4. University of Illinois *	1939				
5. University of Kentucky *	1939				
6. Louisiana State University *	1937				
7. University of Nebraska *	1937				
8. University of Notre Dame					1939
9. Temple University					1937
10. University of Utah	1937				
11. Utah Agricultural College *		1938			
12. Washington State College *		1938			
13. Wayne University			1934		
14. University of West Virginia *	1939				

* Land Grant Institution   October 19, 1939

TABLE 7

Total Enrollment of all Students and Number of Schools Reporting November 1, 1932, to November 1, 1938.

YEAR	NUMBER OF SCHOOLS REPORTING	TOTAL	MEN	WOMEN
1932	24	3112 (a)	433	2679
1933	25	5255 (a)	523	4732
1934	29	6602	1104	5498
1935	31	6612 (a)	1084	5528
1936	33	6779 (a)	1143	5611
1937	32	6422 (a)	1122	5300
1938	35	6109	1179	4930
1939	37	5839	1221	4618

(a) Incomplete because of "not reported" items.
1936 total includes 25 for whom sex was not reported.

TABLE 8

Total Number of Students Majoring in Social Work and Number of Full-Time and Part-Time Students as of November 1, 1932, to November 1, 1939.

YEAR	TOTAL	FULL-TIME	PART-TIME
1932	2863	1534	1329
1933	3467	1655	1812
1934	5259	2712	2547
1935	5296	2561	2735
1936	5118 (a)	2545	2573 (a)
1937	5034 (a)	2562 (a)	2472
1938	4956	2356	2600
1939	5103	2560	2543

(a) Incomplete because of "not reported" items.

TABLE 9

Full-Time Students Majoring in Social Work and Number Who are Graduate, Undergraduate, and Otherwise Classified as of November 1, 1932, to November 1, 1939.

YEAR	TOTAL	GRADUATE	UNDERGRADUATE	OTHER
1932	1534	936	563	35
1933	1655	1015	621	19
1934	2712	1940	746	26
1935	2561	1797	739	25
1936	2545	1864	663	18
1937	2562	1985	566 (a)	11
1938	2356	2147	193 (b)	16
1939	2560	2417	137	6

(a) Undergraduates taking professional curriculum, 301; pre-professional curriculum, 265.

(b) Undergraduates taking professional curriculum only are included.

TABLE 10

Descriptive Titles of Degrees Offered in Schools of Social Work, 1938.

1. MASTER OF ARTS—Bryn Mawr College, University of Chicago, University of Cincinnati, University of Denver, Fordham University, Indiana University, University of Iowa, National Catholic School of Social Service, Northwestern University, the University of Washington............ 10
2. MASTER OF ARTS IN SOCIAL WORK—University of Minnesota 1
3. MASTER OF ARTS IN SOCIAL ADMINISTRATION—Ohio State University 1
4. MASTER OF SCIENCE—Simmons College 1
5. MASTER OF SCIENCE IN SOCIAL WORK—Boston College, Catholic University, University of North Carolina, St. Louis University, and College of William and Mary........................ 5
6. MASTER OF SCIENCE IN SOCIAL SERVICE—Boston University 1
7. MASTER OF SCIENCE IN SOCIAL ADMINISTRATION—

University of Louisville, University of Pittsburgh, Western Reserve University............ 3
8. MASTER OF SOCIAL SCIENCE—Smith College....... 1
9. MASTER OF SOCIAL SERVICE—University of Buffalo, Jewish School of Social Work 2
10. MASTER OF SOCIAL WORK—Atlanta University, Carnegie Institute of Technology, Loyola University, University of Michigan, Ohio University, Pennsylvania School, University of Southern California, Tulane University, Washington University 9
                                                     —
                                                    34

TABLE 11

Descriptive Titles of Certificates and Diplomas Offered in Schools of Social Work, 1938.

1. DIPLOMA—Atlanta; New York School of Social Work 2
2. DIPLOMA IN SOCIAL WORK—Fordham; National Catholic School of Social Service.............. 2
3. DIPLOMA IN SOCIAL SCIENCE—Toronto.......... 1
4. CERTIFICATE IN SOCIAL ECONOMY—Bryn Mawr College 1
5. GRADUATE CERTIFICATE IN SOCIAL WORK—University of Buffalo 1
6. PROVISIONAL PROFESSIONAL CERTIFICATE IN SOCIAL ADMINISTRATION—University of Louisville...... 1
7. CERTIFICATE A AND CERTIFICATE B—Graduate School for Jewish Social Work............... 1
8. CERTIFICATE IN SOCIAL WORK—University of Minnesota; University of Oklahoma; Pennsylvania School of Social Work; * College of William and Mary 4
9. CERTIFICATE IN SOCIAL SERVICE—University of California 1
10. GRADUATE OF SCHOOL—Smith College........... 1
                                                    —
                                                    15

* Pennsylvania School of Social Work also grants Advanced Curriculum Certificate.

TABLE 12

Number of Students Who Received Degrees, Diplomas or Certificates in Social Work During Previous Academic Year, According to Enrollment of November 1, 1932, to November 1, 1938.

		DEGREES			DIPLOMAS, CERTIFI-
YEAR	TOTAL	B.A. *or* B.S.	M.A. *or* M.S.	PH.D.	CATES
1932	624 (a)	283	166	5	171 (b)
1933	730	255	186	3	286
1934	719	299	146	4	270
1935	840	312	234	5	289
1936	1176 (c)	413	352	2	409
1937	1054	226	437	8	383
1938	1220 (d)	222	592	6	400

(a) One student counted under M.S. degree and also under certificate.

(b) Not including certificate in Public Health Nursing.

(c) Incomplete because of "not reported" items.

(d) Autumn term 1937 through summer session 1938.

Illustrative Sequence of Study

UNIVERSITY OF CHICAGO[1]

A suggested professional program for six quarters of work to indicate the general plan of professional education.

First Year Program

FIRST QUARTER	SECOND QUARTER	THIRD QUARTER
The Child and the State; Child Welfare Problems; Social Case Work I; Social Statistics; or Field Work; Medical Lectures; or Social Psychiatry[2]	Social Case Work II; The Law and Social Work; Field Work (Family); Medical Lectures;[2] or Behavior Disorders of Children; or Public Assistance	Public Welfare Admis.; Child Welfare Case W. or Psychiatry in C.W.; Field Work (Family Welfare Advanced, or Child Welfare, or Medical Social, Soc. Psychiatric or Probation Unit); Community Organization

Second Year Program

FOURTH QUARTER	FIFTH QUARTER	SIXTH QUARTER
Social Work and the Courts; Methods of Soc. Investigation; Case Work Elective; Field Work (Med. Social, Psychiatric, Special Children's Service or Probation Unit)	The Family and the State; Case Work Elective; Social Research (Field Investigation, Group Inquiries) or Public Admis.; Field Work (Advanced)	Social Insurance; Case Work Elective or Adminis. Regulation; History of Am. Philanthropy; Soc. Welf. & Eng. Phil.; Soc. Research (Field Investig., Group Inquiries), or Field Work

1. University of Chicago Announcements, May 10, 1939, pp. 7-8.
2. These courses may be taken on a non-credit basis by students who are registered for full-time work.

300 Education for the Public Social Services

UNIVERSITY OF DENVER[1]

Plan of Work

"During the first year the student is expected to obtain the basic requirements for the general field; in the second year greater opportunity is open to select courses in his field of special interest. The first year's work will usually include the first and second courses in social case work, introductory courses in the allied fields of medicine, psychiatry and law, and a general course in child welfare, in community organization, and in public welfare.

"The field practice in case work should, if possible, be undertaken during the first quarter in order that the requirements in this field may be completed before the student enters upon the research for his dissertation. One quarter of field work is prerequisite to the second course in case work. Fifteen hours a week is the minimum field work requirement.

"The second year will include the courses in the history of social work, in social administration, and in research and elective courses in theory and practice.

"A sequence of courses has been arranged, designed to equip students who desire to prepare themselves for the field of administration and who are adapted to that phase of work. Administration in public welfare and in private social agencies to be effective requires education in social work as well as in special techniques of administration.

"The curriculum may be divided into seven major groups of courses: history and survey; social treatment in family and child welfare; medical and psychiatric information; public welfare and law; social organization and administration; social research; and field work."

1. University of Denver Bulletin, 1939-1940; April 25, 1939, p. 6.

Appendix B

NATIONAL CATHOLIC SCHOOL OF SOCIAL SERVICE[1]

Family Welfare Sequence

First Year

FIRST SEMESTER [2] *

Religious Concepts for Social Work
Current Economic Problems
Social Case Work I
Medical Lectures I
Nutrition
Community Organization
Field Work (Case Work)

SECOND SEMESTER

Principles of Catholic Social Work
Social Ethics
Social Case Work II
Medical Lectures II
Child Welfare
Psychiatry
Group Work
Public Welfare Organization
Seminar in Research
Field Work (Case Work)

Second Year

FIRST SEMESTER

* Administration of Social Agencies [2]
* Legal Aspects of Social Work
* Statistics
* Thesis Seminar
* Advanced Psychiatry I
* Comparative Social Philosophies
** Substitute Parental Care [3]
** Community Organization II
** Advanced Medical Information
* Field Work (Family Welfare Agency)

SECOND SEMESTER

* Seminar in Family Welfare [2]
* Seminar in Ethical Problems in Social Work
* Advanced Psychiatry II
* Standards of Living
* Case Work in Public Assistance
** Public Welfare Administration [3]
** Juvenile Delinquency
** Clinical Problems of Childhood
** Current Economic Legislation
* Field Work (Family Welfare Agency)
* Research

1. Catalogue, 1939-1940, p. 17.
2.* Required.
3.** Elective.

UNIVERSITY OF PITTSBURGH[1]

Group Work Sequence

First Year

FIRST SEMESTER

Group Work I
Creative Arts I
Social Psychiatry I
Community Organization II
State and Social Welfare
Field Work

SECOND SEMESTER

Group Work II
Social Psychiatry II
Methods of Social Research
Creative Arts II
Elective
Field Work

Second Year

Group Work III
Administration of Social Agencies
Case Work for Group Workers
History of Social Work
Thesis
Field Work

Group Work IV
Supervision
Community Organization I
Elective
Thesis
Field Work

SIMMONS COLLEGE

First Year Program

Class Work

The following courses are required of all first year students:

Social Agencies
Community Organization (2)
Social Case Work (2)
Medical Lectures (2)
Principles of Human Behavior
Clinical Psychiatry

Methods of Social Research
Statistical Methods
Statistics of Social Work
Public Welfare Administration
(2)

Elective Courses offered: Child and the State; Social Insurance; Food in Relation to Family Life; and Personal and Social Adjustment of Children.

1. Tentative Outline of Courses, University of Pittsburgh, 1939. (mimeo.)

Field Work

Second Year Program

"The School offers to students who have completed the professional work required in the one-year program, described above, advanced work in community organization, medical social work, psychiatric social work, and social research. Students who are interested in children's or family work are encouraged to take the second year of education in the psychiatric social work field." Bulletin, 1939, pp. 18-20.

TULANE UNIVERSITY[1]

The Curriculum

Courses considered important for the first-year student include the following: Social Case Work I and II, Medical Information, Psychiatry for Social Workers, The Field of Child Welfare, Juvenile Delinquency, Community Organization, Health Problems, Public Assistance, Public Welfare Administration, Local Government, Social Statistics.

For second-year students, the following professional courses are offered: Social Case Work III, Psychiatry in Case Work, The Individual and Social Adaptation, Behavior Problems and Personality Disorders of Children, Child Welfare Case Studies, Medical Social Work I, Medical Social Work II, Methods of Social Investigation, Research in Social Work, Social Insurance, Administration of Social Agencies, Law and Social Work, History of American Philanthropy and Social Welfare, History of English Philanthropy and Social Welfare.

Field Work courses offered by the school fall into five main divisions: family case work; child welfare work; psychiatric social work; medical social work; and social welfare planning.

1. Tulane University School of Social Work Announcement, 1939-1940. April 1, 1939; pp. 7-10.

UNIVERSITY OF WASHINGTON[2]

Curriculum

Courses considered fundamental for first-year students include the following:

Social Case Work I and II;
Case Work with Psychiatric Interpretation, *or* Child Welfare Casework;
Psychiatric Information for Social Workers I and II;
Medical Information for Social Workers;
Community Organization and/or The Rural Community;
Problems of Public Assistance;
Problems of Child Welfare;
Social Statistics and/or Methods of Social Research;
Group Work and/or Social Aspects of the Law;
Field Work I, II, and III

"During the second year of graduate study increasing attention is given to field work experience; and additional courses are required in the administration of social agencies, social legislation, the history of social work, social research, and specialized case work."

THE AMERICAN ASSOCIATION OF SCHOOLS OF SOCIAL WORK

Constitution and By-Laws

Constitution

ARTICLE I—NAME

The name of this Association shall be The American Association of Schools of Social Work.

ARTICLE II—PURPOSE

The purpose of this Association shall be, through conference and research, to develop standards of education for professional social work.

2. Bulletin, 1939, p. 8.

ARTICLE III—MEMBERS

There shall be two kinds of membership in the Association, namely, One-Year Schools and Two-Year Schools, but at no time shall the number of One-Year Schools exceed one-half the number of Two-Year Schools in the membership of the Association.

Educational institutions in the United States of America and the Dominion of Canada shall be eligible for membership in this Association, as hereinafter specified in the By-Laws.

ARTICLE IV—OFFICERS

The officers of the Association shall be a President, Vice-President, and a Secretary-Treasurer.

The officers of the Association shall be members of an executive committee which shall be constituted as specified in the By-Laws.

ARTICLE V—AMENDMENTS

The Constitution may be amended at any business meeting of the Association by a two-thirds vote of the members present. All proposed amendments shall be sent to all members of the Association in written form at the time of the call to meeting but not later than sixty days before such meeting is to be held.

Amendments may be proposed by the Executive Committee or on written request of three members through the Secretary of the Association.

ARTICLE VI—MEETINGS

The Association shall hold two business meetings a year: one of which shall be at the time and place of the National Conference of Social Work, and the other, which shall be the annual meeting, shall be at such time and place as may be determined by the Executive Committee.

ARTICLE VII—QUORUM

At any business meeting of the Association two-fifths of the members shall constitute a quorum.

By-Laws

BY-LAW I

ADMISSION TO MEMBERSHIP

Section 1: *Application for admission to the Association*

A. Application for admission may be made at any time, but a period of at least six months must be allowed for consideration of the application by the Association.

B. Applications must be submitted by the Director of the School in the form prescribed by the Executive Committee.

C. No application shall be considered from a school until it has been in existence for at least two academic years.

Section 2: *Admission Requirements*

An educational institution applying for membership in the Association shall meet the following requirements.

A. One-Year Schools. Organization requirements.

    i. A school to be eligible for admission hereafter to the Association as a One-Year member shall maintain the following specific organization and shall be a part of a college or university which is on the list of Colleges and Universities approved by the Association of American Universities and shall have:

    ii. An organic grouping of relevant courses of instruction into a separate curriculum for the stated purpose of professional education for social work;

    iii. An administrator or director chosen or appointed as the executive head of the school, who is empowered, in coöperation with the faculty of the school, to exercise control over admission requirements to courses of instruction within the limits of university regulations. Criteria for determining qualifications for the Director shall include professional experience, graduate study, and familiarity with problems of education.

    iv. A suitable faculty which may be composed of full-time and part-time instructors, provided that at least two persons shall give their full-time to the work of the school;

a. Instruction in fundamental social work methods and the practice of social work shall be given by persons who have had valid and authoritative experience in social work;

b. Instruction in other courses in the curriculum shall be given by persons equally qualified in their respective fields;

v. The school shall have an annual budget for teaching and administrative salaries which can be shown to be adequate to carry out the program of the school;

vi. The school shall furnish satisfactory assurance, in writing, of continued maintenance from a responsible college or university covering a period of not less than three years following the date of admission.

B. *Two-Year Schools.* Organization requirements.

i. A school to be eligible for admission hereafter to the Association as a Two-Year member shall maintain the following specific organization and shall be a part of a college or university which is on the list of Colleges and Universities approved by the Association of American Universities and shall have:

ii. An organic grouping of relevant courses of instruction into a separate curriculum for the stated purpose of professional education for social work;

iii. An administrator or director chosen or appointed as executive head of the school, who is empowered, in coöperation with the faculty of the school, to exercise control over admission requirements to courses of instruction. Hereafter, criteria for determining qualifications for the Director shall include professional experience, graduate study, full-time responsibility to the school, and familiarity with problems of education.

iv. A suitable faculty which may be composed of full-time and part-time instructors, provided that hereafter at least three persons give their full time to the work of the school;

a. Instruction in fundamental social work methods and the practice of social work shall be given by persons who have had valid and authoritative experience in social work;

b. Instruction in other courses in the curriculum shall be given by persons equally qualified in their respective fields;

v. The school shall have an annual budget for teaching and administrative salaries which can be shown to be adequate to carry out the program of the school;

vi. The school shall furnish satisfactory assurance, in writing, of continued maintenance from a responsible college or university covering a period of not less than three years following the date of admission.

C. *Admission Requirements for Students in One-Year and Two-Year Schools*

On and after October 1, 1939, at least 90 percent of the total number of students enrolled in courses in subjects in the professional curriculum for which credit is given toward a degree or certificate shall have received a Bachelor's degree or its academic equivalent in an approved college or university.

D. *Curriculum Requirements*

i. A One-Year school shall provide a curriculum consisting of not less than one academic year of work in graduate professional social work, the courses to be drawn from the basic minimum curriculum of the Association unless given in addition to this curriculum, as hereinafter provided; and,

a. Shall present an approved program of field work under the educational direction of the school;

b. The field work shall be planned and supervised experience in the practice of social work as social work is carried on currently by recognized social agencies.

ii. On and after October 1, 1939, a Two-Year school shall provide a curriculum consisting of not less than two academic years of study in graduate professional social work, including the course of study which covers the basic minimum curriculum of the Association as hereinafter provided; and,

   a. Shall present an approved program of field work under the educational direction of the school;

   b. The field work shall be planned and supervised experience in the practice of social work as social work is carried on currently by recognized social agencies.

iii. The basic minimum curriculum of the Association shall be the minimum curriculum adopted by the Association in December 1932, and as subsequently amended. The minimum curriculum may be amended at any business meeting of the Association by a majority vote of those present and voting provided that notice of the proposed change has been sent to member schools, thirty days before the meeting.

Section 3: *Election*

A school to be a member of this Association must be elected to membership at a regular business meeting of the Association on the recommendation of the Executive Committee.

Section 4: *Payment of Dues*

Upon election to membership, the school must pay the prescribed dues of the Association.

Section 5: *Review*

A school meeting the foregoing requirements of the Association shall be admitted into the Association as a Provisional Member with all the rights and privileges of full membership. At the end of three years of such Provisional Membership, the work of the school shall be reviewed by the Executive Committee, and if found satisfactory, the Executive Committee shall recommend the school for Full Membership at the next meeting of the Association.

Section 6: *Re-admission to Membership*

A school formerly holding membership in the Association shall meet the requirements prescribed for new members. Such a school may be admitted at any business meeting of the Association to provisional membership upon recommendation of the Executive Committee, and the requirement under Section 1, C of this By-Law may be waived.

Section 1

Schools having full membership in the Association shall be subjected to review by the Association.

Section 2

Member schools shall maintain the same standards as are required from schools applying for admission, except where otherwise provided in these By-Laws. Schools that are members of the Association, at the adoption of this By-Law, which do not meet the standards of the Association, shall have three years in which to modify their program in order to meet the Association's requirements.

Section 3

Member schools may be dropped from the Association either because of unsatisfactory standards or because of inactivity provided;

A. That the Executive Committee study the situation of the school and present its findings to the Association with recommendations for action;

B. That the school in question be notified that its case is to be considered, and be given a hearing before the Executive Committee if desired;

C. That the school be given an extension of time, not to exceed one year from the date of notification of unsatisfactory standards, if in the judgment of the Executive Committee such extension is desirable and justified;

D. That a school be dropped from membership at a regular meeting of the Association, and that such action shall require a vote of a majority of the member schools before becoming effective.

ELECTION AND DUTIES OF OFFICERS

Section 1

Officers shall be elected annually and shall hold office for one year. Officers shall be elected by the Association at its annual meeting.

Section 2

The annual meeting of the Association shall be held at a time and place determined by the Excutive Committee.

Section 3

The duties of officers shall be such as normally pertain to their respective offices.

BY-LAW IV

Section 1

The officers of the Association and four members at large shall constitute an Executive Committee. The retiring President of the Association shall be a member of the Executive Committee for one year following his retirement from office.

Section 2

Two members of the Executive Committee shall be elected annually and shall hold office for two years.

A member of the Executive Committee shall be ineligible for re-election until one year has elapsed after the expiration of his term of office.

Members of the Executive Committee shall be elected by the Association at its annual meeting.

Section 3

The duties of the Executive Committee shall be:

A. To conduct the business of the Association between meetings.

B. To appoint such committees as may be necessary to this end.

Section 4

A nominating committee of three shall be elected at each annual meeting to serve for one year, whose duty it shall be to nominate its successors and the officers of the Association. The Nominating Committee shall submit its report in writing to member schools thirty days in advance of the meeting at which election is to take place.

VOTING BODY

Section 1

A member shall nominate to the Secretary of the Association in advance of the meeting of the Association the person to represent said member at that meeting.

Section 2

In all matters of decision by the Association each member school shall have one vote.

BY-LAW VI

DUES

Section 1

The annual dues shall be as follows:

A. The annual dues shall be $75 for One-Year Schools and $100 for Two-Year Schools, payable at the beginning of the fiscal year.

B. The dues shall be increased according to the following schedule: for all schools reporting a full-time enrollment as of November 1 in the preceding fiscal year,

    i. Of 100 to 149, an additional $50 for the given fiscal year;

    ii. Of 150 to 199, an additional $100 for the given fiscal year;

    iii. Of 200 or over, an additional $200 for the given fiscal year.

C. Additional dues provided in sub-section B shall be payable at the same time as annual dues.

Section 2

Any member of this Association that has not paid membership dues before the expiration of the fiscal year shall be automatically dropped from membership at the end of the fiscal year, and it shall be the duty of the Treasurer so to notify such member of this action by Registered Mail within ten (10) days from the expiration of said fiscal year. Such member shall be automatically reinstated upon payment of the dues in arrears before the expiration of thirty (30) days from the receipt of said notification.

BY-LAW VII

FISCAL YEAR

The fiscal year shall be the calendar year.

BY-LAW VIII

AMENDMENTS

By-Laws may be amended at any business meeting of the Association by a majority vote of members present at the meeting, provided that the proposed amendment has been submitted to the members with the call to meeting at least thirty days prior to the date of such meeting.

(Constitution adopted December 29, 1931, and amended to
June 4, 1941)

Minimum Curriculum as Adopted at the December
1932 Meeting of

THE AMERICAN ASSOCIATION OF SCHOOLS
OF SOCIAL WORK

With the Accompanying Statement:

That a School offering this curriculum shall be permitted
to grant a provisional certificate approved by the American
Association of Schools of Social Work to any student who
at the end of one graduate year of study, shall have completed this curriculum.

		Semester Hours	Quarter Hours
GROUP A (all required)	Case Work	2 or 3	3 or 4
	Medical Informa- tion	2 or 3	3 or 4
	Psychiatric Infor- mation	2 or 3	3 or 4
		Not less than 6 nor more than 9	Not less than 9 nor more than 12
GROUP B (2 courses required)	Community Or- ganization	1, 2, or 3	2, 3, or 4
	Specialized Case Work	1, 2, or 3	2, 3, or 4
	Group Work	1, 2, or 3	2, 3, or 4
		Not less than 4 nor more than 6	Not less than 6 nor more than 9
GROUP C (2 courses required)	Field of Social Work	2 or 3	2, 3, or 4
	Public Welfare Administration		
	Child Welfare	2 or 3	2, 3, or 4
	Problems of La- bor or Industry		
		Not less than 4 nor more than 6	Not less than 6 nor more than 9

		Semester Hours	Quarter Hours
GROUP D (1 course required)	Social Statistics Social Research Social Legislation Legal Aspects of Social Work or Social Aspects of Law	2 or 3	3 or 4
		TOTAL 20 or 22	TOTAL 30

In this group two courses may be substituted giving in combined credit no more than the credit allowed for one course.

FIELD WORK

NOT MORE THAN TEN SEMESTER OR FIFTEEN QUARTER *CREDITS* OF FIELD WORK

Note: There should be not *less* than one semester credit or two quarter credits in any course.

INDEX

ADMINISTRATION of social services, content of courses in, 18, 182-184; problems of future for, 230-233

Adult education, part of public school program, 4

Aged, aid for. *See* Old Age Insurance; Public Assistance; Unemployment Compensation.

Agencies for social work, and school curriculum, 19-20; and field work of schools, 22-23; private, 23, 32; coöperation of on post-entry education, 27; for unemployment compensation, 55; attitude toward organization and procedure, 83-86; structure and function of, 174-176ff; selection of for field work, 210; and state administration of public welfare, 246-280

American Association of Medical Social Workers, study made by, 34

American Association of Schools of Social Work, advisory committee of, v; study committee of, vi-vii; executive committee of (1938-40), vii-viii; research staff of, viii; survey of aims of, x, xi; adopts two-year curriculum, 25; sponsored by Rockefeller Foundation, 33; original plan of, 44; curriculum of

member schools of, 47-48; decision of on status of professional curriculum, 51; table of member schools of, 292-293; table of tentative member schools of, 294; constitution and by-laws of, 304-313; minimum curriculum adopted by, 313-314; mentioned, 21. *See also* Curriculum.

American Public Welfare Association, study made by, 34

American Red Cross, influence on social work, 46

Atlanta University, mentioned, 49n

BASIC case work, course in, 18. *See also* Curriculum.

Benson, George C. S., mentioned, 42

Bernstein, Saul, mentioned, 42

Blind, aid to, 5, 12, 57. *See also* Public Assistance.

Boston College, mentioned, 49n

Boston School of Social Work, mentioned, 46

Boston University, mentioned, 49n

Bryn Mawr College, mentioned, 49n, 50n

Bureau of Prisons, analysis of administration of, 253-254

Bureau of Public Assistance, advisory committee on training and personnel of, 15

Business administration, and social work, 44

CALIFORNIA, state civil service requirement, 133n
Carnegie Institute of Technology, mentioned, 49n
Case work, in Public Assistance,
78; definition of, 99; content
of courses in, 190-193; suggested changes in courses in,
193-194. *See also* Curriculum.
Catholic University, mentioned,
49n
CCC, and Public Assistance, 77
Chicago School of Civics and
Philanthropy, mentioned, 46
Child health care. *See* Public
Health.
Child Welfare Services, professional education for, 14, 17;
personnel policies of, 16, 132-
133; non-federal programs
of, 59-60; scope and function of, 59-60, 78-81, 111;
and juvenile delinquency, 70;
importance of public relations in, 79; relation to other
public institutions, 80-81,
102; special skills needed in,
101-102; training needs for
administration of, 122-123;
residence requirements for
personnel in, 140-141; salary
levels for personnel in, 144-
145; staff development for
personnel in, 155-156; possibilities for promotion in,
159-160; table of employee
distribution in, 290-291. *See
also* Curriculum; Dependent
children; Personnel.
Civil Service. *See* Merit system.

Claims administration. *See* Old
Age Insurance; Unemploy-
ment Compensation.
College of William and Mary,
mentioned, 50n
Community organization, definition of, 197; content of
courses in, 197-200, 213-215;
suggested changes in courses
in, 200. *See also* Curriculum;
Personnel; Schools of social
work.
Crippled children, aid to, 30,
60.
Curriculum, survey of, 13-14,
17-19; course in community
organization, 18; case work in,
18; recommendations for, 18-
20, 215-220; for one-year program, 21, 48n; and faculty
leadership, 23-24; for two-
year program, 25, 48n; for
graduate study, 21, 27-28,
48, 172, 240-241; extension
courses in, 26-27; attitude
toward, of services, 103;
job analysis course in, 118;
elementary statistics in, 118;
fundamental concept of, 170-
172; scope of basic, 173; classification of subject matter in,
173-174; inter-relation of
courses in, 177-178; and university administrations, 179-
180; content of practice
courses in, 186-200; illustra-
tive sequence of study in, 299-
304

DEPENDENT children, aid to,
under Public Assistance, 5, 12,
57; under Child Welfare,
80

Depression, 1930, influence of, on development of social work schools, 47

ECONOMICS, need for knowledge of in services, 18, 118
Employment counselling, mentioned, 4
Employment Service, beginnings of, 5; requirements of for personnel, 16-17; function of, 72-74; table of personnel distribution in, 287-288-289. *See also* Unemployment Compensation; United States Employment Service.
Engineering, and social work, 44
Extension courses. *See* Curriculum.

FACULTY, impact of services on, 235-236
Farm Security Administration, analysis of scope and function of, 264-267
Field work, training center establishment for, 18; placement in, 19; relationship with schools, 22-23, 63; definition of, 203; philosophy of, 204-206; content and scope of courses in, 206-210; suggested changes in content of courses in, 211-212. *See also* Agencies.
Fordham University, mentioned, 49n

GRADUATE School for Jewish Social Work, mentioned, 49n
Graduate study. *See* Curriculum.

Graham, George, study of public administration by, 181
Grants-in-aid, federal to state, 54-57
Group work, in curriculum, 18; definition of, 195; content of courses in, 196-197

HARRISON, Frances N., mentioned, 42
Hatch Act, application to public social services, 87
Hathway, Marion, mentioned, 42
Housing, under federal program, 5, 7; content of course in, 180. *See also* United States Housing Authority.

INDIAN Affairs. *See* Office of Indian Affairs.
Indiana University, mentioned, 49n
Industrial hygiene. *See* Public Health.
In-service training, 145ff
Institutes of Public Administration, purposes of, 178
Insurance, commercial, and social work, 87-88. *See also* Old Age Insurance; Personnel.

JUNIOR Civil Service Examiner, register of, and old age insurance, 124
Juvenile delinquency. *See* Child Welfare Services.

KAHN, Dorothy C., mentioned, 42

LABOR laws. *See* Law.
Labor relations, understanding

Labor relations—*cont'd*
of necessary in unemploy-
ment compensation, 98-99
Lansdale, Robert T., men-
tioned, 42
Law, in social work, 44; interpretation in employment
services, 74-76; understanding
of necessary in individual
services, 82; labor, 118
Loyola University, mentioned,
49n

MARGARET Morrison College
of Carnegie Institute of Technology, mentioned, 50n
Medical information, content
of course in, 186-187
Merit system, for recruitment of
personnel in services, 28, 34n,
133-137, 167-168; recommendations for improvement of,
28-29; made basis for personnel selection in all states, 34n;
report on by Social Security
Board, 226n
Missouri School of Social Economy, mentioned, 46
Montreal School of Social
Work, and McGill Univer-
sity, 49n
Mother's assistance, first act for,
passed, 5; in Pennsylvania, 8;
principle of, 8; discussed at
White House Conference, 62;
mentioned, 30. *See also* Public Health; Vocational guidance.

NATIONAL Catholic School
of Social Service, sequence of
social work courses in, 301;
mentioned, 49n

National Conference of Social
Work, classified services, 176
National Youth Administra-
tion, analysis of administra-
tion of, 263-264
New York School of Philan-
thropy, mentioned, 46
New York School of Social
Work, mentioned, 49n
Northwestern University, men-
tioned, 49n
Nursery schools, mentioned, 4

OFFICE of Indian Affairs,
analysis of administration of,
258-260
Ohio State University, mentioned, 49n
Old age assistance, concept of,
8-9
Old Age Insurance (Old Age
and Survivors' Insurance),
professional education for,
14; personnel policies of, 15;
salary levels for personnel in,
16, 141-142; and schools, 17-
18; replaced by Old Age and
Survivors' Insurance, 34n;
function and scope of, 52-53,
67-71; definition of, 53; claims
administration in, 68-69; special skills needed for, 95-96;
duties of personnel in, 106-
107; bases of personnel selection for, 124-127; training
needs for administration of,
114-117; residence requirements for personnel in, 137-
139; staff development for
personnel in, 145-147; possibilities for promotion in, 157;
applicants' eligibility for, 228;
change in benefits law for,

Old Age Insurance—cont'd 229; table of employee distribution in, 282-283

PENNSYLVANIA School of Social Work, mentioned, 49n

Personnel, survey of requirements for, 15-18, 124-179; recommendations of study committee for, 16-17; salary discrepancies in, among services, 16; leaves of absence for, 24, 145ff; great demand for, 31; and understanding of community, 100; federal leadership in, 160-166. See also Child Welfare; Old Age Insurance; Public Assistance; Unemployment Compensation.

Philadelphia Training School for Social Work, mentioned, 46, 46n

"Poor relief," mentioned, 4

President's Reorganization Plan, mentioned, 57n

Professional certification, recommendation, for, 17

Professional education, desirability of, 14; facilities for and enrollment, 21; annual expenditure for, by schools, 26; history of, 46-52. See also Curriculum; Public social work.

Psychiatric information, content of courses in, 187-188; analysis of courses in, 189n

Public Assistance, services under, 12; personnel policies of, 15, 159; salary levels for personnel in, 16, 143-144; scope and function of, 57-60, 76-78; 107-110; determination of

eligibility for, 77; special skills needed in, 99-100; training needs for administration of, 119-122; staff development for personnel in, 152-155; residence requirements for personnel in, 139-140; possibilities for promotion in, 159; content of courses in, 179. See also Curriculum; Personnel.

Public Health, program of, 4; analysis of administration of, 274-279

Public recreation, mentioned, 4

Public schools, and social services, 272-273

Public social services, basic concept of, 9-10; recommendations for, 14-15; development of, since 1930, 31-33; and Hatch Act, 87; relation to of local, state, and regional units, 111-112; training needs for executive leadership in, 113ff. See also Agencies; Social service.

Public Welfare, salaries in, 16; basic curriculum and, 18, 19; content of courses in, 178, 180-181. See also Curriculum.

REORGANIZATION Act, 1939, mentioned, 57n

Report of the Committee on Economic Security, mentioned, 227

Research, definition of, 220; scope and content of courses in, 201-203

Residence requirements, survey of, 16. See also Child Welfare; Old Age Insurance; Person-

Residence requirements—*cont'd* nel Public Assistance; Unemployment Compensation.

Rockefeller Foundation, grant to American Association of Schools of Social Work, 33

Rural social work, and curriculum, 18; and land grant colleges, 32; in child welfare, 59; and location of social work schools, 217-218

ST. LOUIS University, mentioned, 50n

Schools of social work, recommendation for joint planning with services, 20; choice of students, 24; enrollment in, 50-51, 295-298; and public opinion, 63; training facilities offered by, 39-41; relation to services, 61-64; and related schools, 62; impact of services on one-year type, 233-234; impact of services on students of, 236-239; relationship with communities, 241-242; problems of future, 243-245; table of title and degrees offered by, 296-297. *See also* Curriculum; Professional education.

Simmons College, sequence of social work courses in, 302-303; mentioned, 50n, 59n

Smith College, mentioned, 50n

Social Hygiene. *See* Public Health.

Social Security Act, effects integration of public social work, 5; services established under, 12, 34; personnel under, 12; amendment, August, 1939; 34n; provisions for Old Age Insurance, 52; amendment regarding old age insurance, 52n; provisions for Unemployment Compensation, 54; provisions for Public Assistance, 58; provisions for Child Welfare, 59; amendment regarding merit systems, 224; philosophy of, 227-228. *See also* Social Security Board.

Social Security Board, on training and personnel for social work, 15; location of central office of, 53, 53n; Second Annual Report, quoted, 67n; duties of Regional Office of, 106; Fifth Annual Report, quoted, 225n

Social Security numbers, assignment of, 67

Social service, concepts of, 6-7; philosophy of, 7-10; knowledge of Organizations needed for, 82-83; development of, 225-226; in public schools, 272-274. *See also* Public social services; Social work.

Social work, fundamental beliefs of, 10; personnel requirements for, 15-18; salary discrepancies in, 16; basic curriculum for, 44; philosophy of education for, 45-52; need in, for understanding human behavior, 89-95; necessity for professional attitude in all services of, 89; general function and scope of services in, 52-60; historical development of, 175-176. *See also* Public social services, Social service.

Staff workers courses, mentioned, 238n

State Employment Service, first established, 5n. *See also* Employment Service.

TRAINING needs, discussed, 33-38, 114-123. *See also* Curriculum; Public social services.

Transient families, aid to, 80

Tulane University, sequence of social work courses in, 303; mentioned, 5on

UNDERGRADUATE training, mentioned, 14. *See also* Curriculum.

Unemployment Compensation, professional education for, 14; requirements for service in, 15, 16-17, 128-132; and schools, 17-18; relation to Employment Service, 54ff; federal-state relationship in, 54-55; scope and function of, 55, 72-76, 107; number of personnel in, 56-57; classification of applicants for, 72; duties of claims examiner in, 74-76; special skills needed in, 96-99; training needs for administration of, 117-122; and public relations, 118; residence requirements for personnel in, 138-139; salary levels for personnel in, 142-143; staff development for personnel in, 147-152; possibilities for promotion in, 158-159; channels for use of, 229-230; table of personnel distribution in, 284-286. *See also* Employment Service; Personnel.

United States Children's Bureau, services under, 79n; mentioned, 15

United States Employment Service, issues job descriptions, 77; evolution of, 57n. *See also* Employment Service.

United States Housing Authority, study of training needs for, 34; analysis of administration of, 267-272. *See also* Housing.

United States Veteran's Administration, analysis of scope and function of, 255-256

University of Buffalo, mentioned, 49n

University of California, mentioned, 49n

University of Chicago, sequence of social work courses in, 299-300; mentioned, 49n

University of Denver, sequence of social work courses in, 300; mentioned, 49n

University of Iowa, mentioned, 49n

University of Michigan, mentioned, 49n

University of Minnesota, mentioned, 49n

University of North Carolina, mentioned, 49n

University of Pittsburgh, sequence of social work courses in, 302; mentioned, 5on

University of Oklahoma, mentioned, 49n

Universtiy of Southern California, mentioned, 6on

University of Washington, sequence of social work courses in, 304; mentioned, 49n

324 Index

VOCATIONAL guidance, part of public school, 4; needed in unemployment administration, 97, 117; in service to mothers, 101; mentioned, 18. *See also* Vocational Rehabilitation.

Vocational Rehabilitation, analysis of administration of, 256-258

WASHINGTON University, mentioned, 50n

Western Reserve University, mentioned, 50n

White House Conference, 1909, 8; 1930, 62

Workmen's Compensation, first act for, passed, 5; fundamental concept of, 8; analysis of administration of, 247-252

Works Progress Administration, under Public Assistance, 77; analysis of function and scope of, 260-263

www.ingramcontent.com/pod-product-compliance
Lightning Source LLC
Chambersburg PA
CBHW021808270326
41932CB00007B/104